Egyptian Mysteries Volume 1: Principles of Shetaut Neter

Cruzian Mystic Books / Sema Institute of Yoga
P.O.Box 570459
Miami, Florida, 33257
(305) 378-6253 Fax: (305) 378-6253

© 2004-2006 By Reginald Muata Abhaya Ashby

All rights reserved. No part of this book may be used or reproduced in any manner whatsoever without written permission (address above) except in the case of brief quotations embodied in critical articles and reviews. All inquiries may be addressed to the address above.

The author is available for group lectures and individual counseling. For further information contact the publisher.

Ashby, Muata
Egyptian Mysteries: Volume 1, Shetaut Neter ISBN: 1-884564-41-0

Temple of Shetaut Neter-Aset
INTERNET ADDRESS: www.Egyptianyoga.com
E-MAIL ADDRESS: Semayoga@aol.com

BASED ON THE VIDEO PRESENTATION

INTRODUCTION TO SHETAUT NETER

By

Sebai Maa
(Dr. Muata Ashby)
2003

SEMA UNIVERSITY

www.SemaUniversity.org

The Sema University School of Kemetic Culture and Ancient Egyptian Mysteries offers online studies leading to Associate and Bachelor degrees.

ASSOCIATE DEGREE
You may earn an Associate degree in Kemetic studies by completing 5 courses over a period of 1-1/4 years. Those who complete the Associate Degree are granted a certificate with the title of Teacher of Kemetic Culture

BACHELOR DEGREE
You may earn an Bachelor degree in Kemetic religion or philosophy within 2 years by concentrating in specific areas of study like:

	Degree Concentration area	Degree Concentration area	Degree Concentration area	Degree Concentration area	Degree Concentration area
Degree title	*Kamitan African Theology* *33 credit*	*Sema (Yoga) & Health Practitioner* *30 credit*	*Kamitan African Philosophy of Religion and Ethics* *27 credit*	*Comparative Religion and World Religion* *24 credit*	*Interdisciplinary Kamitan Studies* (Student may combine electives to create a program of their choice with approval of their mentor.) *24 credit*
FOCUS OF THE DEGREE PROGRAM	Understanding the nature of Kamitan religion and its special concept of theism the nature of the Divine and its relationship to the Self as well as the main religious Kamitan paths to spiritual enlightenment.	Understanding the nature of Kamitan disciplines of SEMA or Yoga the sciences for attaining spiritual enlightenment through cultivation of body mind and soul.	Understanding the nature of Kamitan philosophy psycho-mythology and wisdom for transforming and enlightening the mind to attain higher consciousness.	Understanding the nature of world religion and its dept to Kamitan religion as well as discovering the true meaning of religion and how to get to the source and true purpose of religion: Spiritual enlightenment and human peace.	Student must complete the core courses and then choose at least 5 electives from the other degree programs

Those who complete the Bachelor degree program receive a Diploma and the title of Basu (instructor, teacher) in their chosen area of concentration.

<u>**ONLINE:**</u> The program is delivered online and via correspondence. The student receives lesson plans and interactive contact via the internet and can communicate with Sebai Dr. Muata Ashby, mentors and other students.

<u>**ACCESS TO STUDENT ONLY AREAS**</u> of the Sema University Web site containing special lectures, access to online conferences on philosophy, meditative practice, and more.

Begin your studies at any time of the year and start your path of self-discovery, learn how to promote the Kemetic path in your community and promote the upliftment of humanity through Ancient Egyptian Spirituality

www.SemaUniversity.org

OPENING PRAYER

Hetep Hetep Hetep Hetep
Om Amun Ra Ptah Om Amun Ra Ptah Om Amun Ra Ptah Om Amun Ra Ptah

Hetep

Om Amun Ra Ptah is a brief prayer to the great trinity of Neterian Theology.

The Book of Shetaut Neter

NETERIANISM
Vol. 1

Introduction to the Egyptian Mysteries

Sema Institute of Yoga

Sema (☥) is an Ancient Egyptian word and symbol meaning *union*. The Sema Institute is dedicated to the propagation of the universal teachings of spiritual evolution which relate to the union of humanity and the union of all things within the universe. It is a non-denominational organization which recognizes the unifying principles in all spiritual and religious systems of evolution throughout the world. Our primary goals are to provide the wisdom of ancient spiritual teachings in books, courses and other forms of communication. Secondly, to provide expert instruction and training in the various yogic disciplines including Ancient Egyptian Philosophy, Christian Gnosticism, Indian Philosophy and modern science. Thirdly, to promote world peace and Universal Love.

A primary focus of our tradition is to identify and acknowledge the yogic principles within all religions and to relate them to each other in order to promote their deeper understanding as well as to show the essential unity of purpose and the unity of all living beings and nature within the whole of existence.

The Institute is open to all who believe in the principles of peace, non-violence and spiritual emancipation regardless of sex, race, or creed.

Egyptian Mysteries Volume 1: Principles of Shetaut Neter

About the Author

Who is Sebai Muata Abhaya Ashby D.D. Ph. D.?

Priest, Author, lecturer, poet, philosopher, musician, publisher, counselor and spiritual preceptor and founder of the Sema Institute-Temple of Aset, Muata Ashby was born in Brooklyn, New York City, and grew up in the Caribbean. His family is from Puerto Rico and Barbados. Displaying an interest in ancient civilizations and the Humanities, Sebai Maa began studies in the area of religion and philosophy and achieved doctorates in these areas while at the same time he began to collect his research into what would later become several books on the subject of the origins of Yoga Philosophy and practice in ancient Africa (Ancient Egypt) and also the origins of Christian Mysticism in Ancient Egypt.

Sebai Maa (Muata Abhaya Ashby) holds a Doctor of Philosophy Degree in Religion, and a Doctor of Divinity Degree in Holistic Health. He is also a Pastoral Counselor and Teacher of Yoga Philosophy and Discipline. Dr. Ashby received his Doctor of Divinity Degree from and is an adjunct faculty member of the American Institute of Holistic Theology. Dr. Ashby is a certified as a PREP Relationship Counselor. Dr. Ashby has been an independent researcher and practitioner of Egyptian Yoga, Indian Yoga, Chinese Yoga, Buddhism and mystical psychology as well as Christian Mysticism. Dr. Ashby has engaged in Post Graduate research in advanced Jnana, Bhakti and Kundalini Yogas at the Yoga Research Foundation. He has extensively studied mystical religious traditions from around the world and is an accomplished lecturer, musician, artist, poet, screenwriter, playwright and author of over 25 books on Kamitan yoga and spiritual philosophy. He is an Ordained Minister and Spiritual Counselor and also the founder the Sema Institute, a non-profit organization dedicated to spreading the wisdom of Yoga and the Ancient Egyptian mystical traditions. Further, he is the spiritual leader and head priest of the Per Aset or Temple of Aset, based in Miami, Florida. Thus, as a scholar, Dr. Muata Ashby is a teacher, lecturer and researcher. However, as a spiritual leader, his title is *Sebai,* which means Spiritual Preceptor.

Sebai Dr. Ashby began his research into the spiritual philosophy of Ancient Africa (Egypt) and India and noticed correlations in the culture and arts of the two countries. This was the catalyst for a successful book series on the subject called "Egyptian Yoga". Now he has created a series of musical compositions which explore this unique area of music from ancient Egypt and its connection to world music.

Who is Hemt Neter Dr. Karen Vijaya Clarke-Ashby?

Karen Clarke-Ashby (Seba Dja) is a Kamitan (Kamitan) priestess, and an independent researcher, practitioner and teacher of Sema (Smai) Tawi (Kamitan) and Indian Integral Yoga Systems, a Doctor of Veterinary Medicine, a Pastoral Spiritual Counselor, a Pastoral Health and Nutrition Counselor, and a Sema (Smai) Tawi Life-style Consultant." Dr. Ashby has engaged in post-graduate research in advanced Jnana, Bhakti, Karma, Raja and Kundalini Yogas at the Sema Institute of Yoga and Yoga Research Foundation, and has also worked extensively with her husband and spiritual partner, Dr. Muata Ashby, author of the Egyptian Yoga Book Series, editing many of these books, as well as studying, writing and lecturing in the area of Kamitan Yoga and Spirituality. She is a certified Tjef Neteru Sema Paut (Kamitan Yoga Exercise system) and Indian Hatha Yoga Exercise instructor, the Coordinator and Instructor for the Level 1 Teacher Certification Tjef Neteru Sema Training programs, and a teacher of health and stress management applications of the Yoga / Sema Tawi systems for modern society, based on the Kamitan and/or Indian yogic principles. Also, she is the co-author of "The Egyptian Yoga Exercise Workout Book," a contributing author for "The Kamitan Diet, Food for Body, Mind and Soul," author of the soon to be released, "Yoga Mystic Metaphors for Enlightenment."

Hetep -Peace be with you!

Seba Muata Ashby & Karen Ashby

TABLE OF CONTENTS

Sema Institute of Yoga 3
About the Author 4
PART 1: INTRODUCTION 8
Where Was Shetaut Neter Practiced in Ancient Times? 11
   The Term Kamit (Qamit, Kamit, Kamit) and Its Relation to Nubia and the term "Black" 11
Who Was the Founder of Neterianism? 14
      Khepri and the Creation Myth 15
Who and What Were the Ancient Kamitans and Nubians? 19
   The Relationship between Nubia and Egypt 20
      The Nubian Gods and Goddesses in the Kamitan Paut 22
   The Importance of Religion 27
When Was Shetaut Neter First Practiced? 29
   A Most Ancient Tradition 32
      The Stellar Symbolism related to the Pole Star and the Opening of the mouth and Eyes
      Ceremony in Ancient Egypt 32
      Opening of the Mouth with the Imperishable Stars 38
      Basic Timeline of Kamitan History 42
What is Shetaut Neter? 43
      Etymology of the term Shetaut Neter 44
      Who is Neter? 45
      Who Are the Neterians? 45
      What is the Essential Philosophy of Shetaut Neter? 46
   The Pursuit of Happiness 47
   Forgiveness, Hope, Redemption and Healing the Errors of the Past To Become Free from the
   Past 48
   What is The True Purpose of Life? 52
      The Kamitan (Neterian) philosophy of teaching: 53
   The Philosophy of the Afterlife 54
   Nehast: The Great Spiritual Awakening 56
   Six Main Traditions of *Shetaut Neter* 57
   Anthropomorphic and Zoomorphic iconography in Neterian Religion 60
      The Stages of African Religion 63
      Sacred Scriptures of Shetaut Neter 68
Part 2: The 4 Neterian Principles: Introduction to Neterian Spirituality 69
      Great Truth #1: 70
      Great truth #2: 73
      Great Truth # 3 74
      Great Truth #4: 75
   The Creation of The Universe 78
      The Memphite Tradition 80
      The Memphite Tradition 80
      The Theban Tradition 81
      The Goddess Tradition 82
      THE FIRST KING AND QUEEN OF KAMIT AND THE ASARIAN RESURRECTION
      MYTH TO BE KNOWN BY ALL NETERIAN FOLLOWERS 83

- The Importance of the Asarian Resurrection Myth and its Teaching 86
- The Neterian Eucharist 88
- The Temples of Asar 88
- Opening the Mouth 88
- The Aton Tradition 89
- The Fundamental Principles of Shetaut Neter 90
  - Basic Tenets of Neterian Religion 90
  - The Great Awakening of Neterian Religion 90
  - The Oneness of Humanity 90
  - One God for All Human Beings 90
- How to Become a Qualified Aspirant 97
  - Devotional Worship of the Divine 99
  - Sema Tawi Philosophy 106
  - Tjef Neteru Sema Paut Ritual Postures of Enlightenment 108
- The Serpent Power: The Most Ancient Discipline 111
  - History of The Serpent Power and Yoga of Life Force Development for Spiritual Enlightenment in Ancient Egypt 111

PART 3: How to Be a Disciple of Shetaut Neter: Egyptian-African Mysteries? 113
- What Are The Disciplines of Shedy? 113
- Yoga in Ancient Egypt 114
- What is Egyptian Yoga? 114
  - The Term "Egyptian Yoga" and The Philosophy Behind It 114
- The Discipline of Wisdom: Listening to the Teachings 116
- The Discipline of Devotion and Love 117
- The Discipline of Meditation 118
- The Discipline of Righteous Action 119
  - Importance of Maat Philosophy 119
  - Karma and Reincarnation 123
- The Discipline of Neterian Tantric Philosophy 125
- The Prt M Hru and The Mysteries of Life and Death 126
  - Mystery Of The Elements of the Human Personality 126
    - (1) THE KHU or AKHU: 127
    - (2) THE BA: 127
    - (3) THE SAHU: 128
    - (4) THE KHAIBIT: 128
    - (5) THE AB: 128
    - (6) THE SEKHEM: 129
    - (7) The KA: 129
    - (8) THE REN: 129
    - (9) THE KHAT: 130
  - More Mystical Implications of Name and Word 130
    - The Importance of the Spiritual Name 130
    - The Prt M Hru and The Readings for the Guidance of the Dying Person and their Relatives 131
    - The Body of the Deceased, the Metaphysics of the Astral Plane and Transcending Beyond 132
    - Architecture of Heaven, Hell and the Transcendental Realms 134
    - The Amenta, The Beautiful West 135

Part 4: Initiation Into Shetaut Neter	136
The Ancient Egyptian Precepts of Initiatic Education	136
The Importance of Good Association	136
How to Approach a Spiritual Preceptor	137
The Tradition of Initiation	**140**
Initiation With a Spiritual Preceptor	142
What are You Being Initiated Into?	142
What is the Philosophy of Shems?	143
INDEX	145
Other Books by Muata Ashby	151

Music Based on the Prt M Hru and other Kamitan Texts......**Error! Bookmark not defined.**

PART 1: INTRODUCTION

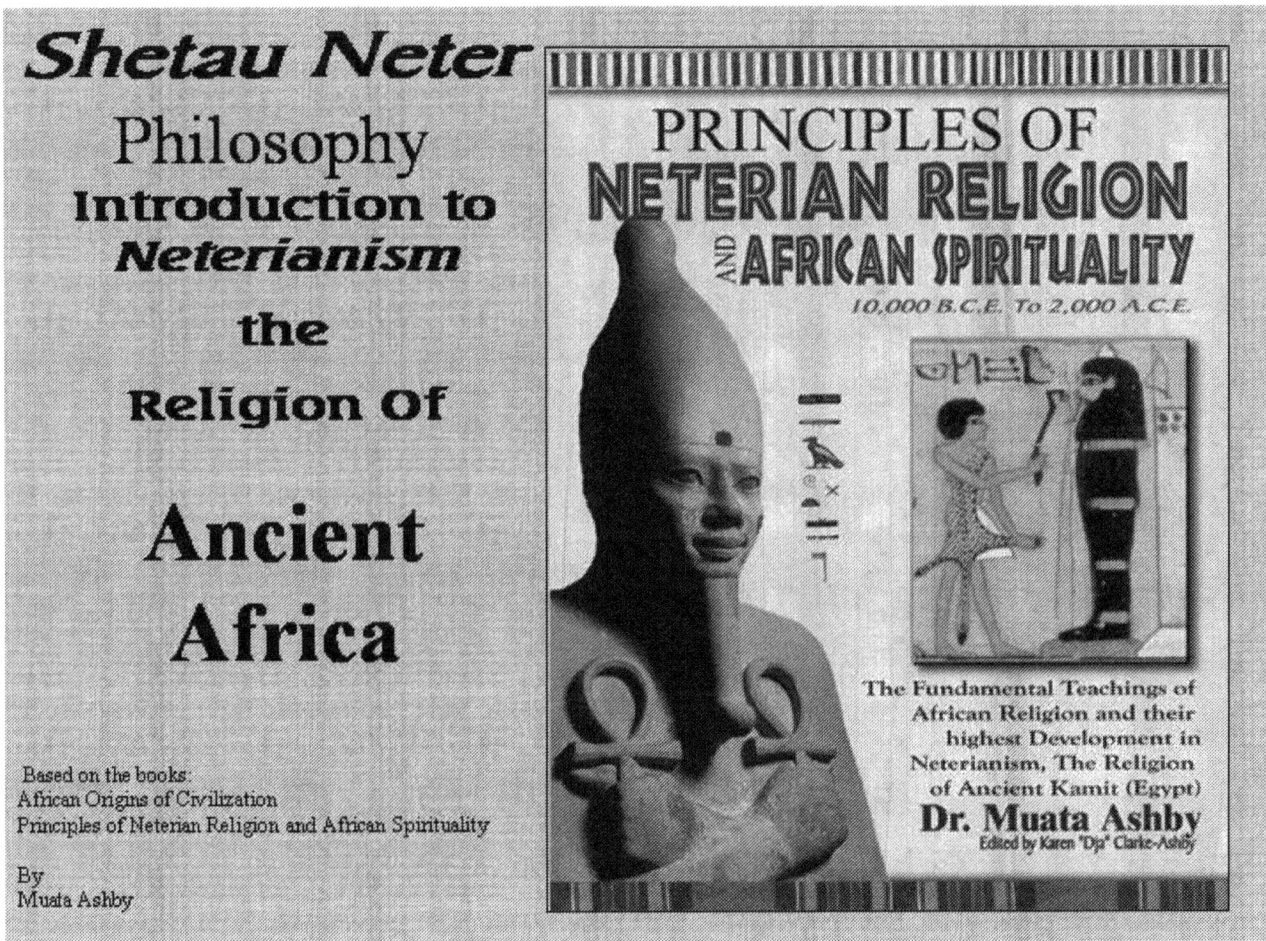

(Slide #1)

Shetaut Neter is the name or ancient African term that most likely you have heard translated as the "Egyptian Mysteries." You probably know that the Egyptian Mysteries is something that was practiced an Kamit (ancient Egypt). In general (orthodox) western culture, it is often related as something mysterious, something occult, something shrouded in history, in darkness. People are oftentimes told that they should shy away from it or that they should fear it. This is one of the great hoaxes that have been perpetrated on ancient Egyptian spirituality and African Culture. The importance of African philosophy is not only for African culture in Africa, but African Culture outside of Africa, the latter relating to all humanity in the larger sense. Most people in the world are following spiritual traditions and philosophies in ways that are leading them into ignorance, darkness, stress and strife. Those are not humanistic traditions, traditions that are based on truth and universal spirituality. We need to rectify this. Firstly, this philosophy is for all people. Our own Kamitan scriptures state this point. Shetaut Neter (The Egyptian Mysteries) is a universal teaching to improve life, and promote peace and prosperity for all. All people are part of the human family, spiritually and physically. Genetics has shown that all human beings, regardless of if one's ancestry is from Africa, Asia, Europe or the Americas in more recent times, all originated from Africa. Therefore, all human beings are Africans, sharing in the legacy and heritage of Africa. This fact was well recognized in ancient times. Therefore, Neterianism does not support any form of racism, sexism or notion of superiority of any individual, gender or group of humans being over another.[i]

Egyptian Mysteries Volume 1: Principles of Shetaut Neter

So, this study is to serve as an introduction to Neterian religion and African spirituality and culture. It will be presenting information not previously addressed in detail in our previous books, and specifically will be addressing the Principles to Neterian Religion and African Spirituality.

Who are we?
Not a church-Not a cult-Not New Age-Not Masons, etc
We are an Kamitan-African Religion

Sema Institute	Temple of Shetaut Neter-Aset
• Sema University • Bachelor Degree Program • Book store • Audio tapes • Video	• Priesthood • Spiritual counseling • Initiations • Spiritual worship programs

(Slide #2)

Lets begin here, with "Who are we?" What is the Sema Institute all about? What is Neterianism? Is it a philosophy, a school, a cult, or a religious program? What is it?

If you are going to the class to study Neterian philosophy under, you go out into the street and someone asks you, "What are you up to? You go to this place for a couple of hours. What are you doing over there? Something mysterious? Something wild? Or something crazy? What is it that you are doing? What are you going to tell them; I am in a cult? Or I am doing some secret philosophy.

Neterianism is not a church. Neterianism is not a cult. Neterianism is not New Age spirituality…trying to put all the spirits together and trying to say "Oh, we are all one". New Age spirituality is really a reaction to the oppression of Orthodox Religion, an attempt to move away from religion all together. Thus, it is not an authentic spiritual movement, but in a sense, more like a new form of limited religious practice.

True religion (authentic spiritual movement) is a process that leads you through three steps: myth, ritual and mysticism. If one's religion does not have these three steps, then one is not practicing true religion. If a religion has a myth and its followers practice ritual(s) relating to that myth, if that is the extent of the religion, only containing dogmas and stories in which its followers must have faith, then that religion is not reaching a

Egyptian Mysteries Volume 1: Principles of Shetaut Neter

mystical level of oneness with all creation. Such a religion stays at the level of ritual, and leads to conflict with other religions that have different rituals...each fighting with the other over which is the holiest and or true ritual, and which is the only true myth. This is a source of strife between religions.

Practicing Neterianism means that one is practicing Kamitan African Religion. That is how you can define it. There are two branches to our organization. One is the Sema Institute. Under this branch we have Sema University, where we now have an Associate Degree program for advanced education, the bookstore, audio tapes, video tapes...everything that relates to the academic-educational aspect of the Sema Institute.

Secondly, we have the Temple of Shetaut Neter/ Temple of Aset. This includes everything related to priesthood, spiritual counseling, initiations, and spiritual worship programs. I want you to understand it this way, so that you can realize that the teaching can be approached as a philosophy of life, a spiritual philosophy or as a religion, a spiritual religious process. So when someone asks you, what you are practicing, how will you answer? What would a person practicing Yoruba religion say if asked this question? What would a person practicing Voodum say if asked this question? They would respond, "I am practicing African Religion" or "I am practicing Yoruba." Thus, if you choose to join the practice, you can say I am practicing Neterianism.

It is very important for you to realize this term "Shetaut Neter" comes directly from the scriptures of Ancient Africa...from the Medu Neter itself. It is not a made up term. It is not a fabricated term for modern times. It is the actual term.

The term Neterianism is derived from the term Shetaut Neter. Neterianism means that it relates to the Neter. And who is the Neter? We will discuss this shortly.

In ancient times, Shetaut Neter was practiced in the land that is currently in modern times called "Egypt," but the African name is "Kamit."

However, it must be clearly understood that in Neterian Theology there are two kinds of Mysteries, the lower and the higher. The lower Mysteries are worldly, practical branches of learning, the areas that help human beings to improve their lives and learn about the world around them. The lower mysteries offer limited insight because they only use physical, empirical means for the researches. Examples of the lower mysteries include mechanics, engineering, astronomy, literature, mathematics, physiology, etc. The higher Mysteries are the disciplines or sciences that promote insight into the nature of self and the revelation of the Mysteries of life, the Mysteries of the universe. The higher Mysteries answer questions such as "Who am I? Where did I come from? Why am I here? What is life? What or who is God?," etc. This book does not deal with the lower mysteries. However, certain knowledge of the lower Mysteries is necessary to pursue the higher Mysteries. One could not study the Mysteries if one could not understand a certain level of mathematics, language, etc.; a certain level of maturity, stability and intellectual capacity are necessary to pursue higher spiritual attainment, and the lower Mysteries provide that foundation. By being proficient in one of the lower Mysteries, you can get a reasonably well paying job, and be pay your bills. Then you can also to afford to buy spiritual books, to read them and then reflect on their meaning. Stability and financial capacity gained from being proficient in the lower Mysteries allows you to think without the pressure of financial burdens, purchase the materials necessary for the practice, visit spiritual centers, confer with spiritual teachers, etc. So this book is for those who are ready and able to pursue the higher Mysteries of life, the mystical, metaphysical disciplines that lead to attaining transcendental consciousness, enlightenment, the Great Spiritual Awakening.

Where Was Shetaut Neter Practiced in Ancient Times?

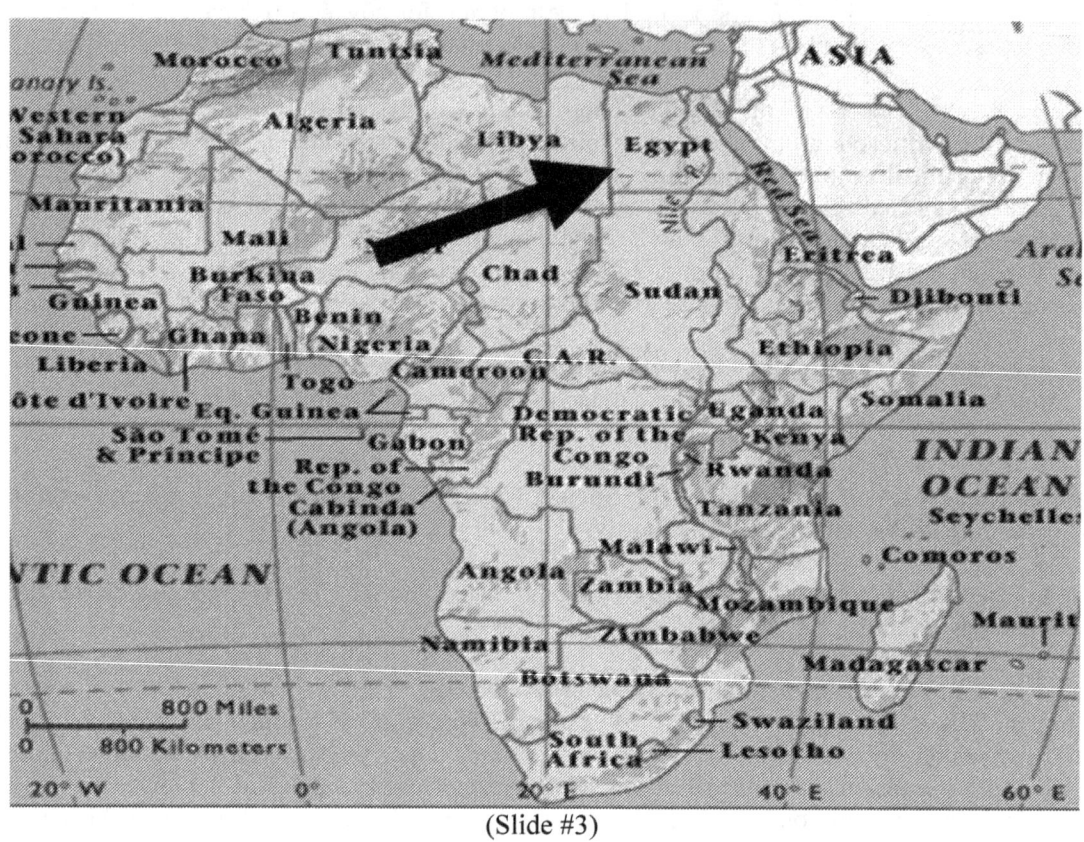

(Slide #3)

In ancient times Neterianism, was practice in the land of Kamit and the land of Kush. Kamit is located in the Northeastern corner of Africa. A civilization began to appear along the Nile River more than 12,000 years ago; this civilization became the Kamitan society. The Kamitan themselves say that they came from the south, from the land of Kush, originally as colonists.

The Term Kamit (Qamit, Kamit, Kamit) and Its Relation to Nubia and the term "Black"

In ancient times, the land of Kush was known to the ancient Greeks as Ethiopia. Today it is called Sudan. As we will see, the terms "Ethiopia," "Nubia," "Kush" and "Sudan" all refer to "black land" and/or the "land of the blacks." In the same manner we find that the name of Egypt which was used by the Ancient Egyptians also means "black land." The hieroglyphs below reveal the Ancient Egyptian meaning of the words related to the name of their land. It is clear that the meaning of the word Qamit is equivalent to the word Kush as far as they relate to "black land" and that they also refer to a differentiation in geographical location, i.e. Kush is the "black land of the south" and Qamit is the "black land of the north." Both terms denote the primary quality that defines Africa, "black" or "Blackness" (referring to the land and its people). The quality of blackness and the consonantal sound of K or Q as well as the reference to the land are all aspects of commonality between the Ancient Kushitic and Kamitan terms.

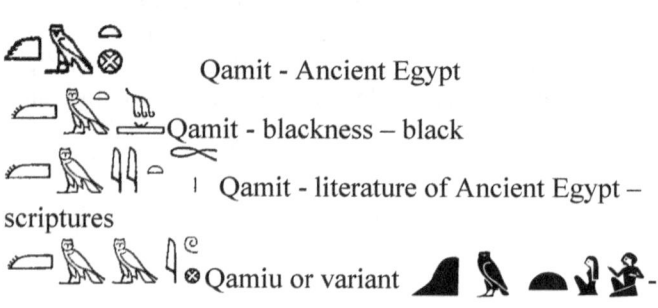

Ancient Egyptians-people of the black land.

Egyptian Mysteries Volume 1: Principles of Shetaut Neter

How to understand the country of Egypt and Ethiopia

The Terms "Ethiopia," "Nubia," "Kush" and "Sudan"

The term "Ethiopian," "Nubian," and "Kushite" all relate to the same peoples who lived south of Egypt. In modern times, the land which was once known as Nubia ("Land of Gold"), is currently known as the Sudan, and the land even further south and east towards the coast of east Africa is referred to as Ethiopia (see map).

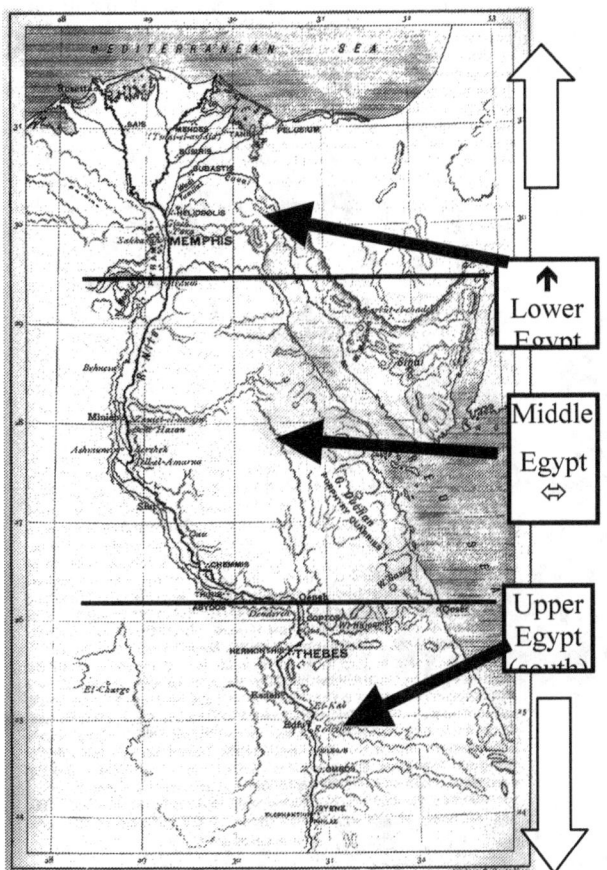

Recent research has shown that the modern Nubian word *kiji* means "fertile land, dark gray mud, silt, or black land." Since the sound of this word is close to the Ancient Egyptian name Kish or Kush, referring to the land south of Egypt, it is believed that the name Kush also meant "the land of dark silt" or "the black land." Kush was the Ancient Egyptian name for Nubia. Nubia, the black land, is the Sudan of today. Sudan is an Arabic translation of *sûd* which is the plural form of aswad, which means "black," and ân which means "of the." So, Sudan means "of the blacks." In the modern Nubian language, nugud means "black." Also, nuger, nugur, and nubi mean "black" as well. All of this indicates that the words Kush, Nubia, and Sudan all mean the same thing — the "black land" and/or the "land of the blacks."[iii] So, the differences between the term Kush and the term Kam (Qamit, Kamit, Kemit - name for Ancient Egypt (previously described) in the Ancient Egyptian language) relate more to the same meaning but different geographical locations.

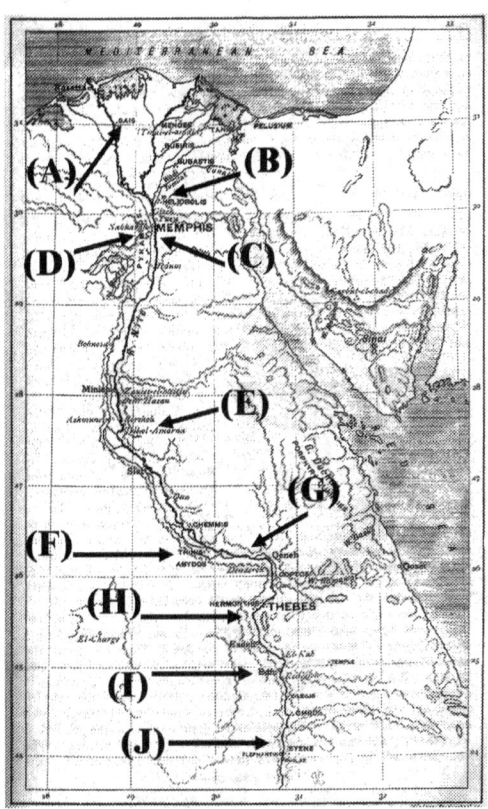

Above- The Land of Ancient Egypt-Nile Valley - The cities wherein the theology of the Trinity of Amun-Ra-Ptah was developed were: A- Sais (temple of Net), B- Anu (Heliopolis-temple of Ra), C-Men-nefer or Hetkaptah (Memphis, temple of Ptah), and D- Sakkara (Pyramid Texts), E- Akhet-Aton (City of Akhnaton, temple of Aton), F- Abdu (temple of Asar)-Greek Abydos, G- Denderah (temple of Hetheru), H- Waset (Thebes, temple of Amun), I- Edfu (temple of Heru), J- Philae (temple of Aset). The cities wherein the theology of the Trinity of Asar-Aset-Heru was developed were Anu, Abdu, Philae, Denderah and Edfu.

The flow of the Nile brought annual floods to the Nile Valley and this provided irrigation and new soil nutrients every year that allowed for regular crops when worked on time. This regularity and balance of nature inspired the population to adopt a culture of order and duty based on cosmic order: Maat. This idea extends to the understanding of Divine justice and reciprocity. So if work is performed on time and in cooperation with nature, there will be order, balance and peace as well as prosperity in life.

Egyptian Mysteries Volume 1: Principles of Shetaut Neter

Kamit (Egypt) is located in the north-eastern corner of the continent of Africa. It is composed of towns along the banks of the Hapi (Nile River). In the north there is the Nile Delta region where the river contacts the Mediterranean Sea. This part is referred to as the North or Lower Egypt, "lower," because that is the lowest elevation and the river flows from south to north. The middle of the country is referred to as Middle Egypt. The south is referred to as Upper Egypt because it is the higher elevation and the river flows from there to the north. The south is the older region of the dynastic civilization and the middle and north are later.

So the original Ancient Egyptians, ancient Africans, were people of African descent, related to the people of Kush. Thus, Neterianism (Shetaut Neter) is not a religion that was brought into Africa from Asia Minor, Europe or from any place else. The Shetaut Neter tradition is an indigenous African Religion. It is the very beginning…the first religion.

The Sphinx and its contemporary architecture throughout Kamit give us the earliest history, the earliest recorded evidence of the practice of religion anywhere in the world. The Sphinx has now been proven to be the earliest example of the practice of religion in human history, 10,000 BCE.

The next religion appears in India at about 2,500 to 3,000 BCE. We have shown in the book *African Origins* that there was a direct relationship between the Indians and the Ancient Egyptians/Ancient Africans, so much so that the basic tenants of Hinduism and Buddhism can be directly correlated to Shetaut Neter.

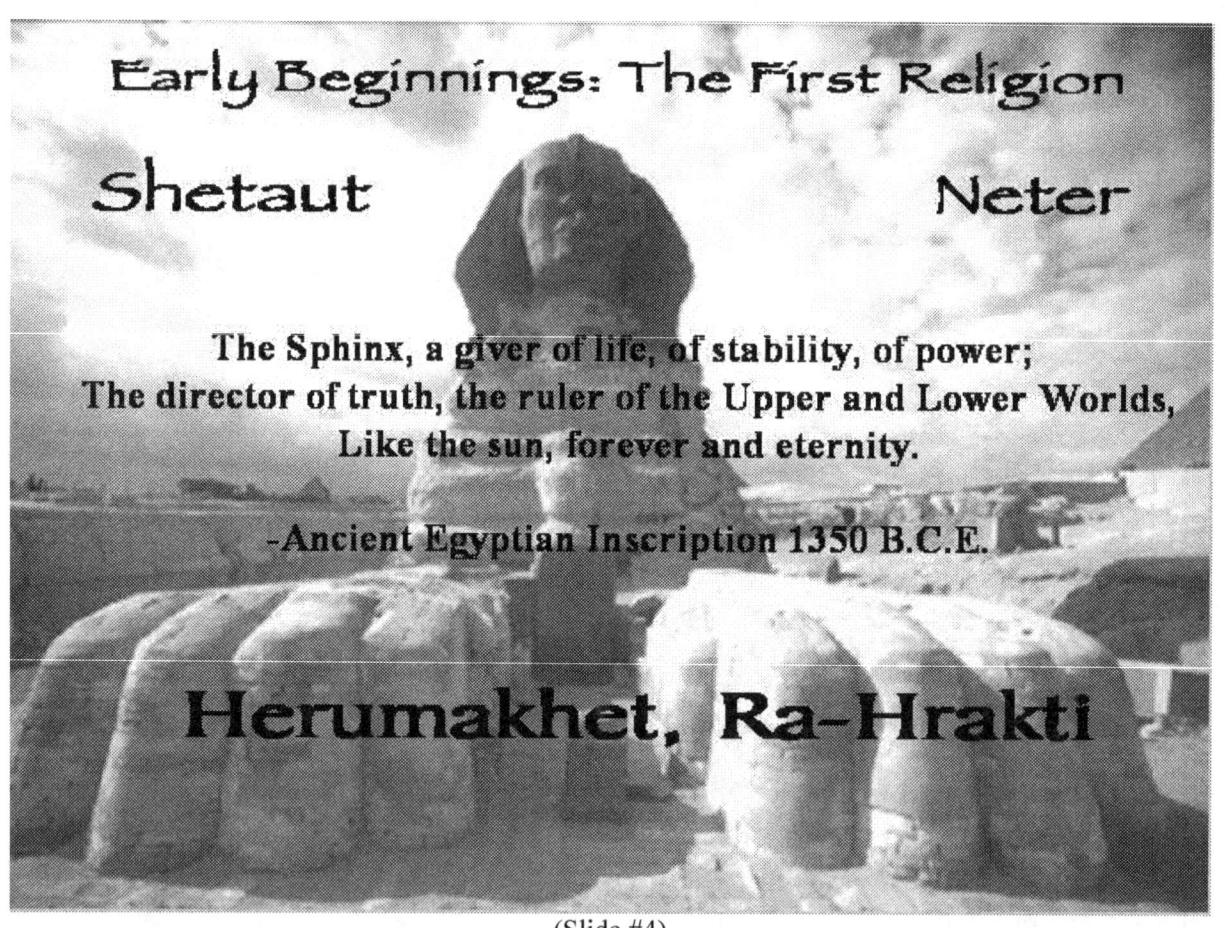

(Slide #4)

The following quote was written about the Sphinx:

> "The Sphinx, the giver of life, of stability, of power, the director of truth, the ruler of the Upper and Lower worlds, like the sun, forever and eternity."

Another misconception that is pervasive is that we don't know anything about the Sphinx. First of all, *Herumakhet*, is the correct name, not Sphinx. Sphinx is the Greek term. Herumakhet means Heru in the Horizon. Another Ancient Kamitan name for the Sphinx is Harakti.

These names or these words, especially Ra Harakti, are used extensively in the Pyramid Text, the earliest spiritual text in the world. So we have extensive knowledge about the Sphinx and the Neterian philosophy.

Note the headdress on Herumakhet. The headdress is basically a reproduction or a metaphor for a lion's mane. The lion represents the astronomical symbol of Leo that was in the procession of the Equinoxes at the time of the creation of the Sphinx, which is 10,000 BCE. This correlates to geological evidence about the age of Harakti.

Who Was the Founder of Neterianism?

KHPR

One of the most important questions in life for followers of any religion is who started it? In order to understand who founded Neterianism, the teaching of Shetaut Neter, we must also understand the origins of creation. In the sacred scriptures of Shetaut Neter we are told that Creation is a cycle. That is, that Creation occurs cyclically. God brings creation into existence and then dissolves it again.

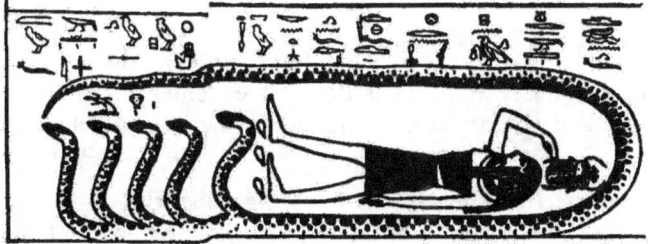

The Sun-god of night surrounded by the five-headed serpent of 'Many Faces'. On his head is the beetle of Khepri the the rising sun of the following day.

The current cycle of Creation began around the year 36,000 B.C.E. In the beginning there was nothing more than a watery mass, a primeval ocean, called Nun. Nun is the body of Khepri. Prior to the creation, Khepri remained in a recumbent posture. He rested on the back of the great serpent *Asha-hrau* ("many faces"). From that Nun the Divine Spirit arose by stimulating Asha-hrau to move and churn the ocean. Then he named himself Khepri, Creator.

Khepri called out his own name and *dchn* – vibrations were infused in the ocean and waves vere formed. Just as there are many waves in the ocean with many shapes and sizes, the objects of the world came into being in the form of elements, Ra (fire), Shu (air-space), Tefnut (water), Geb (earth), Nut (ether). Everything in creation emanates from the Nun or primordial ocean, and expresses in the form of elements in succeeding levels of denseness. These elements also manifest in the form of the opposites of Creation (man-woman, up-down, white-black) which appear to be exclusive and separate from each other, but which are in reality complements to each other.

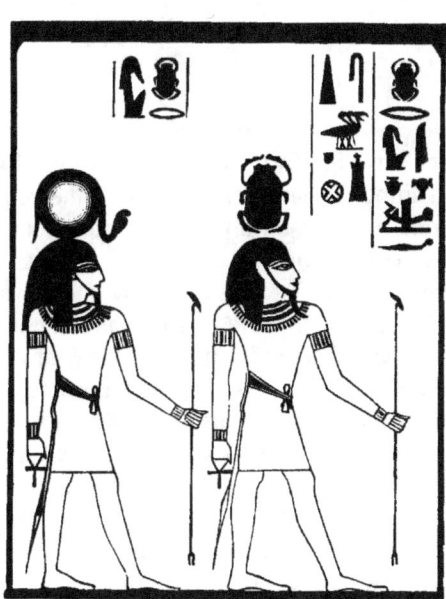

ABOVE: LORD KHEPRI, FOUNDER OF NETERIANISM

Khepri and the Creation Myth

Khepri congealed the Nun, his own body, into all the forms of Creation. The first spot that was congealed from the Nun is called ◯◯◯ *Benben*, the first place, the Ben-Ben dot, •, of Creation. That dot is the center point in the symbol of Khepr-Ra ☉. That dot is the very point at the top of the Pyramid 🦉▽△ *mr*- Obelisk, 〰️▯ *tekhnu*. The pyramid-obelisk symbolizes the mound that formed from that initial spot. Khepri sat atop the hill of Creation and all solid ground took form underneath him.

Khepri then bought forth Creation by emerging in a boat. The Nun waters lifted him and his boat up with his great arms. He brought nine divinities with him in that boat, lesser gods and goddesses, to help him sustain the Creation and lead human beings on the righteous path to life and spiritual enlightenment.

Having created Creation, Khepri now sails the ocean, which has now become Creation itself, with his divinities, on the divine boat. Khepri-Ra and the *pauti*, Company of gods and goddesses, travels in the Boat of Millions of Years, which traverses the heavens, and thereby sustains creation through the wake of the boat that sends ripples (vibrations) throughout Creation.

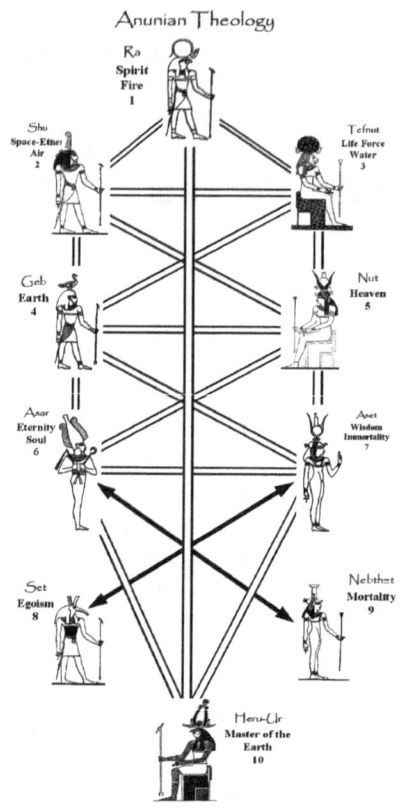

The act of "Sailing" signifies the motion in creation. Motion implies that events occur in the realm of time and space relative to each other, thus, the phenomenal universe comes into existence as a mass of moving essence we call the elements. Prior to this motion, there was the primeval state of being without any form and without existence in time or space. The gods and goddesses of the boat form the court of Kheper-Ra. As Ra, the Supreme Being governed the earth for many thousands of years. He created the world, the planets, the stars and the galaxies; he also created animals, as well as men and women. In the beginning, men and women revered the Divine, but after living for a very long time, they began to take Ra for granted. They became arrogant and vain. Ra sent his daughter, Hetheru, to punish them, but she forgot her way and became lost in the world. Then He left for his abode in heaven and gave the earthly throne to his son Shu, and daughter, Tefnut. After a long period of time, they turned over the throne to their children, Geb and Nut. After some time again, Geb and Nut gave the throne to their children, Asar and Aset, and so on in a line of succession throughout history, down to the Pharaohs of Kamit.

Egyptian Mysteries Volume 1: Principles of Shetaut Neter

Lord Khepri manifests as Neberdjer, "All-encompassing Divinity." Aspirants are to say:

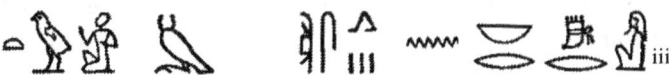iii

tu-a m shems n Neberdjer

*"I am a follower of Neberdjer*iv

er sesh n Kheperu

in accordance with the writings of Lord Kheperu"

So, the Shetaut Neter "Mystery teachings" were originally given by the Creator, Khepri. In this capacity he is known as  *Shetaut Kheperu*, "hidden Creator of forms." Lord Djehuti codified these Mystery teachings into the hieroglyphic texts, and these teachings were passed down to succeeding generations of divinities, sages and priests and priestesses throughout history.

So Lord Khepri imparted his knowledge to the divinities, and especially to his son Djehuti. Thus, Lord Khepri, the Self Created Divinity, is the founder of Shetaut Neter. The codifier was his first main disciple, Djehuti. Djehuti has the body of a man and the head of an Ibis bird. He also has another form as a baboon. The teaching that Lord Khepri gave to Djehuti became known as *Shetitu* and it was conveyed through the *Medu Neter* (hieroglyphic texts).

"Medu Neter"

The teachings of the Neterian Traditions are conveyed in the scriptures of the Neterian Traditions.

Above: A section from the pyramid of Teti in Sakkara Egypt, known as the "Pyramid Texts" (Early Dynastic Period) showing the cross

The Medu Neter was used through all periods by priests and priestesses – mostly in monumental inscriptions such as the Pyramid texts, Obelisks, temple inscriptions, etc. – since Pre-Dynastic times. It is the earliest form of writing in known history.

Thus, these Shetaut (mysteries- rituals, wisdom, philosophy) about the Neter (Supreme Being) are related in the writings of the hidden teaching. And those writings are referred to as *Medu Neter* or "Divine Speech," the writings of the god Djehuti (Ancient Egyptian god of the divine word). *Medu Neter* also generally refers to any Kamitan hieroglyphic texts or inscriptions. The term Medu Neter makes use of a special hieroglyph, which means "*medu*" or "staff - walking stick-speech." This means that speech is the support for the Divine,. Thus, just as the staff supports an elderly person, the hieroglyphic writing (the word) is a prop or support (staff) which sustains the Divine in the realm of time and space. That is, these Divine writings (*Medu Neter*) contain the wisdom which enlightens us about the Divine, *Shetaut Neter*. If *Shetitu* is mastered through the study of the Medu Neter then the spiritual aspirant becomes Maakheru or true of thought, word and deed, that is, purified in body, mind and soul. The symbol medu is static while the symbol of Kheru is dynamic.

The term Maakheru uses the glyph kheru, which is a rudder – oar (rowing), and a symbol of voice, meaning that purification occurs through the righteous movement of the word, when it is used (rowing-movement) to promote Maat (virtue, order, peace, harmony and truth). So Medu Neter is the potential word and Maa kheru is the perfected word.

The hieroglyphic texts (Medu Neter) become useful (Maakheru) in the process of religion when they are used as ▦ *hekau* - the Ancient Egyptian "Words of Power." They are to be ▦ *Hesi*, chanted and ▦ *Shmai*- sung, and thereby one performs ▦ or ▦ *Dua* or adoration of the Divine. The divine word allows the speaker to control the gods and goddesses, who actually are the cosmic forces in Creation. Human beings are a higher order beings, and they can attain this higher state of consciousness if they learn about the nature of the universe and elevate themselves through virtue and wisdom.

Above: Lord Djehuti imparted the teaching he learned from Khepri to goddess Hetheru (here in the form of a cow goddess). She became lost in the world and forgot her true identity. He showed her how to discover her true Self, how to know herself and how to find her way back to heaven, to her father Ra. Here Djehuti is shown presenting to Hetheru, the healed right eye of Ra, her true essence.

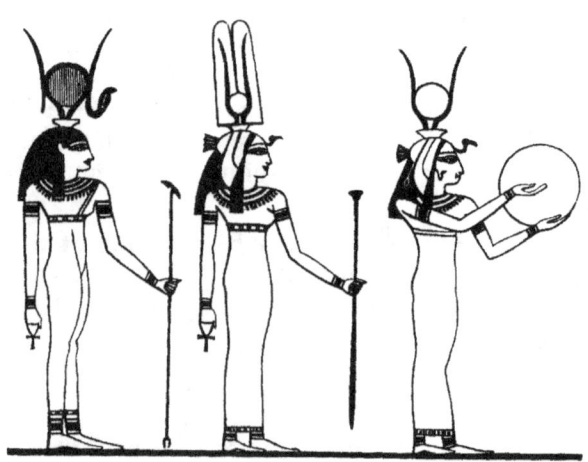

Above: Hetheru as Queen

Lord Khep-Ra knew that human beings needed guidance, so he sent his great grandchildren, Asar and Aset, to be teachers and role models for human beings on earth. Lord Djehuti also imparted the hidden knowledge of life to Aset and Asar, so that they would lead people on earth in a righteous manner, showing them the path of peace, prosperity and spiritual enlightenment. Asar and Aset established the Shetaut Neter, "Divine Mysteries," ritual worship and Ancient Egyptian religion. When human beings become too involved in the world they forget their true nature, and so the Temple, ▦ *Het Neter* {House of the Divinity {God(dess)}-Temple}, was created, where the pressure of the world can be relieved, and an association with something other than the worldly perspective (i.e., with Divinity) can occur.

Temple of Aset, Egypt, Africa

Such a place and its teaching are needed so that the mind can become aware of higher possibilities and turn away from ▦ *umt-ab-* "mental dullness" due to ▦ *Khemn*, "ignorance," and be led to ▦ *Nehast* –"Resurrection, spiritual awakening," ▦ *Akhu*, "enlightenment" and so that human beings may become ▦ *Sheps-* "nobility, honor, venerable-ness, honored ancestors."

Egyptian Mysteries Volume 1: Principles of Shetaut Neter

Above: *Aset nurses baby Heru*

So, Aset learned the Mystery teachings from Lord Djehuti. Aset is the ancient African prototype of the mother and child which is popular all over Africa, and also in Christian and Indian iconography with the birth of Jesus and Krishna, respectively. The mother is the first teacher. Aset not only raised Heru, but also initiated him into the mysteries of life and creation, with the teaching she learned from Djehuti and Khepri, in order to enlighten him and make him strong for the battle of life.

Heru is the redeemer, the challenger, the one who stands up for his father, Asar, and liberates him from the imprisonment of death. Heru represents spiritual aspiration and success in the spiritual path. Heru reestablishes order after defeating the evil Set, and takes the throne of Kamit. In his form as Heru Behdet, Heru is a warrior. He fights for truth, justice and freedom for all.

Heru, the redeemer, the warrior, the greatest advocate of Asar (the soul) and triumphant aspirant is the one who leads the aspirant to the initiation hall. As seen above, Heru is often the one shown leading the aspirant by the hand, into the inner shrine. In rituals, the priest wears a Heru mask in the context of a ritual theatrical ceremony of the temple that is meant to awaken the glory of the Neterian teaching in the heart of the aspirant.

From the Prt M Hru (Book of the Dead) Chapter 4: Ani and his wife worship Lord Khepri in his boat.

Who and What Were the Ancient Kamitans and Nubians?

(Slide #5) Slide of Tomb Painting from Tomb of Huy

"And upon his return to Greece, they gathered around and asked, "tell us about this great land of the Blacks called Ethiopia." And Herodotus said, "There are two great Ethiopian nations, one in Sind (India) and the other in Egypt."

Recorded by Egyptian high priest *Manetho* (300 B.C.)
also Recorded by *Diodorus* (Greek historian 100 B.C.)

Who were the Ancient Egyptians, and what did they look like? And why should we study about them? In order to understand Kamit, it is necessary to understand the origin of the ancient Kamitans in the land of Kush, (Nubia) and their relation to the other peoples of Africa. In the slide the four men in the front are Ancient Egyptians; above two in the rear are Nubians. The most important aspect of this slide is that you can see the that hue of skin of both groups is exactly the same... i.e., there is no difference. There is much more information about this given in the book *African Origins*.

This slide came from a tomb painting from one of the early European Explorers who opened the tomb in the early 1800's, before there was photography. He made this painting. And if you realize that, if anyone should have an agenda for showing things other than how they appeared, it should have been some of the early Egyptologists, but they did not do that. That came mostly from the later Egyptologists. If you go to the tomb were this picture comes from now, it is much degraded because of pollution and vandalism.

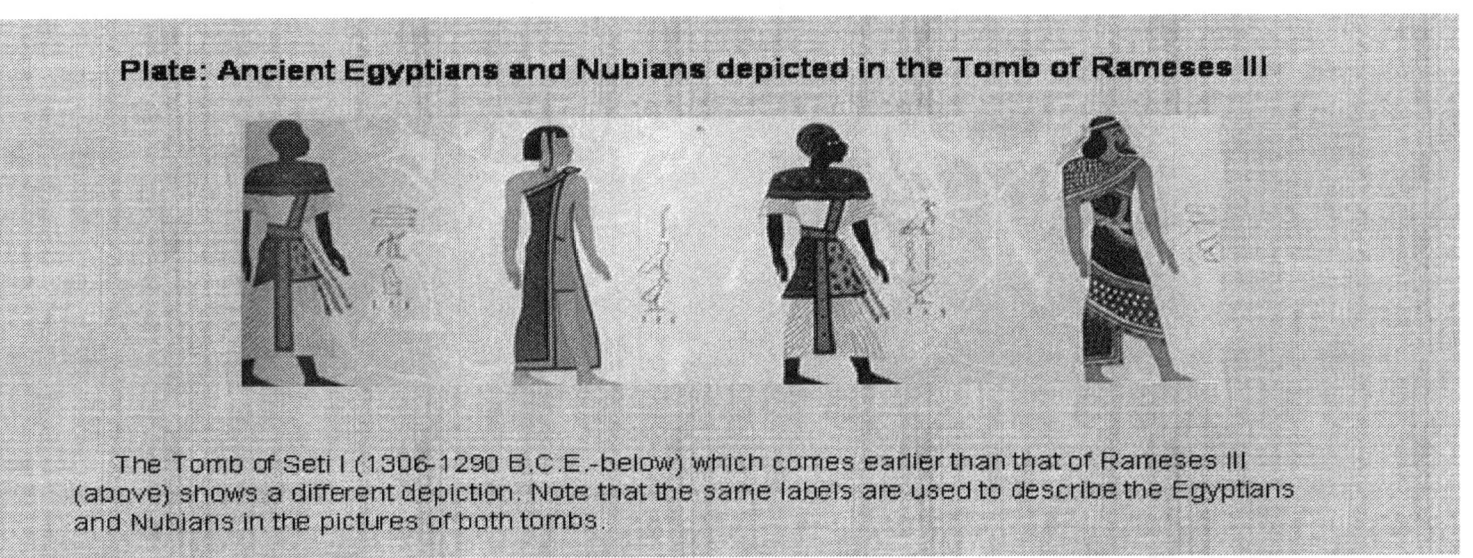

(Slide #6)

The slide above comes from the Tomb of Rameses III. It is important because it shows that the ancient Egyptians recognized the different skin colorations of other peoples in ancient times and saw themselves as being equal to the Nubians. Also it shows that there was a concept of ethnicity, but not racism. This is very important, because it has lessons for present day society. It shows that the ancient Africans had a higher culture and understanding of humanity than present day so called advanced civilization.

The Relationship between Nubia and Egypt

Diodorus Siculus (Greek Historian) writes in the time of Augustus (first century B.C.):

"They also say that the Egyptians are colonists sent out by the Ethiopians, Asar having been the leader of the colony. For, speaking generally, what is now Egypt, they maintain, was not land, but sea, when in the beginning the universe was being formed; afterwards, however, as the Nile during the times of its inundation carried down the mud from Ethiopia, land was gradually built up from the deposit...And the larger parts of the customs of the Egyptians are, they hold, Ethiopian, the colonists still preserving their ancient manners."

The situation between Ancient Egypt and Nubia may be likened to that of England and the United States. Far from being a racial issue, it so happened that the child, Kamit, grew to such stature and glory, that it surpassed the parent. Due to certain cultural differences that developed between the countries, there was a vying over control of trade in Africa, just as two siblings quarrel over clothing or jewelry. The true state of affairs between the two countries became evident when Kamit was besieged and occupied by foreign conquerors. The Nubians lent their support as allies, if not as family members coming to the rescue of kin in trouble, to restore Kamit to her former glory in the Late Period of Kamitan history.

At around 2000 B.C.E., the Nubian Kingdom of Kerma or Karmah grew in power and ambition, and became an economic competitor with Kamit. When Kamit experienced a period of social upheaval beginning around 1,700 B.C.E., when the Hyksos (Asiatics most likely from present-day Syria) conquered lower (northern) Egypt, armies of upper or southern Kamit withdrew from lower Nubia and Karmah took over this region. However, soldiers from Karmah fought on both sides in the warfare between the Kamitans and the Hyksos, pointing to the fluidity of the situation in Nubia and the ambivalence of the Nubians in that period. The Kamitans began a national war of liberation by around 1570 B.C.E. They waged war first against Karmah, because during the conflict with the Hyksos, the Kamitan Pharaoh Kamose intercepted a message from the Hyksos ruler to the new king of Karmah. This message invited Karmah to join forces with Hyksos to conquer Kamit, and they would share its spoils between them.

Kamit moved to reconquer lower Nubia to prevent such an alliance, and then the Kamitans drove the Hyksos from Kamit. Kamit then occupied Nubia for approximately 500 years, and the Nubians (or Kushites) absorbed Kamitan culture.[v] This period also marked the beginning of the New Kingdom era in Ancient Egyptian history, a period marked by a re-flowering in Kamitan culture. In the New Kingdom and Late Periods of Ancient Egyptian history, the Nubians adopted the worship of the Kamitan deity, Amun, particularly in his ram form, and also the architectural style of Kamit (pyramid with attached chapel in the characteristic form with two pylons). The Nubians also adopted the art of building pyramids, but most of these were for use as tombs, somewhat like the pyramid tombs of the Ancient Egyptian Old Kingdom Period (not the Great Pyramids at Giza). This building boom was especially marked during the Meroitic Period of Nubian history. Thus, there are a larger total number of pyramids in Nubia than in Egypt itself.

Below: Typical Egyptian New Kingdom Period Temple.

Below: (A)- Nubian Meroitic Period Temple complete with pylons. Below: (B)- Typical Egyptian New Kingdom Period Temple.

(A)

(B)

Above-(A): Pyramid temple Nubian Meroitic (last Nubian capital 4th century B.C.E. to 3rd century A.C.E.). Above (B): Pyramid tomb of Nubian King and Egyptian Pharaoh Taharka- Late Period 25 Dynasty –8th century B.C.E.

Below: Nubian Meroitic Period Temple complete with pylons.

(A)

(B)[vi]

Egyptian Mysteries Volume 1: Principles of Shetaut Neter

The Nubian Gods and Goddesses in the Kamitan Paut[vii]

Left: The God Amun in the form of the Ram headed man.

While the Kamitan divinity Amun was popular in Nubia, this popularity was amplified in the later periods of Nubian history which began with the New Kingdom Period in Kamit. The Nubian preference was the ram-headed man while the preference in Kamit was either the ram in a completely zoomorphic (animal) form or the divinity as a man (with the body and head of a man {anthropomorphic}).

If we look further back however, we will discover that the mythic association between the Kamitans and the Nubians in Pre-Dynastic times is supported by the earliest writings of Ancient Egypt. Firstly, the god Bas (Basu, Bes), who is usually referred to as a "Sudani" (Nubian) god, is also equated by the Ancient Egyptian scriptures and iconography with the Kamitan divinity Heru. The following panel shows this link most succinctly.

Figure- Above: (A) -Heru as a Divine child, master of nature, controller of beasts (evil, unrighteousness, the lower self), wearing mask of Basu. Above (B) – Basu as the dwarf with the characteristic Nubian plumes as headdress.

In anthropology, pigmies are known as members of any of various peoples, especially of equatorial Africa and parts of southeast Asia, having an average height less than 5 feet (127 centimeters).[viii] In the ancient period, the pigmies of Nubia were renowned for knowing "the dance of the God" and for being jovial but forthright people. In this vein they were renowned musicians and lovers of play and festivity, but also leaders in wars of righteousness and protectors of children. These are all attributes of Basu. Basu also appears in the Pyramid Texts along with the other gods and goddesses of Kamit. The Pyramid Texts are the earliest known extensive writings about the myth and philosophy of Kamit. Therefore, any divinity that is mentioned in those texts emerges with the same importance of the other Kamitan gods and goddesses, depending on the interrelationships provided in the text itself. Thus, at the inception of Kamitan history the Nubian gods and goddesses are present, further proving the predynastic and early dynastic links. The system of Neteru (gods and goddesses) of Kamit may be divided into the following groups for easy understanding.

Transcendental
Divinities: Neberdjer, Heru – beyond the cosmos, beyond time and space

⇕

Cosmic
Divinities: Ex. Asar, Aset, Amun, Ra, Net, etc.—universal worship

⇕

Natural
Divinities: Geb, Nut, Shu, Tefnut, etc.— divinities symbolizing the cosmic forces of nature

⇕

Local (worldly)
Divinities: worshipped at the particular nome (city-town) but not nationally throughout Egypt

⇕

Legendary
Divinities: – original divinities of the ancient period that gave rise to the ones worshipped in the later forms

Egyptian Mysteries Volume 1: Principles of Shetaut Neter

Above left: Kamitan depictions of the Kamitan/Nubian God Bas as the Harpist. Above right: The Kamitan/Nubian god Bas in the form of the all-encompassing divinity, Neberdjer.[ix]

Bas and a host of other Nubian divinities can be seen as the legendary divinities which appear in the early Kamitan texts, but later take on new Kamitan forms, under which their worship continues. Bas, for example, continues to be worshipped as Heru. Bas also figures prominently as a part of the Kamitan concept of the transcendental divinity, *Neberdjer*. The iconography of Bas in the form of Neberdjer (above right) closely follows that of the representation of Heru as the Divine Child (previous page) in the following respects. Both are regarded as the all-encompassing Divinity, masters of the animal forces. In the picture of Heru above (previous page), this is symbolized by Heru holding and standing on the animals; his nudity is a symbol of transcendentalism (unconditioned consciousness). The Bas mask he wears is a symbol of the wonderful and magnificent nature of the Divine, who manifests as a dwarf, and at the same time as a personality overflowing with joviality and life.

Neberdjer (Above right) represents all of the forces of the other divinities including Ra, Amun and Heru, thus symbolizing non-duality and Supreme Divinity. This Being is in control of the seven eternal animal forces (seven animals encircled by the serpent with its tail in its mouth-symbolizing eternity).

Other Nubian divinities which were mentioned in the Ancient Egyptian Pyramid Texts include:

Aahs

The Nubian divinity Aahs is referred to as the "Regent of the land of the south."

Ari Hems Nefer

The Nubian divinity *Ari Hems Nefer* is referred to as the "beautiful womb." *Ari Hems Nefer* was a divinity of the area 15 miles south of the modern Egyptian city of Aswan, where the temple of Aset is located. In ancient times it was known as *Pilak* or the limit or southern border of Egypt. Today it is called Philae.

or

The Nubian divinity **Meril** is referred to as the "beloved lion" divinity of the city of Kalabshah (city located 35 miles south of the modern Egyptian city Aswan), where the temple of Khnum is located. In ancient times it was known as Elephantine by the Greeks or the first cataract of Egypt. Today it is called Aswan.

Symbol A , Symbol B ,

Symbol C

The symbols above for the Nubian divinity **Dudun** show the association with one of the oldest most worshipped and most powerful divinities of Kamit, Heru, whose symbol is the falcon (hawk). Symbol A shows the characteristic Heruian icon, the hawk, perched on the divine solar boat. Symbol B shows one of the full spellings of the name including the phonetic signs and again, including the hawk, this time perched on the standard, meaning *Dudun Sa Heru:* "Dudun the son of Heru." Symbol C shows one of the full spellings of the name including the phonetic signs and this time showing the symbol of the two lands, meaning *Dudun Sa Tawi* "Dudun the son of the two lands (i.e. Nubia and Egypt)." The divinity Dudun was important in Kamitan spirituality even into the late period. The evidence of this can be found in the fact that it was Dudun who symbolically burnt the special Nubian incense through which the royalty of Kamit was to be purified for induction to the high offices, including the throne of rulership. Pharaoh Djehutimes III built temples to Dudun in Nubia at *el-Lessya* and *Uronarti*. Below we see the symbols of Heru used in Kamit. Notice the correlation to the symbols of Dudun.

variant form

The symbols of Heru and those of Dudun are a perfect match. Therefore, Dudun was the name for the same divinity which was called Heru in Kamitan religion. Another strong correlation between Nubian and Kamitan religion is the dwarf figure. We have already been introduced to Basu. This quality of stature and Nubian features is also present in the figure of Asar in his aspect of Ptah-Seker-Asar.

23

Ptah-Seker-Asar (as Pigmy)   **Goddess Mut (below), the Mother of Asar and Aset**

Above far-left The god Asar. Middle- is Ptah-Seker-Asar as an average sized man. Far right- The god Ptah of Memphis.

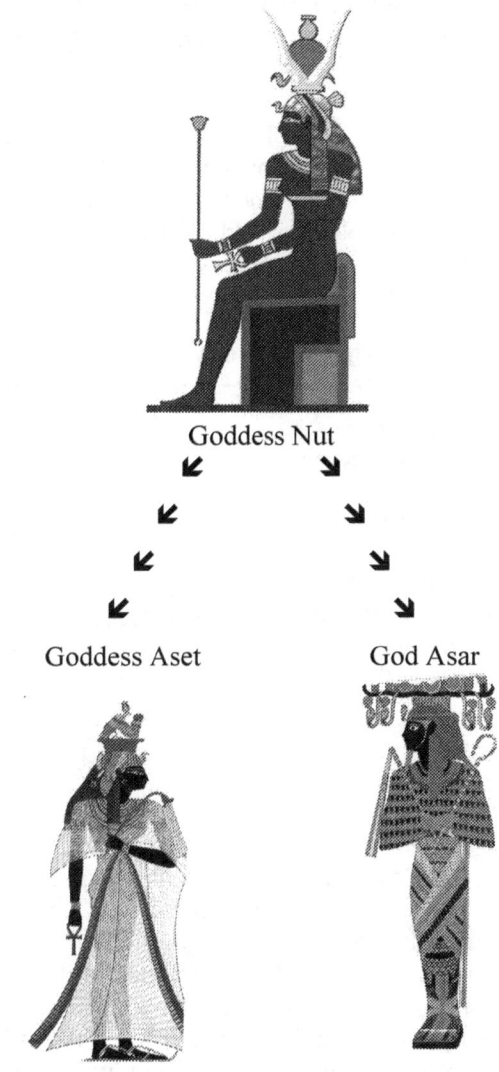

Ptah-Seker-Asar unites the three main spiritual traditions of the early Dynastic Period in ancient Kamit, that of Ra, Asar, and Ptah. Asar is part of Anunian theology, which is centered on the divinity Ra, and Ra is associated with the even earlier Heru as the all-encompassing Divinity. Also, Asar is associated with the divinity Heru, as Heru is Asar's son in the Asarian mystical tradition. Ptah is the central divinity in the theology of the Ancient Egyptian city of *Mennefer* (also Het-Ka-Ptah), known as Memphis. He is associated, in his work of Creation, with the Divinity Tem, who is a form of Ra. Therefore, the dwarf figure of Ptah-Seker-Asar is one of the elements that united the culture of Nubia with that of Kamit. Also the religious iconography of Basu as the dwarf and the characteristic Nubian plumed headdress comes into the later Dynastic Period. Therefore, the impact of Nubian spirituality was felt all the way from the commencement of Kamitan religion through the late period.

In Kamitan philosophy, blackness is used as a descriptive nomenclature of the people, certain of the gods and goddesses, as well as the concept of the transcendental, and not as a racial feature.

In the Temple of Denderah in Kamit, it is inscribed that the goddess Nut gave birth to the goddess Aset there, and that upon her birth, Nut exclaimed: *"As"* (behold), *I have become thy mother."* This was the mythic origin of the name "Ast," (Aset) later known as Isis to the Greeks and others. It further states that *"she was a dark-skinned child and was called Khnemet-ankhet"* or "the living lady of love." Thus, Aset also symbolizes the "blackness" of the vast un-manifest regions of existence. In this capacity she is also the ultimate expression of the African ideal prototype of the Christian Madonna, especially in statues where she is depicted holding the baby

Egyptian Mysteries Volume 1: Principles of Shetaut Neter

Heru in the same manner Mother Mary is portrayed holding baby Jesus in the later Christian period. Her identification is also symbolized in her aspect as *Amentet*, the Duat, itself.

Ament means "hidden." It is a specific reference to the female form of the astral plane or Netherworld known as *Amenta* (Amentet, Amentat) or the Duat. Like her husband Asar, who is known as the *"Lord of the Perfect Black,"* Aset is the Mistress of the Netherworld (Amentet, Amentat). Thus, Aset also symbolizes the "blackness" of the vast unmanifest regions of existence (the unmanifest). Upon further reflection into the mythology it becomes obvious that since Asar is the Duat, and since the goddess Amentet is also Amentat or the realm of Asar, they are in reality one and the same (both the realms and the deities). So Aset and Asar together form the hidden recesses of Creation. In essence they are the source of Creation, and are therefore both simultaneously considered to be the source of the Life Force, which courses through Creation.

Chronology of Nubian History

8,000 B.C.E.	Pottery and community found at Karmah
2,000 – 1550 B.C.E.	Karmah Period
1549 – 850 B.C.E.	Unification with Kamit (Ancient Egypt) Period
850 – 270 B.C.E.	Napata Period
716 B.C.E.	25th Dynasty – beginning Nubian rulership of Egypt Period
270 B.C.E. – 350 A.C.E.	Meroe Period Independent Nation
1st century B.C.E.– 1st century A.C.E.	Judaism introduced– some Kushites adopt Judaism
3rd –6th century A.C.E.	Christianization Period – some Kushites adopt Christianity
1000 A.C.E.	Islamization Period, Axum city - Kushites and Arabs Merge

Summary

Thus, it is clear that the Ancient Egyptians, while recognizing the geographical differences between their land and the land of the Nubians (Kamit in the north and Kush in the south), also recognized the similitude of the lands. In effect, the name of lands of Kamit and Nubia actually mean the same thing "black land" or "land of the blacks." The different words used to identify the two cultures (Kush and Kamit) simply denote the relative geographical locations and the ethnic (tribal) differentiation of inhabitants. The ethnic differences here do not relate to race or religion as these have been shown to be the same, but of customs and traditions that developed independently due to differences in distance from each other. This is discussed for the purpose of showing an underlying unity while at the same time denoting the practical differences of the two lands. This of course points to the underlying ethnic homogeneity between the two peoples, and at the same time acknowledges the cultural differences which developed due to the language changes and the accelerated development of the Ancient Egyptians.

Another force which spurred the Ancient Egyptians to develop at a faster pace, was the interaction they had with the Asiatic peoples. Since the Ancient Egyptians were geographically located closer to Asia Minor, they encountered more Asiatics and later, Europeans than the Ethiopians, who were in an area that afforded them a relative form of seclusion. Some of the interactions were peaceful while others were hostile. This prompted (stimulated) the Ancient Egyptians to mature and advance in the areas of building technology, warfare and social as well as spiritual philosophy.

Recent archaeological finds have revealed that the region's people were producing sophisticated ceramics by 8000 B.C.E. Indeed, it seems likely that Nubia contributed as much to Kamit's development as Kamit did to Nubia's.[x] Nubian-Egyptian pottery from the Pre-Dynastic Period is the link between the Ancient Nubian (Ethiopians), the Ancient Egyptians and the Ancient Indus Valley culture (Indians in India), as this form of pottery (black and red) has only been discovered in these areas.

Plate 1: Pre-Dynastic-Ancient Egyptian Neolithic Period Grave-including black and red pottery. (British Museum-Photo by M. Ashby)

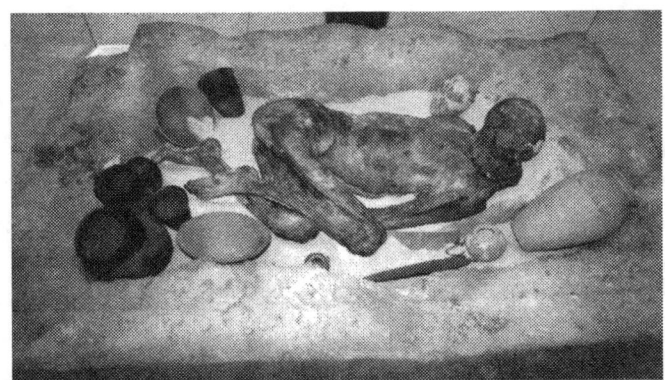

The foundations of Egyptian religion were evident as far back as the Pre-Dynastic era (prior to 4,500 B.C.E.) as religious amulets from that era have been found spread throughout the region (Kamit-Kush). In the early period, the dead were buried in cemeteries, along with pots and other domestic implements, from a period known as "Badarian." Many of these pots found in graves show a boat with a palm branch at the bow and two cabins, over which at least one of them, is the emblem of a divinity.[xi]

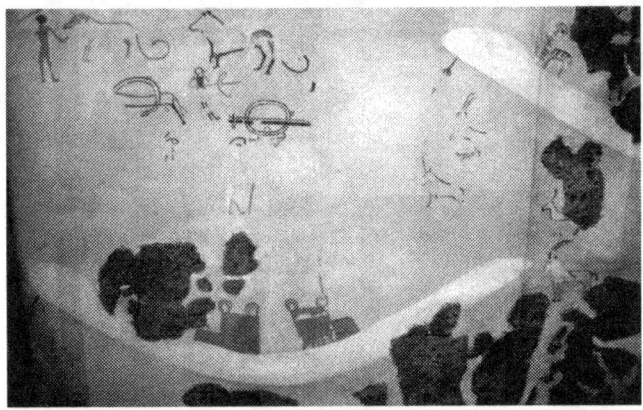

Pre Dynastic Egyptian painting of boat and ibex

The distinctive pottery of this period has been compared and likened to that of the later finds in the Indus Valley. On some of the pottery designs were painted. Some were first in white with a dark red background, and later in red on a light background. There were two periods of development in the Pharaonic system of rule in northeast Africa. The first period developed prior to 10,000 B.C.E. as attested by the headdress of the Great Sphinx. The second period is the late Pre-Dynastic Period (prior to 5000 B.C.E.). There is some evidence that the Pharaonic system of rule (kings and queens as spiritual leaders-head of religion) emerged in the Pre-Dynastic Period in Nubia (Kush) prior to its development in Kamit. The difference between the monarchy of Ancient Nubia and the Pharaonic system of Ancient Egypt may be seen in the domain of rulership. In Kamit, the Pharaonic system developed into an empire when the "two lands" (Upper and Lower Egypt) were consolidated. Kamit had 42 monarchies (referred to as nomarchs since they ruled over nomes or municipalities), but what made the Pharaonic rule different is that it was rulership that united all of the separate nomes.

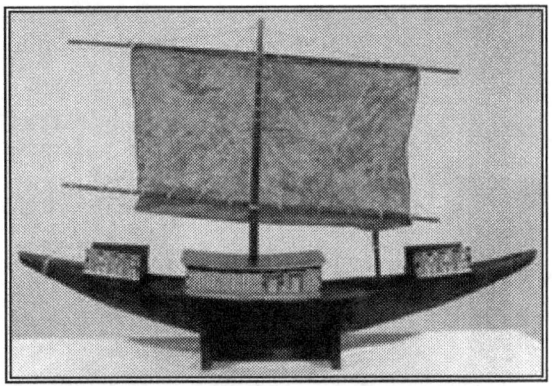

Ancient Egyptian Dynastic era boat

So the Pharaoh was not just a king, but also an emperor. When we speak of a breakdown in the Pharaonic rule in the times when Kamit was not completely overpowered, we are only speaking of the loss of Pharaonic rule and not necessarily a total crash of the society. It would be as if the President of a country lost power temporarily but the governors of the cities or states remained in power, and later conspired to bring back order by pooling resources such as personnel and material in order to rebuild the government. This is what happened during the invasions of the Hyksos as well as the Assyrians. This was the state of affairs during the "Intermediate" periods between the Old and Middle Kingdom Periods, and between the Middle and New Kingdoms. The Ancient Egyptians were not strong enough to overcome the second Assyrian attack, and there was never a second opportunity to overthrow them since Alexander the Great defeated them and took their place. There was still not enough strength to overcome the Greeks, but also there was lesser need, since the Greeks upheld the Kamitan culture and religion. Thus, the Kamitan culture remained relatively intact under the Greeks as compared to the conditions imposed by the Hyksos and Assyrians. These conditions however, would not remain the same under the control by the Roman-Christians, and the later Arab-Muslims who actively sought to stamp out the old religion. Nubia was the last place where Ancient Egyptian religion was practiced, and thus, also the last place where Kamitan religion was practiced that converted to Judaism, Christianity and Islam. Today, the Nubians living in southern Egypt consider themselves ethnically as Nubian, and at the same time nationally as Egyptian, and spiritually as Muslim.

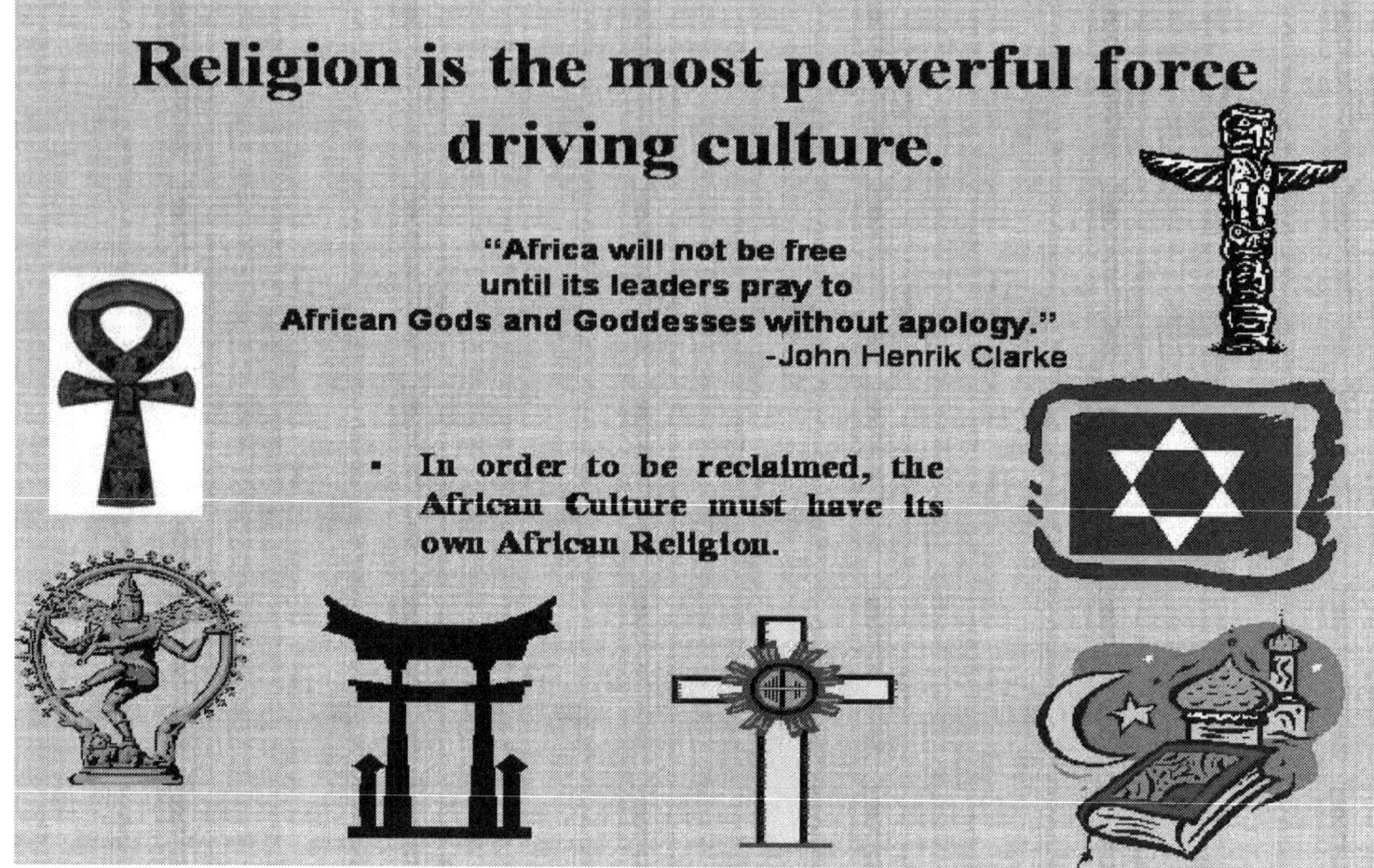
(Slide #7)

The Importance of Religion

Religion is the most powerful force driving culture. Why do we have to go through some of these discussions about religion? It is because most persons have learned what religion is through Western culture, and this has led them to an erroneous concept and practice of religion. So before we can embark on a discussion of what religion is supposed to be, we first need to discuss the three steps of religion, and to set forth the understanding that what we are practicing here, Neterianism, goes back to the source of Ancient African Spiritual tradition.

Religion is the most important force behind culture, and culture is everything that a human being cares about, everything a human being does and the way they do it. If you want to be spiritually liberated, then as a human being you need to worry about culture, you need to think about your culture.

With respect to the culture with which you identify yourself, is it a culture of civilization or a culture of degradation? Is it a culture of wisdom or a culture of ignorance? Degradation and ignorance... this is what is cultivated here in the West by watching television, football, basketball, the entertainment tonight shows, promoting wealth for some and poverty for others, seeking power over nature and destroying the environment, eating fast foods and processed foods, wondering what J-Lo[xii] is doing, etc. As a practitioner of Neterianism, you need to wonder about what you are doing in your lives today, right now. Forget about J-Lo.

And as John Henrik Clarke said, "Africa will not be free until its leaders pray to African Gods and goddesses without apology." This means African leaders must stop looking to outside sources of spirituality to legitimize themselves or legitimize their culture. Ultimately it is not going to work because they are serving cross purposes.

Egyptian Mysteries Volume 1: Principles of Shetaut Neter

In order to be successful, the legacy of our ancestors must be lived, and not just studied and revered. In most of the lectures that are given on Ancient Egypt, the presenters are filling you with the wonder of how great African Culture was, and all the history… don't you long for something more than that? How is that going to help you in your life? You attend such a lecture for an evening and it makes you feel better, but does it really help you improve your life situation? I can tell you how it actually helps you. It makes you feel better so you can go on with your life and think you are accomplishing something, and think that you are getting somewhere in life, and think that you are elevating yourself. And year in and year out the speakers come in and tell you the same thing, and all the while, your life remains essentially the same. Meanwhile, African culture, and the general culture as well, continue to degrade. And we wonder why.

(Slide #8)

Consider Herumakhet, the Sphinx. If we don't take care of the Herumakhet, it becomes covered over by sand and other debris, and this is the same as our legacy. It must be uncovered and cleansed continuously, so that we may continue to benefit from its glory; that is what allows us to elevate ourselves. That is what allows us to become great and to remain great in our own right.

This is a picture (upper right side of Slide #8) from the early explorers in the 1800's showing how the Sphinx appeared to them at that time. Since the influx of Muslims to Egypt at about 800-1000 A.C.E. and again with greater ferocity in the early 1800's A.C.E., there has been vandalism on the Sphinx and other monuments of Ancient Egypt. There are several pictures that exist from the last two to three hundred years that bear this out.

When Was Shetaut Neter First Practiced?

Before the Songai Empire
 Before Timbuktu
  Before the Mali Empire
  Before the Ghana Empire
   Before Islam
    Before Christianity
     Before the Sumerians
      Before the Greek Civilization
       Before the Roman Empire
        Before Hinduism
         Before Buddhism
          Before Europe
           Before The United States

THERE WAS

KAMIT

Egyptian Mysteries Volume 1: Principles of Shetaut Neter

When Was Neterian Religion Practiced?

Time-line of Major World Religions

10,000 B.C.	6000 B.C.	4500 B.C.	4000 B.C.E	3500 B.C.E	3000 B.C.E	2500 B.C.E	2000 B.C.E	1500 B.C.E	1000 B.C.E	500 B.C.E	0	500 B.C.E
Ancient Egyptian Religion												Coptic Period to Present
Pre-Dynastic Era		Old Kingdom				Middle Kingdom			New Kingdom	Nubian Period	Assyrian Period	Persian Period
↑ Shetaut Neter Begins Here			Indus Valley Culture				Aryan India			Hinduism India present		
								Minoan Greek				
										Classical Greek		
										Taoism to present		
										Buddhism to present		
			Pre-Judaic Pre-Islamic	Arabian Canaan Babylonian Syrian Religions						Pre-Islamic Allah		
				Sumerian Religion								
										Judaism to present		
											Christianity to present	
												Islam to present

(Slide #9)

When was Neterian religion practiced? This (above) is a timeline of world religions, and on the far-left in 10,000 BCE we have Ancient Egyptian Religion in its earliest recorded history. This is the earliest physical evidence of Ancient Egyptian Religion, not that it is the beginning of Ancient Egyptian Religion, but the earliest physical evidence. We will use this benchmark of the earliest physical evidence available. Other cultures and other spiritual traditions may say they were there 100,000 years ago or 50,000 years ago; however, there is no physical evidence to back that up.

The earliest physical evidence for other spiritual traditions comes no earlier than 7,000 B.C.E., but this is in the form of artifact, not in the form of a complete and extensive spiritual philosophy, spiritual literature with a defined ontology[xiii] and epistemology[xiv]. That does not happen until much later coming down to 1,500 BCE.

So all the religions you know of in the world today begin after that point. The Indus valley culture begins around 2,500 B.C.E. Then comes the Aryan civilization of India; later in Asia Minor (now called the Middle East) the Sumerians and Judaism come in, then in the east, Buddhism, Taoism, down to Classical Greek culture in Europe, and Hinduism in India, then Christianity and Islam which are two of the latest world religions that have come about.

This timeline gives you a graphic, visual idea of how ancient what we are talking about is, and we have shown through the research that this development in Ancient Kamit is actually is a perfection of African spiritual teachings. The same teachings that you find in Ancient Kamit, you find generally throughout African Religion.

Egyptian Mysteries Volume 1: Principles of Shetaut Neter

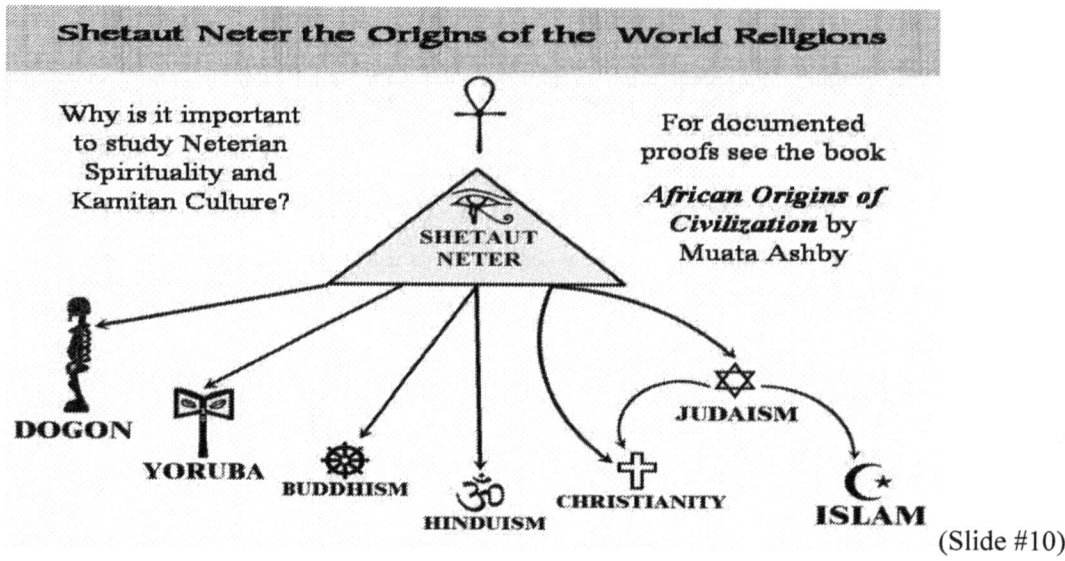

(Slide #10)

Shetaut Neter is the origin of the present day world religions. Why is it important to study Neterian spirituality and Kamitan culture? It is important because documented proof by others and myself has shown that Shetaut Neter has influenced Dogon spirituality, Yoruba religion, Buddhism, Hinduism, and Christianity. It has influenced Christianity directly and also through influences in Judaism. And through these influences, it has influenced Islam as well. I have documented these influences and traced them, and others have also done this. What I have done is added original research and also I have compiled the research of other scholars as well.

Christianity is directly based on Neterian Religion. However, the current form of Christianity that is practiced is not the original form that originated in Kamit; this is the source of problems that we have in Christianity today. In the Jewish Holy Scriptures, the Old Testament, it is stated that they emerged from Egypt with Moses and the Bible says, "Moses was skilled in all the magic of the Egyptians." It is understood that he was an Egyptian priest. This explains the varied correlations that can be made between ancient Egyptian religious traditions and rituals and those of the Jews. For example, the Jewish tradition originally describes God as the "Elohim" which is a general Hebrew term that is used in the Old Testament meaning any divine being, but more importantly, it is used frequently in reference to The God of the Israelites. Actually the term means gods (and goddesses) (plural), implying that Divinity is multifaceted. The Jewish term Elohim is correlated to the Neterian (Ancient Egyptian Religion) term "Neter" which means "The God." Neter manifests as "neteru" or the "gods and goddesses."

The Jews developed a philosophy of a devil (Satan) as rival to God Almighty. Prior to that development there was no such model in ancient religions. Christianity later adopted that concept of a devil since they adopted the Old Testament as the starting point of their religion. The Ancient Egyptian God Set represents egoism, lower desires, chaos and negativity. Set is the Divinity from which many scholars, including myself, believe the early Jews confused and developed their concept of Satan. Actually one of the names of Set is Setek or Sutek. "Sutek" and "Satan" are very similar. This idea of a devil was a new concept in spirituality that emerged with Judaism and a few other traditions, such as Zoroastrianism. Other Jewish traditions adopted from Ancient Egyptian culture include the tradition of three-fold daily worship (based on Anunian Theology of ancient Egypt), the tradition of bathing the body of the deceased before burial, the concept of monotheism, and the precepts of righteous (ethical) action (Ten Commandments).

There are several direct correlations between Christianity and the Ancient Egyptian traditions. These adoptions are attested to by the early Christian writers and scholars, who admit the cooptation of the ancient Egyptian and Greek symbols and traditions, and some of the philosophies, in order to attract the followers of what they termed "Pagan" traditions (i.e., non-orthodox Christian traditions) to the new religion, Orthodox Christianity. While all of the correlations between Ancient Egyptian religion and Christianity are too numerous to include here, the most prominent ones will be briefly described. The orthodox Christians adopted the Ancient Egyptian winter solstice celebration of the birth of the Neterian god Heru on December 25th as the birthday of the Christian savior, Jesus. Other adoptions include the concept of the resurrection, the Eucharist, the cross, the Trinity, the Mother and Child iconography, the concept of anointing the Christ, the persecution of Jesus upon his birth, and the concept of Baptism. These are all fundamental Christian concepts and symbols still in use today, which were in existence previously in Ancient Egyptian/African religion, some of which contain some of the original African-Neterian values. Our books, *The Mystical Journey From Jesus to Christ* and *African Origins* go into more details on this topic.

A Most Ancient Tradition

The Stellar Symbolism related to the Pole Star and the Opening of the mouth and Eyes Ceremony in Ancient Egypt

Herodotus, in his books of history, quoted one of his guides as having told him that Kamitan history had lasted for a period of time during which, "the sun had twice risen where it now set, and twice set where it now rises."[xv]

"This remark Schwaller de Lubicz interpreted as a description of the passage of one and a half precessional cycles. This would place the date of foundation (of ancient Egypt) around 36,000 BC, a date in broad agreement with the other sources."[xvi]

There are three constellations that circulate around the North Pole of the planet earth. These are Draco, Ursa Major and Ursa Minor. The Great Pyramid was discovered to have a shaft that points to the North Pole. Precession is the slow revolution of the Earth's axis of rotation (wobbling) about the poles of the ecliptic. The *ecliptic* is a great circle inscribed on a terrestrial globe inclined at an approximate angle of 23°27' to the equator and representing the apparent motion of the sun in relation to the earth during a year. It is caused by lunar and solar perturbations acting on the Earth's equatorial bulge and causes a westward motion of the stars that takes around 25,868 years to complete.[xvii] During the past 5000 years the line of direction of the North Pole has moved from the star Thuban, or Alpha (a) Draconic, in the constellation Draco, to within one degree of the bright star Polaris, also known as Alpha (a) Ursae Minors, in the constellation Ursa Minor (Little Dipper), which is now the North Star. Polaris is a binary star of second magnitude, and is located at a distance of about 300 light-years from the earth. It is easy to locate in the sky because the two stars opposite the handle in the bowl of the dipper in the constellation Ursa Major (Big Dipper), which are called the Pointers, point to the star Polaris.[xviii]

Figure below: The Neterian Zodiac and the Precession of the Equinoxes and the History of Ancient Egypt

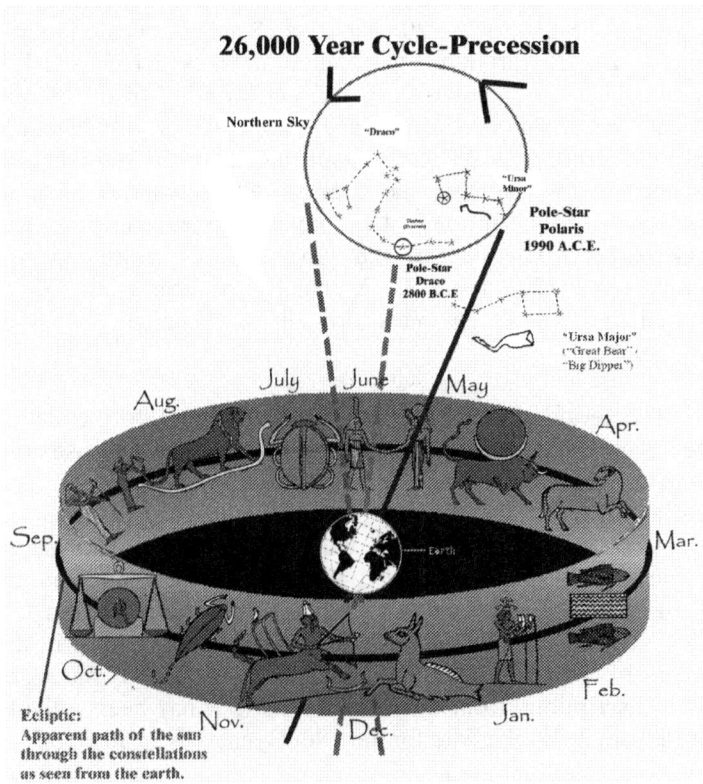

The Zodiac is an imaginary belt in the celestial sphere, extending about 8° on either side of the ecliptic. The ecliptic is a line that traces the apparent path of the Sun among the stars. It is believed that the width of the zodiac was originally determined so as to include the orbits of the Sun and Moon and of the five planets that were believed to have been known by people in ancient times (Mercury, Venus, Mars, Jupiter, and Saturn). The zodiac is divided into 12 sections of 30° each, which are called the signs of the zodiac. Because of the precession of the equinoxes about the ecliptic, a 25,920-year cycle or "Great Year" period, the first point of Aries retrogrades about 1° in 72 years, so that the sign Aries today lies in the constellation Pisces. In about 13,061 years, when the retrogression will have completed the entire circuit of 360°, the zodiacal signs and constellations will again coincide. It is believed that the zodiacal signs originated in Mesopotamia as early as 2000 B.C.E. and the Greeks adopted the symbols from the Babylonians and passed them on to the other ancient civilizations. The Chinese also adopted the 12-fold division, but called the signs rat, ox, tiger, hare, dragon, serpent, horse, sheep, monkey, hen, dog, and pig. Independently, the Aztec people devised a similar system.[xix]

The calendar based on the Great Year was also used by the Ancient Egyptians. The Great Year is founded on the movement of the earth through the constellations known as the *Precession of the Equinoxes*. It is confirmed from the history given by the Ancient Egyptian Priest Manetho (𓈖𓌃𓏏𓊖-*MernDjehuti*) in the year 241 B.C.E. Each Great Year has 25,860 to 25,920 years and 12 arcs or constellations. Each passage through a constellation takes 2,155 – 2,160 years. These are known as the "Great Months" of the "Great Year." As explained earlier, the current cycle or year began at around 10,858 B.C.E. At about the year 36,766 B.C.E., according to Manetho, the Creator, Ra, ruled the earth in person from his throne in the Ancient Egyptian city of Anu (Greek-Heliopolis-city of the sun). By this reckoning our current year (2,004 A.C.E.) is actually the year 12,862 G.Y. based on the Great Year System of Ancient Egyptian reckoning.

The period of 36,525 years is also 25 times 1,460, which is the cycle of the helical rising of Sirius (when Sirius rises not only in the east but on the ecliptic, i.e. with the sun). The Sirian calendar was another time reckoning system based on the star Sirius and its relation with the sun of our solar system, which contains a cycle of 1,460 years. An inscription by Censorings informs us that the rising of Sirius occurred in 139 A.C.E. This means that the Sirian cycle also occurred in the years 1321 B.C.E, 2781 B.C.E, and 4241 B.C.E. By means of two inscriptions from the 18th Dynasty, it has been reliably established that the date for the 18th Dynasty is 1580 B.C.E.

According to the reckoning based on the History of *MernDjehuti* (Manetho), if we take the average number of years in the Great Year and add it to the known year of the beginning of the current Great Year we get a total of 36,748 (25,890 + 10,858=36,748). If we compare this number with the history of *MernDjehuti* (Manetho) we find a difference of 18 years, accountable by the deterioration in the translated records and the variance in the number of years in the Great Year cycle. Thus, we have correlations that support the History and the practice of reckoning time by the Great Year. So we have reliable confirmations that the Sirian calendar was in use in Ancient Egypt at least as early as 4241 B.C.E.[xx] and that a greater form of reckoning, the Great Year, corroborates the History of *MernDjehuti* (Manetho) which takes Ancient Egyptian chronology and civilized use of mathematics, astronomy and time reckoning back to 36,748 B.C.E. This longer duration cycle system of time reckoning was supported by recent discoveries.

"That the Egyptians handled astronomical cycles of even greater duration is indicated by inscriptions recently found by Soviet archeologists in newly opened graves during the period of their work on the Aswan Dam.[xxi] Here the cycles appear to cover periods of 35,525 years, which would be the equivalent of 25 cycles of 1461 years. The apparent discrepancy of one year in this recording of cycles is due to the Sothic cycle of 1460 years being the equivalent of a civil cycle of 1461 years. According to Muck (researcher), there were three main cycles: one of 365 X 4 = 1460; another of 1460 X 25 = 36,500; and a third of 36,500 X 5 = 182,500 years."[xxii]

In a brilliant discovery by Joseph Campbell in relation to the same great age period being used in India, Iceland and Babylon and the unlikelihood of this arising by chance.

"There are, however, instances that cannot be accounted for in this way, and then suggest the need for another interpretation: for example, in India the number of years assigned to an eon[xxiii] is 4,320,000; whereas in the Icelandic *Poetic Edda* it is declared that in Other's warrior hall, Valhall, there are 540 doors, through each of which, on the "day of the war of the wolf,"[xxiv] 800 battle-ready warriors will pass to engage the antipodes in combat.' But 540 times 800 equals 432,000!

Moreover, a Chaldean priest, Broses, writing in Greek ca. 289 B.C., reported that according to Mesopotamian belief 432,000 years elapsed between the crowning of the first earthly king and the coming of the deluge.

No one, I should think, would wish to argue that these figures could have arisen independently in India, Iceland, and Babylon."[xxv]

When we compare the Indian, Icelandic and Babylonian system of Ages of time with that of Ancient Egypt some startling correlations can be observed; the same numbers appear.

Egyptian Mysteries Volume 1: Principles of Shetaut Neter

Ancient Egyptian Age	Ancient Indian Age
25,920 Great Year	------------------------------------
25,920 ÷ 6 = 4320	432,000 Kali Yuga – Iron Age
	4,320,000 Maha Yuga – Great Age or Cycle
25,920 ÷ 4 = 8640	864,000 Diaper Yuga – Copper Age
25,920 ÷ 2 = 1296	1,296,000 Treta Yuga – Silver Age
25,920 ÷ 15 = 1728	1,728,000 Satyr Yuga – Golden or Truth Age

The *Royal Papyrus of Turin* gives a complete list of the kings who reigned over Upper and Lower Egypt from Menes to the New Empire, including mention of the duration of each reign. Before the list comes a section devoted to the Pre-Dynastic era. This section lists the kings who reigned before Menes, and the duration of each reign, establishing that there were nine Dynasties. According to Schwaller de Lubicz, some of these were called:

> ... the (venerables) of Memphis, the venerables of the North, and finally the *Shemsu-Hor,* usually translated as the 'Companions of Horus'.

Fortunately, the last two lines have survived almost intact, as have indications regarding the number of years:

venerables Shemsu-Hor, 13,429 years
'Reigns up to Shemsu-Hor, 23,200 years (total 36,620) (before) King Menes.[xxvi]

The Turin Papyrus names the following neteru (gods and goddesses) as rulers in the Pre-Dynastic ages:
Ptah, Ra, Shu, Geb, Asar, Set, Heru, Djehuti, Maat

In support of the above, Diodorus of Sicily reports that several historians of his time reported that Kamit was ruled by gods and heroes for a period of 18,000 years. After this Kamit was ruled by mortal kings for 15,000 years.[xxvii] While it is true that this account differs with that of *MernDjehuti* (Manetho) and the Turin Papyrus, the inescapable fact remains that every account refers to ages of rulers that go back beyond 30,000 B.C.E. as the earliest period of record keeping. The implications are far reaching. Consider that if we were to add the figure above for the period prior to the first king (King Menes) of our era and use the first confirmed date for the use of the calendar (4240 B.C.E.) we indeed would have a date over 40,000 B.C.E. for the beginnings of Ancient Egyptian history (36,620+4240).

Picture Below (A) -The Great Heru m akhet (Sphinx) of Egypt-with the Panel of Djehutimes between its Paws. (19th century rendition of the Sphinx)[xxviii]

Picture : Below (B)-The Great Heru m Akhet (Sphinx) of Ancient Egypt.

(A)

(B)

Egyptian Mysteries Volume 1: Principles of Shetaut Neter

Plate: The Great Sphinx, covered in sand - Drawing by early Arab explorers[xxix]

The Sphinx is the oldest known monument and it relates to the solar mysticism of Anu as well as to the oldest form of spiritual practice known. From it we also derive certain important knowledge in reference to the antiquity of civilization in Ancient Egypt. The picture of the Great Sphinx above-right appeared in 1876. Notice the broad nose and thick lips with which it is endowed. Any visitor to Egypt who examines the Sphinx close up will see that even with the defacement of the nose, it is clearly an African face, and not an Asiatic or European personality being depicted. Many early Egyptologists also concluded this upon gazing at the monument; this picture is but one example of their conviction on the subject.

Figure below: The Per-Aah (Pharaoh) Djehutimes IIII (Thutmosis) makes offerings to the Great Heru m Akhet (Sphinx)

The Heru-em-akhet (Horemacket Ra-Herakhti (Herukhuti, Heruakhuti - Great Sphinx) Stele is a panel placed directly in front of the chest of the monument in between the two front paws. The inscription that survived with the Ancient Egyptian Sphinx also has serious implications for the revision of the dating of Ancient Egyptian history. It recounts the story of how the prince Djehutimes IIII (Thutmosis IV- 18th Dynasty 1401-1391 B.C.E.) fell asleep at the base of the Sphinx on a hot day and the spirit of the Sphinx came to him. The Sphinx offered him kingship and sovereignty over the world if Djehutimes would repair him and make devout offerings and worship. Having complied with the wishes of the Divine, to maintain the great monument and sustain the worship of Ra-Herakhti, Djehutimes became king and Kamit prospered under his reign with the favor of the Divine. According to Egyptologist Maspero, this was not the first time that the Sphinx was cleared:

> The stele of the Sphinx bears, on line 13, the cartouche of Khephren in the middle of a gap .... There, I believe, is the indication of an excavation of the Sphinx carried out under this prince, and consequently the more or less certain proof that the Sphinx was already covered with sand during the time of Cheops and his predecessors.[xxx]

R. A. Schwaller de Lubicz reports that legends support the contention that at a very early date in Ancient Egyptian history, the Old Kingdom fourth Dynasty (Cheops {Khufu} reigned 2551-2528 B.C.E., Khephren {Ra-ka-ef} reigned 2520-2494), the Sphinx was already considered ancient and as belonging to a remote past of Ancient Egyptian Culture.

> A legend affirms that even in Cheops' day, the age of the Sphinx was already so remote that it was impossible to situate it in time. This Sphinx is a human and colossal work. There is an enigma about it that is linked with the very enigma posed by the Sphinx itself.

It has been proposed, as a support of the use of the Great Year calendar, that the Ancient Egyptians instituted the use of different symbolisms in religion and government in accordance with the current symbolism of the particular age in question.[xxxi] Thus, during the age (great month) of Leo, the lion symbolism would be used. What is compelling about this rationale is that the new evidence in reference to the age of the Sphinx coincides with the commencement of the New Great Year and the month of Leo, which began in 10,858 B.C.E. However, when it is understood that the damage on the Sphinx would have required thousands of years to produce, and when the history of *MernDjehuti* (Manetho) as well as the conjunction of the Sphinx with the constellation Leo when it makes its heliacal rising at the beginning of each Great Year is taken into account, it becomes possible to understand that the Sphinx was already in existence at the commencement of our current Great Year, and to envision the possibility that the Sphinx was created at the beginning of the previous Great Year anniversary (36,748 B.C.E.).

The Great Sphinx and its attendant monuments as well as other structures throughout Egypt, which appear to be compatible architecturally, should therefore be considered as part of a pinnacle of high culture that was reached well before the Dynastic age, i.e. previous to 5,000 B.C.E. The form of the Sphinx itself, displaying the lion body with the human head, but also with the particularly "leonine" headdress including the lion's mane, was a legacy accepted by the Pharaohs of the Dynastic Period. In the Ancient Egyptian mythological system of government, the Pharaoh is considered as a living manifestation of Heru, and he or she wields the leonine power which comes from the sun, Ra, in order to rule. Thus, the Pharaohs also wore and were depicted wearing the leonine headdress. The sundisk is the conduit through which the Spirit transmits Life Force energy to the world, i.e. the Lion Power, and this force is accessed by turning towards the Divine, symbolized in the form of the sundisk. Hence, this is the reason for the orientation of the Sphinx towards the east, facing the rising sun. All of this mystical philosophy and more is contained in the symbolic-metaphorical form and teaching of the Sphinx. Thus, we have a link of Ancient Egyptian culture back to the Age of Leo and the commencement of the current cycle of the Great Year in remote antiquity.

Heru-m-akhet or "Heru in the Horizon" or "manifesting" in the horizon, the "Sphinx," actually represents an ancient conjunction formed by the great Sphinx in Giza, Kamit and the heavens. This conjunction signals the beginning of the "New Great Year." It has been noted by orthodox as well as nonconformist Egyptologists alike, that the main symbolisms used in Ancient Egypt vary over time. Nonconformist Egyptologists see this as a commemoration of the zodiacal symbol pertaining to the particular Great Month in question. What is controversial to the orthodox Egyptologists is the implication that the Ancient Egyptians marked time by the Great Year, because this would mean that Ancient Egyptian civilization goes back 12 millenniums, well beyond any other civilization in history. This further signifies that all of the history books and concepts related to history and the contributions of Africa to humanity would have to be rewritten. Also, since it has been shown that the Ancient Egyptians commemorated the Zodiacal sign of Leo at the commencement of the Great Year it means that the knowledge of the precession of the equinoxes, the Great Year and the signs of the Zodiac proceeded from Ancient Egypt to Babylon and Greece and not the other way around. The twelve zodiacal signs for these constellations were named by the 2nd-century astronomer Ptolemy, as follows: Aries (ram), Taurus (bull), Gemini (twins), Cancer (crab), Leo (lion), Virgo (virgin), Libra (balance), Scorpio (scorpion), Sagittarius (archer), Capricorn (goat), Aquarius (water-bearer), and Pisces (fishes).

That is precisely what the records reveal. Mentu the bull disappears and is superceded by the ram of Amon. The character of the architecture loses its monolithic simplicity. While still within its recognizable tradition, there is no mistaking a change of 'character'. The Pharaohs incorporate Amon in the names they assume: Amenhotep, Tutankhamun.

Egyptologists attribute the fall of Mentu and the rise of Amon to a hypothetical priestly feud, with the priests of Amon emerging victorious. There is nothing illogical or impossible about this hypothesis, but at the same time there is no evidence whatever to support it.

The evidence shows a shift of symbolism, from duality under Gemini, to the bull, to the ram. These shifts coincide with the dates of the astronomical precession.

Further corroboration of Egyptian knowledge and use of the precession of the equinoxes, and of the incredible coherence and deliberation of the Egyptian tradition, was deduced by Schwaller de Lubicz from a detailed study of the famous zodiac from the Temple of Denderah. This temple was constructed by the Ptolemies in the first century BC, upon the site of an earlier temple. The hieroglyphs declare that it was constructed according to the plan laid down in the time of the 'Companions of Horus' - that is to say, prior to the beginnings of Dynastic Egypt. Egyptologists regard this statement as a ritual figure of speech, intended to express regard for the tradition of the past.[xxxii]

One striking form of symbolism that is seen from the beginning to the end of the Ancient Egyptian history is the Sphinx/Pharaonic Leonine headdress.

Figure Above- The Heru-m-akhet (Sphinx) Pharaonic headdress.[xxxiii]

Figure Below- Drawing of the Sphinx from a sculpture in Egypt

Figure below: Constellation Leo-The Lion

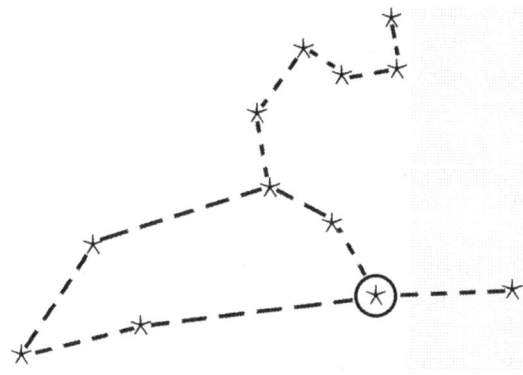

The Great Sphinx faces due east and in the year c. 10,800 B.C.E. a perfect conjunction is created as the Sphinx faces the rising sun and the constellation Leo, the lion.

Below: The Sphinx faces due east at the beginning of the Great year and faces the Constellation Leo as it makes its Heliacal Rising.

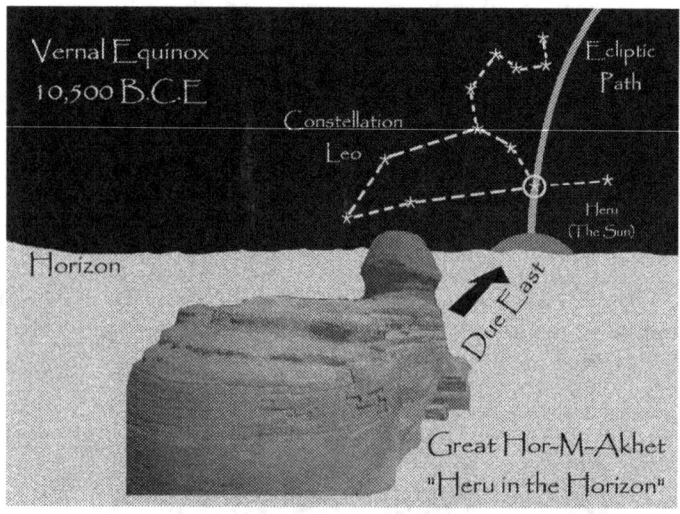

The Sphinx on Earth (Rw or Ru) as a Counterpart to the Sphinx in the Heavens.

The Sphinx on earth as a counterpart to the Sphinx in the heavens (Astral Plane), i.e. the horizon of the earth plane and the horizon of the astral plane. In this view, the Sphinx on earth and the Sphinx in heaven complement each other and form two halves of the akher-akhet symbol, but turned facing each other, looking at the sun which is between them, i.e. turning away from the earth plane and towards the Transcendental Spirit.

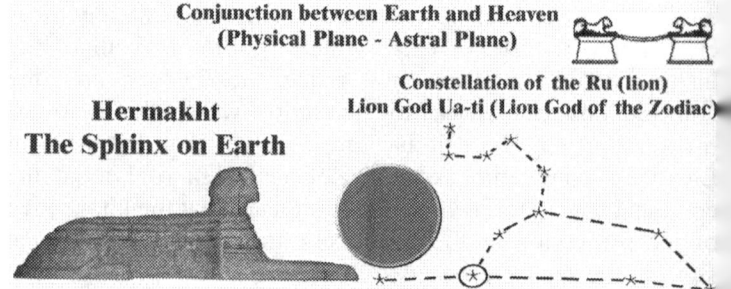

Figure Below- The Ancient Egyptian zodiacal signs for the ages of the Ram, Bull and Lion

Opening of the Mouth with the Imperishable Stars

In the Hermetic Texts, which are the later development in Ancient Egyptian scripture, Hermes, the Greek name ascribed to the Ancient Egyptian god Djehuti, states to his pupil Asclepius (Kamitan Imhotep), *"Did you know, O Asclepius, that Egypt is made in the image of heaven?"*[xxxiv] The Ancient Egyptian Pyramid Texts and the Pert M Heru (Book of Enlightenment) texts contain more references to stellar mysticism. The stellar symbolism of Ancient Egypt relates to the passage of time, but also to mystical awakening and spiritual realization.

> As to these all, Maat and Djehuti, they are with Isdesba[xxxv] Lord of Amentet. As to the divine beings behind Asar, they are again Mseti, Hapy, Duamutf, and Kebsenuf. They are behind the Chepesh[xxxvi] in the northern heavens.
>
> From Prt M Hru Chap. 4, V. 22

The Chepesh has important mystical symbolism. Mythically it represents the foreleg of the god Set which was torn out and thrown into the heavens by the god Heru during their epic battle. A similar teaching occurs in the Babylonian epic of Gilgemesh[xxxvii\xxxviii] when the "foreleg of the Bull of Heaven" is ripped out and thrown at the goddess Ishtar, who was the goddess or Queen of Heaven in Mesopotamia. It symbolizes the male generative capacity and is one of the offerings of Hetep given in Chapter 36 (usually referred to as #30B) of the Pert M Heru (Egyptian Book of the Dead). Its cosmic and mystical implications provides us with insight into Kamitan philosophy as well as ancient history.

Also, in ancient times the Chepesh symbol represented the "Northern path" of spiritual evolution. Since the constellation of the Ursa Major ("Great Bear" or "Big Dipper"), known to the Ancient Egyptians as "Meskhetiu," contains **seven** stars and occupied the location referred to as the "Pole Star." This refers to the fact that as it occupies the pole position, it does not move, while all the other stars in the sky circle around it. This constellation, whose symbol is the foreleg, ⌐⌐, was thus referred to as "the imperishables" in the earlier Pyramid Texts: "He (the king-enlightened initiate) climbs to the sky among the imperishable stars."[xxxix]

Akhemu Seku - never setting stars – imperishable

Akhemu Urdu - never resting stars – setting

The Great Pyramid in Egypt, located in the area referred to as "The Giza Plateau" in modern times, incorporated this teaching. The main chamber in the Great Pyramid incorporates two shafts that pointed in ancient times to the Chepesh (Ursa {Bear} Major {Great} - the foreleg) in the north sky and to Orion (Sahu or Sah), the star system of Asar (Osiris) in the southern sky. The imperishable constellation refers to that which is unchanging, absolute, transcendental and perfect.

Figure below: The Great Pyramid of Egypt with the Mystical Constellations (view from the East) and the Perishable and Imperishable stars.

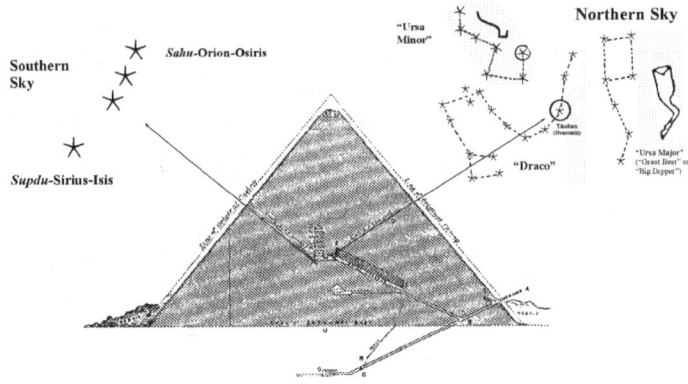

Figure below: The Great Pyramid of Egypt with the Mystical Constellations (view from the South).

Egyptian Mysteries Volume 1: Principles of Shetaut Neter

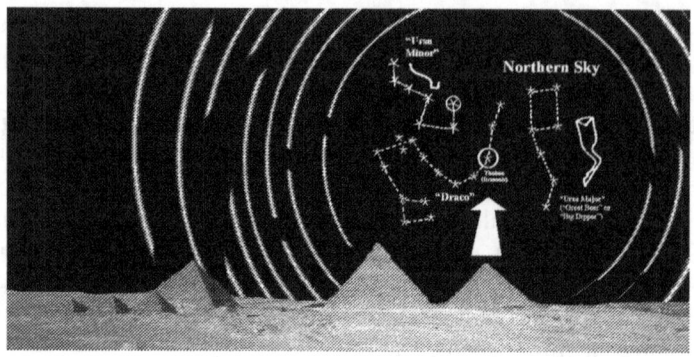

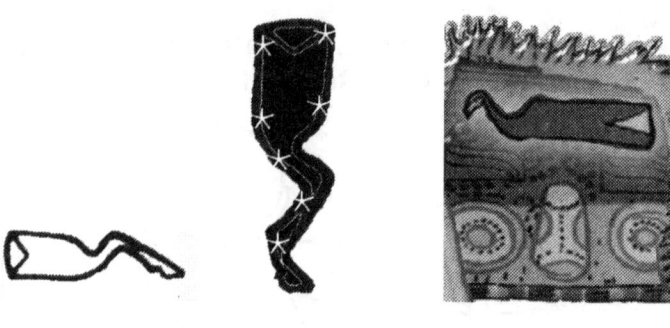

Figure below: The Hetep Offering Slab with the foreleg symbol.

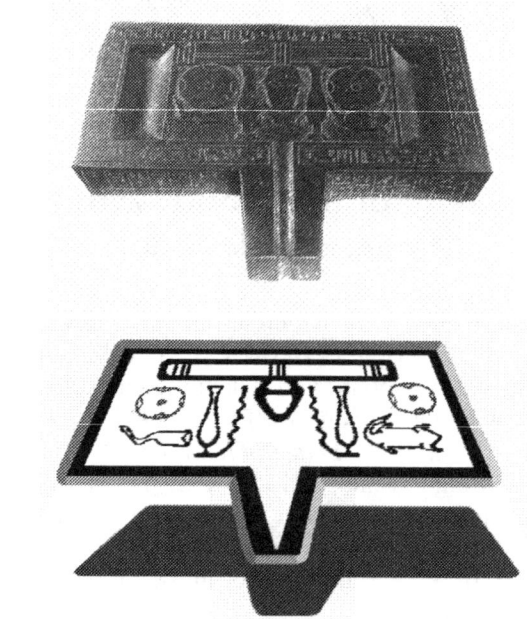

When the Great Pyramids are viewed over the course of one evening, from the south to north, the perishable stars (forming circles, moving below the horizon) can be seen moving around the imperishable stars (those which do not set, that is go below the horizon) in the center. Time lapse photographs of this constellation (Meskhetiu - Ursa Major ("Great Bear" or "Big Dipper"), show it as remaining in the center and other stars moving around it. Also, it does not sink below the horizon and become "reborn" in the eastern horizon each day as do other stars. The Orion constellation refers to that which is changing, incarnating (rising in the east) and becoming. In this manner Asar is reborn through Sopdu (the star Sirius-Aset, Isis) in the form of Heru-Sopdu (Heru who is in Aset), also known as Sirius B. Therefore, mystically, the "Northern Path" is promoted as the path to immortality and enlightenment through the attainment of absolute consciousness which transcends the perishable and ever-changing nature of creation. The "Southern Path" is the process of reincarnation, renewal and repeated embodiment (*uhem ankh* {Kamitan}), for the purpose of further spiritual evolution through self-discovery by means of human experiences. This teaching is also reflected in the zodiac inscription from the temple of Hetheru at Denderah and in the "Opening of the Mouth Ceremony" where a symbol of the imperishable constellation, ⌐, is carried by the priest and is called *Sba ur*. The mystical intent is to open the mind, through mystical wisdom and disciplines, so as to render it *uadjit*, , (universal and infinite, all-encompassing, unlimited) and beyond the fluctuations of egoism, i.e. mortal consciousness.

Used in the Hetep (Hotep) offering table, the leg symbolizes the male gender. The goose symbolizes the female gender. Thus, the initiate offers duality in the form of sex awareness to the divinity in exchange for the realization of non-duality, or the transcendence of gender (dual) consciousness altogether, i.e. the "imperishable" or eternal realization of the Higher Self.

Figure: Below left- Hieroglyph for the Chepesh (foreleg). Center-The Chepesh with constellation.[xl] Right- The Chepesh as part of the Hetep offering in the *Pert M Heru* Texts and temple inscriptions.

Egyptian Mysteries Volume 1: Principles of Shetaut Neter

Figure: Vignettes from the Opening of the Mouth Ceremonies from the Ancient Egyptian texts. (A)- with Chepesh (Chpsh-foreleg), (B) with the Seba (Sba) ur instruments.

"O Initiate, I have come in search of you, for I am Horus; I have struck your mouth for you, for I am your beloved son; I have split open your mouth for you... I have split open your eyes for you... with the Chepch (Chpsh) of the Eye of Heru- Chepesh (Foreleg). I have split open your mouth for you... I have split open your eyes for you... with the adze of Upuaut..... with the adze of iron . . . [PT 11-13]

The opening of the mouth and eyes is a mystical teaching relating to expansion in expression (mouth) and awareness (open eyes). These factors (mouth and eyes) are the signs of the existence of consciousness or its absence. From the passages above we learn that the Priests and Priestesses "open" the mouth and eyes by touching them with the ritual instruments which symbolize the eternal, the absolute, i.e. the expansion of consciousness, immortality and spiritual enlightenment. Also, we learn that the adze instrument (Ursa minor) is actually also the Eye of Heru, which is the greatest offering-eucharist of the Egyptian mysteries. The Eye symbolizes divine consciousness as it is one and the same with Heru, Asar and Ra. Therefore, being touched with these instruments means attaining God (Divine)-consciousness.

Figure below: Human Origins- Modern Human Beings Originate in Africa – 150,000 – 100,000 B.C.E.

The history of modern humanity begins in Africa 150,000 years ago. All the human beings who are alive all over the earth today descend from an original group of human beings who lived 150,000 years ago in central-equatorial Africa. These human beings spread out from there and populated the rest of Africa over the next 50,000 years.

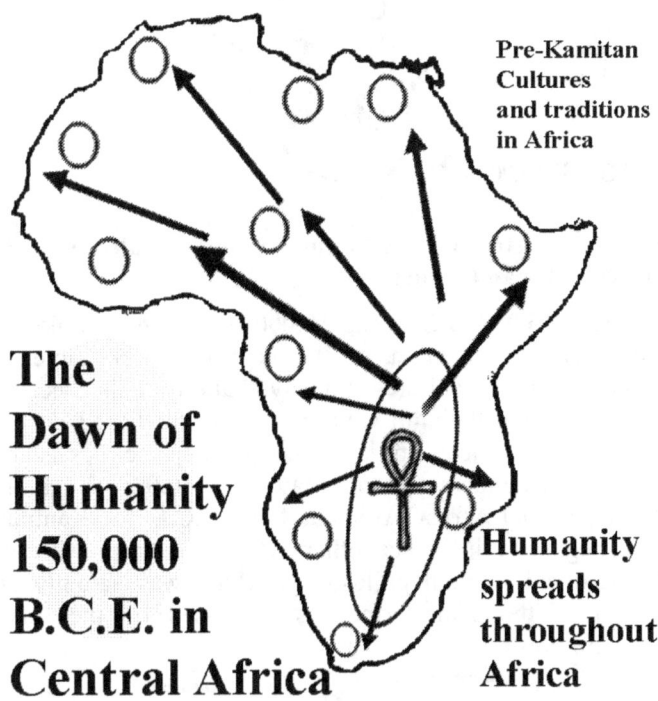

Figure below: Human Cultural Development -Cultures develop throughout Africa – 36.000-10,000 B.C.E.

Over the next 50,000 years (150,000-100,000 B.C.E.) the people who populated Africa developed cultures that took on several unique aspects, but at the same time manifested the principles that they had carried with them from the originating point to their new homes around the continent. These were a set of social (Maat-Ubuntu) and religious (Supreme Being served by lesser gods and goddesses) principles which became the basis of all African religions that would develop thereafter. Over time some of the groups lost contact and different languages developed, but the principles remained the same and became highly evolved in the Kush-Kamit region.

Egyptian Mysteries Volume 1: Principles of Shetaut Neter

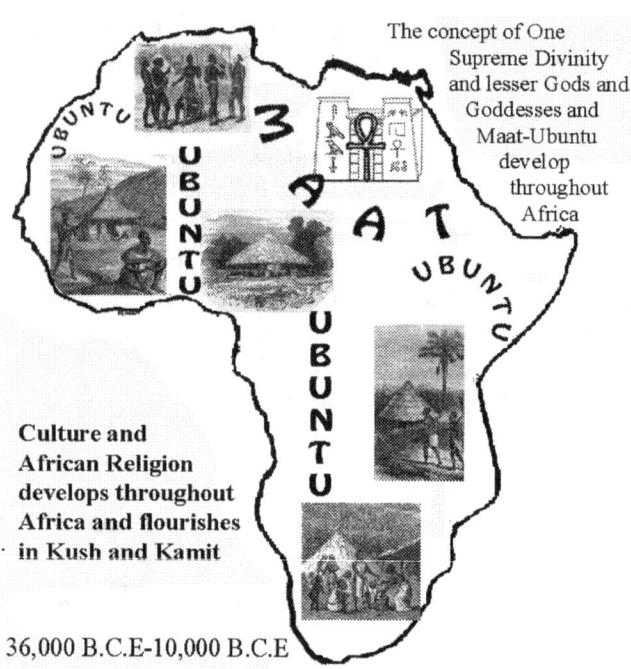

Culture and African Religion develops throughout Africa and flourishes in Kush and Kamit

The concept of One Supreme Divinity and lesser Gods and Goddesses and Maat-Ubuntu develop throughout Africa

36,000 B.C.E-10,000 B.C.E

Figure below: African High Culture- Kamitan Culture Influences African Cultures

Between 36,000 B.C.E. and 10,000 B.C.E. the peoples of the northeastern quadrant of the continent were able to develop advanced culture and civilization. This became known as the Kush-Kamit Civilization. It was based on the same essential African spiritual and social principles as all other African cultures that originated in 150,000 B.C.E. in central-equatorial Africa. At about 4,000 B.C.E. the Kamitan culture began to influence other African nations with its highly evolved African philosophy, which was actually an evolution of the same principles possessed by the other African cultures.

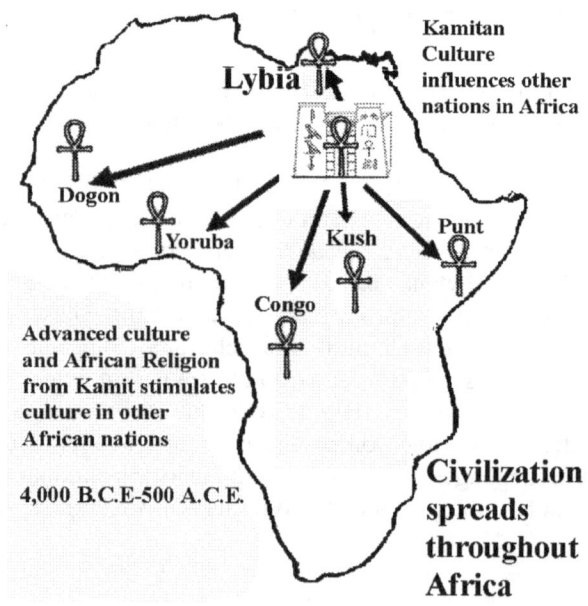

Advanced culture and African Religion from Kamit stimulates culture in other African nations

4,000 B.C.E-500 A.C.E.

Civilization spreads throughout Africa

Figure below: Kamitan Civilization Influences Cultures Outside of Africa 4,000 B.C.E.-500 A.C.E.

At about 3,500 B.C.E. or earlier, the Kamitan culture and civilization began to influence the peoples in Asia Minor (Mesopotamia) and South East Asia (India and China). At about 1,900-1,400 B.C.E. the Kamitan culture and civilization began to influence the archaic Greek culture (Minoans), thereby fomenting the development of culture and spirituality in those areas.

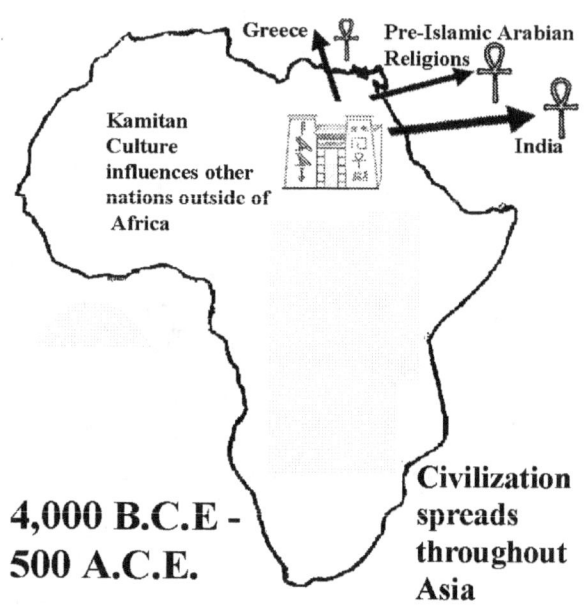

Kamitan Culture influences other nations outside of Africa

4,000 B.C.E - 500 A.C.E.

Civilization spreads throughout Asia

Basic Timeline of Kamitan History

c. 65,000 B.C.E. Paleolithic – Nekhen (Hierakonpolis)
c. 10,000 B.C.E. Neolithic – period

PREDYNASTIC PERIOD

c. 10,500 B.C.E.-7,000 B.C.E. Creation of the Great Sphinx Modern archeological accepted dates – Sphinx means Her-m-akhet or Heru (Horus) in the horizon. This means that the King is one with the Spirit, Ra as an enlightened person possessing an animal aspect (lion) and illuminated intellect. Anunian Theology – Ra - Serpent Power Spirituality

c. 10,000 B.C.E.-5,500 B.C.E. The Sky GOD- Realm of Light-Day – NETER Androgynous – All-encompassing –Absolute, Nameless Being, later identified with Ra-Herakhti (Sphinx)

>7,000 B.C.E. Neterian Myth and Theology present in architecture

OLD KINGDOM PERIOD

5500+ B.C.E. to 600 A.C.E. Amun -Ra - Ptah (Horus) – Amenit - Rai – Sekhmet (male and female Trinity-Complementary Opposites)

5500+ B.C.E. Memphite Theology – Ptah
5500+ B.C.E. Hermopolitan Theology- Djehuti
5500+ B.C.E. The Asarian Resurrection Theology - Asar
5500+B.C.E. The Goddess Principle- Theology, Isis-Hathor-Net-Mut-Sekhmet-Buto
5500 B.C.E. (Dynasty 1) Beginning of the Dynastic Period (Unification of Upper and Lower Egypt)
5000 B.C.E. (4th-5th Dynasty) Pyramid Texts - Egyptian Book of Coming Forth By Day - 42 Precepts of MAAT and codification of the Pre-Dynastic theologies (Pre-Dynastic period: 10,000 B.C.E.-5,500 B.C.E.) Coming Forth By Day (Book of the Dead)
4241 B.C.E. The Pharaonic (royal) calendar based on the Sothic system (star Sirius) was in use.

MIDDLE KINGDOM PERIOD

3000 B.C.E. WISDOM TEXTS-Precepts of Ptahotep, Instructions of Any, Instructions of Amenemope, Etc.
2040 B.C.E.-1786 B.C.E. *COFFIN TEXTS* Coming Forth By Day (Book of the Dead)

1800 B.C.E.-Theban Theology - Amun

NEW KINGDOM PERIOD

1580-1075 BCE NEW KINGDOM
1539-1292 18th (Thebes) Dynasty
1292-1190 19th (Thebes) Dynasty
1190-1075 20th (Thebes) Dynasty

1075-656 BCE 3RD INTERMEDIATE

1075-945 21st (Tanis) Dynasties
45-712 22nd (Bubastis) Dynasties
838-712 23rd Dynasties
727-712 24th (Sais) Dynasties
760-656 25th ("Nubian" or "Kushite") Dynasties

664-332 BCE LATE PERIOD

664-525 26th (Sais) Dynasty
525-405 27th Dynasty (Persian Conquest)
1st Persian occupation
521-486 Darius I
486-466 Xerxes I
409-399 28th (Sais) Dynasty
399-380 29th (Mendes) Dynasty
381-343 30th (Sebennytos) Dynasty
343-332 31st Dynasty (Persian)
2nd Persian occupation

332 BCE-AD HELLENISTIC CONQUEST PERIOD

332-305 32nd Dynasty (Alexandria)("Macedonian")
332-323 Alexander III the Great
305-30 33rd Dynasty (Alexandria)("Ptolemaic")

332 BCE-A.C.E. ROMAN CONQUEST PERIOD
30 BCE-14 A.C.E. Augustus

394 A.C.E. COPTIC CHRISTIAN CONQUEST PERIOD
394 A.C.E. Theodosius adopted Christianity as the state religion of Rome

ARAB AND MUSLIM CONQUEST PERIOD
(c. 700 A.C.E.-present)

What is Shetaut Neter?

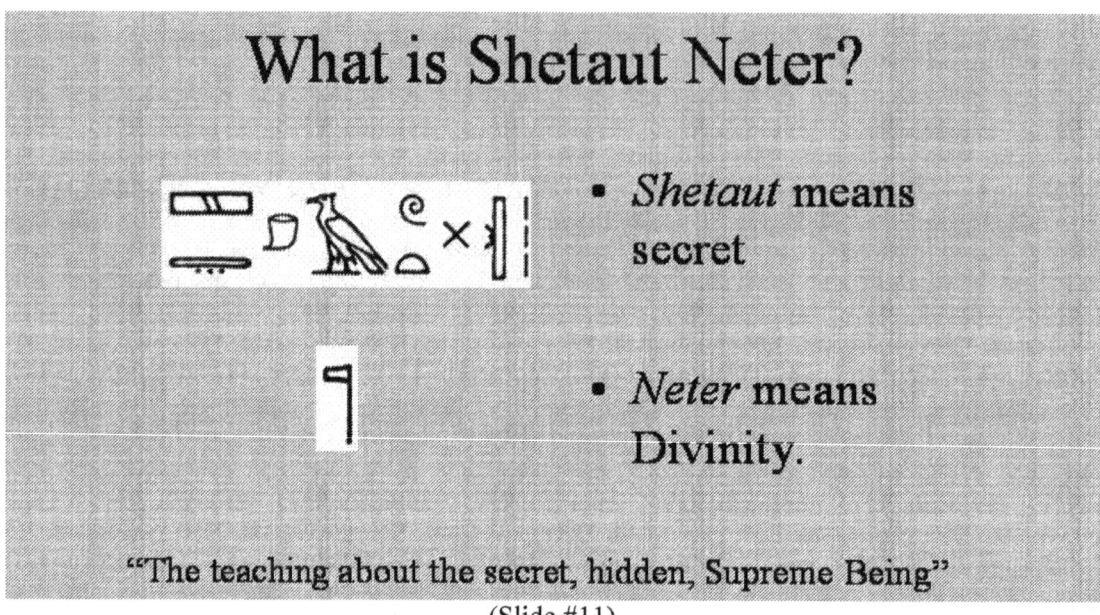

(Slide #11)

Now we will examine the hieroglyphic text definition of Shetaut Neter. "Shetaut" is the first word. It means secret or hidden or mysteries and the flag looking symbol means "Neter." Neter means Divinity. It can mean God or Goddess. It means Divinity in general. "Shetaut Neter" therefore means the teaching about the secret, hidden "Supreme Being," or "Divine Mysteries." This is the earliest term that we have a record of, for the term religion, and it comes from Africa. It is important to acknowledge this, because for many years, most of the western missionaries and scholars were trying to convince African people and others that Africans had/have no word for the term religion, and that African spirituality, therefore, is really a form of, to use the term that a Muslim gentleman told me, "primitive speculation." While visiting Egypt, I was told by a Muslim person that Islam is real religion, Christianity and Judaism are religions too, albeit wrong, and that African spirituality and the Eastern religions (Hinduism, Buddhism, Taoism, etc.) are no more than speculation that are feeble, backward attempts at religion, but not true religion.

What is Neterianism?

The term "Neterianism" is derived from the name "Shetaut Neter." Those who follow the spiritual path of Shetaut Neter are therefore referred to as "Neterians."

- *"Neterianism"*

- When referring to the religion of Ancient Egypt itself the term "Neterianism" will be used. So this term will substitute for or be used interchangeably with the term "Ancient Egyptian Religion" or Kamitan Religion.

- *"Neterian"*

- When referring to anything related to the religion of Ancient Egypt, the term Neterian will be used interchangeably with the terms Shetaut Neter, as it relates to the Kamitan term for religion, "Shetaut Neter."

(Slide #12)

Egyptian Mysteries Volume 1: Principles of Shetaut Neter

What is Neterianism? The term "Neterianism" is derived from the term Shetaut Neter. Those who follow the spiritual path of Shetaut Neter are referred to as "Neterians." When referring to the religion of ancient Egypt, itself, the term Neterianism will be used. This term will be substituted for or will be used interchangeably with the term Ancient Egyptian Religion or Kamitan Religion or spirituality. All these are referring to the same thing: Neterianism, Shetaut Neter, Ancient Egyptian Religion, or Kamitan Religion.

The term "Neterian" means a person who follows Shetaut Neter, and the specific term for that person who is a "follower" is *Shems*. *Shemsu* are persons (plural) who follow Shetaut Neter. They are disciples or followers. This next slide shows the specific Medu Neter scripture that gives us this wisdom of the terms:

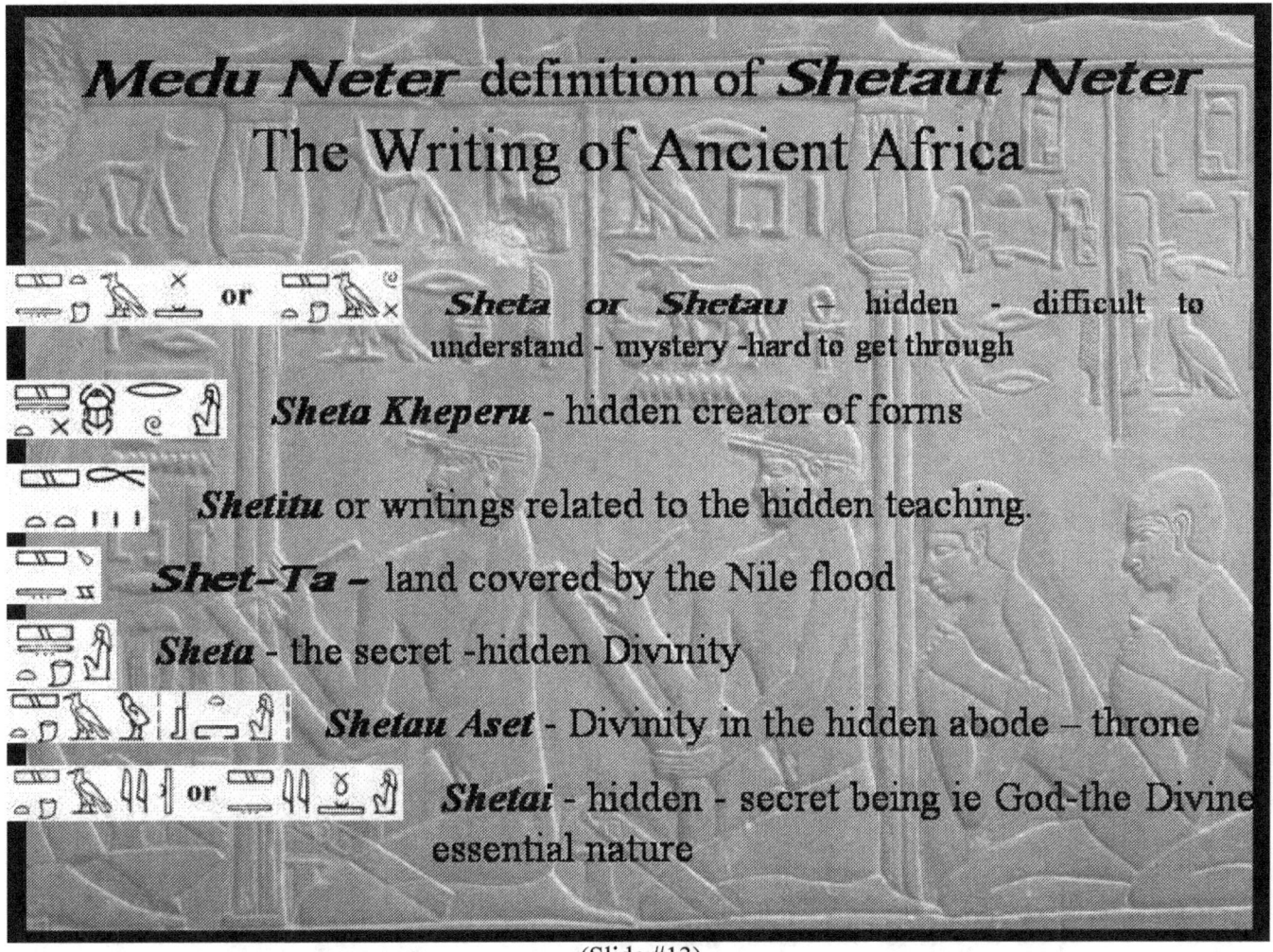

(Slide #13)

Etymology of the term Shetaut Neter

Here we have the term *Shetaut* or *Sheta* meaning "hidden, difficult to understand, hard to get through, a mystery." The term *Shetaut Kepheru*, means hidden, creator of forms; *Shetitu* means: "writings related to the hidden teachings"; *Shet-Ta* means "the land covered by the Nile." When the Nile water is overflowing, the land is covered, so it means covered, or shrouded.

Sheta means "the secret hidden Divinity." *Shetaut Aset* means "the Divinity in the hidden abode or throne;" (Aset means abode or throne). *Shetai* means "hidden secret Being, The Divine essential nature." This is the etymology of the term Shetaut in Shetaut Neter.

Egyptian Mysteries Volume 1: Principles of Shetaut Neter

Who is Neter?

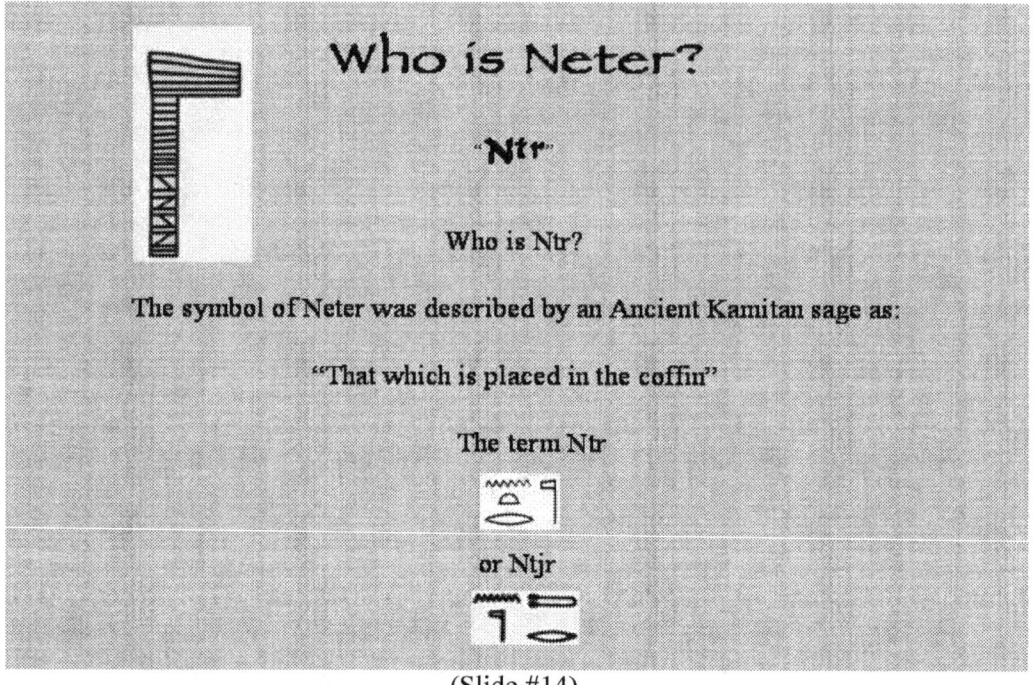

(Slide #14)

The Symbol of Neter (*Ntr*) is the symbol that appears like a flag or hatchet. Another form of the spelling is *Ntjr*. So we can say, Shetaut Neter or Shetaut Ntjr…both of these terms are allowed and proper for our study. So who are Neterians?

Who Are the Neterians?

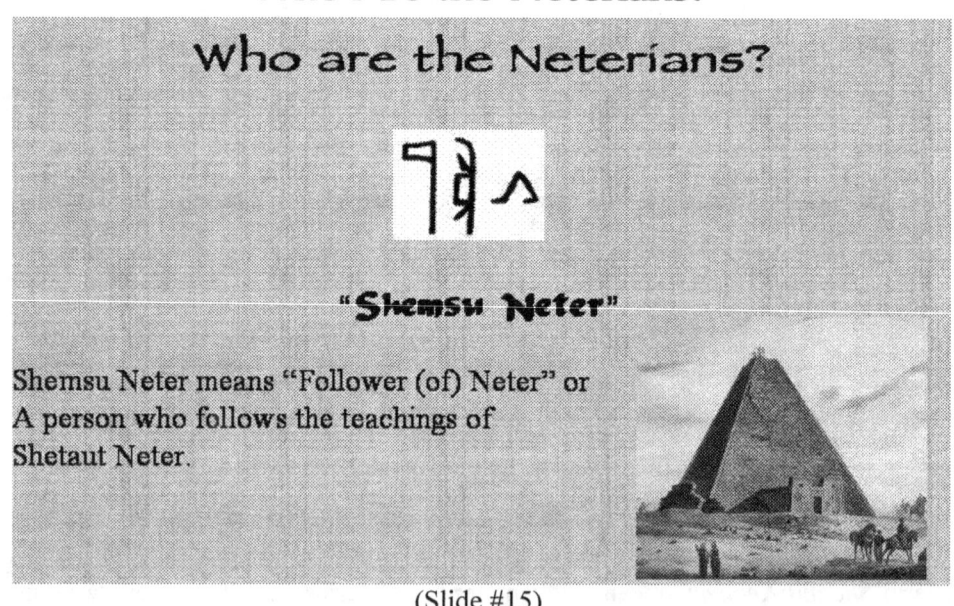

(Slide #15)

In the slide above the first symbol of the term is of course Neter. The Symbols in the term Shems (follower) are the second two symbols, therefore we have "Follower of Neter" …that is, the person who "walks," that is, practices the religion of Shetaut Neter, and who studies the teachings of Shetaut Neter. Also Shems means following or directing the attention and obeying the leader and the teachings of the tradition that is being followed. The following term means *Shemsu Heru* - Followers of Heru. This is the highest kind of title a Neterian aspirant can be given. Such a person is a true follower of the teaching, a true follower of God. Heru means "that which is most high."

> # What is Essential Philosophy of Shetaut Neter?
>
> ## The Spiritual Culture and the Purpose of Life: Shetaut Neter
>
> "Men and women are to become God-like through a life of virtue and the cultivation of the spirit through scientific knowledge, practice and bodily discipline."
>
> -Ancient Egyptian Proverb

(Slide #16)

What is the Essential Philosophy of Shetaut Neter?

We will now go into some of the basic philosophical principles of Shetaut Neter. A Kamitan Proverb states: "Men and women are to become God-like through a life of virtue and cultivation of the spirit through scientific knowledge, practice, and bodily discipline."

This might be referred to as a central purpose, a central goal of the entire process of Shetaut Neter. This is what you are shooting for. Now specifically, what does that mean? That is a matter for much deeper study, for work in the temples, for metaphysics…all of the rest of the teaching that is to be received and some of which has been given through our other books… how to cleanse yourself, how to elevate yourself in consciousness; that is the hard part.

I can tell you that you are the Divine Self a thousand times, but how do you actually have this experience on a perpetual basis? That is the study of the philosophy. That is the practice of the disciplines, and we will discuss a little bit about those as we go along further. This is what our institute and the Temple are all about, disseminating that teachings and assisting in its practice.

But before we go into that, we need to discuss why it is important to study these teachings and disciplines. Why should you not forget all of this and go out to a movie, a party or go do something to get rich so that you may enjoy the pleasures of life? Why should we discuss these things? What should we be discussing, that is what is worthy of being discussed? This goes to the big questions of life. What is my purpose in life? Why am I here? If you are asking those questions, wondering why you are living life as most other people and why you are still unhappy, still depressed, still dissatisfied, frustrated, empty, etc., then you are in a process of desiring to be awakened to the higher realities of life.

The Pursuit of Happiness

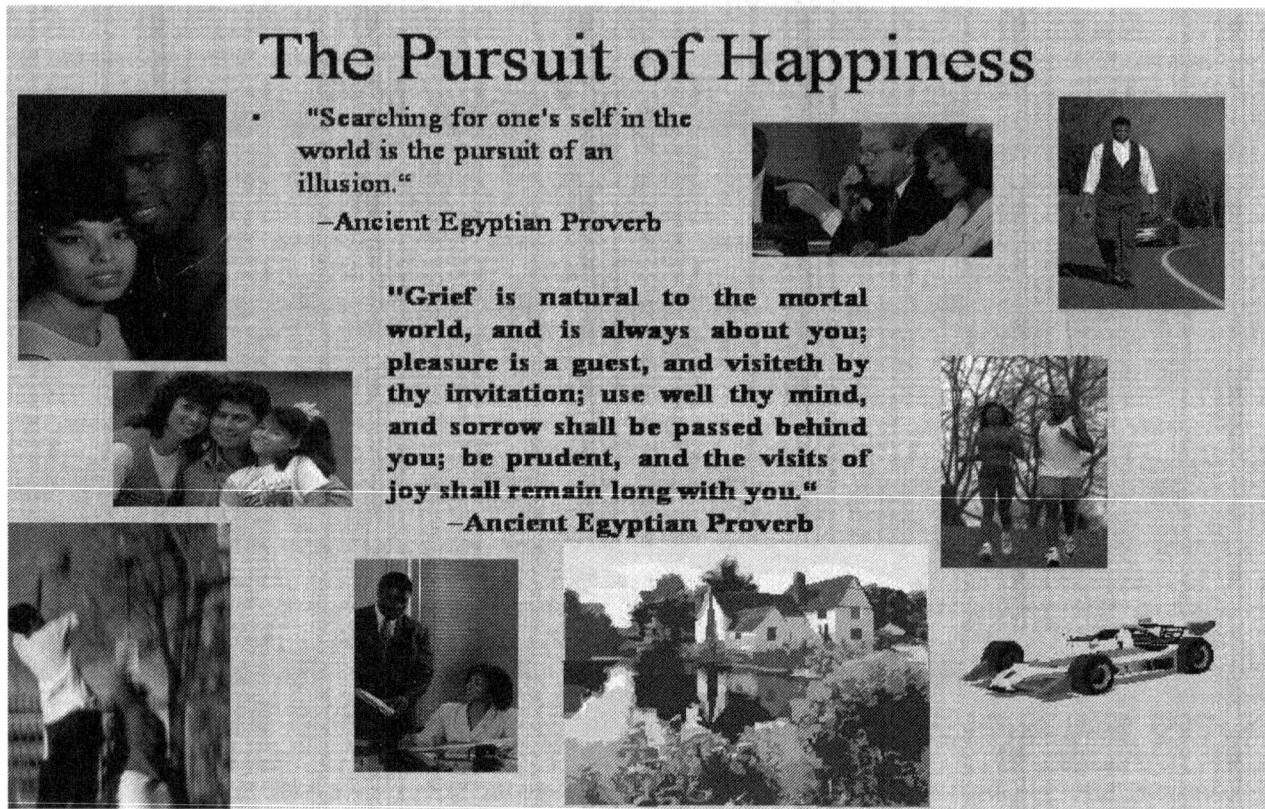

(Slide #17)

Life is really about the pursuit of happiness. But where is true happiness to be found? You might want to pursue a love affair or have love in your life. You might want a family. You might desire to be healthy so you can play with your friends and go to sports events. You might like to have a good job. You might like to have your own house, to have a partner for life. You may like to have a sports car. But with all of these things that you pursue in life to be happy, there is always a problem. Look at the picture above. This is what the gentleman with gas can symbolizes…the problem. You put gas in the car, but then you run out of gas. There is always going to be a running out of gas when one is seeking true (abiding) happiness in the transient pleasures of the world. The lesson is that there is never anything that is permanent, never anything that is wholly as you expect… things always change. You may have a job, but then you realize that somebody else is calling the shots on your job. And you may not like what you are doing in your job. You wish you could change your job, but then you are caught up in mortgages, strife and trouble. This always leads to disappointment and frustration. Life without an authentic spiritual basis will always lead to disappointment. I am not here to tell you that as you practice authentic spirituality, life is going to be wonderful all the time, because you know it already isn't. If you are looking for some kind of a special key or some kind of special words to make life all better, that can only happen with you, when you adopt the teaching correctly, and live in a way that lead you away from strife, unhappiness, and wrong actions. Since the world is always changing and nothing is permanent to the world, this means that you will not have true abiding happiness in the world. But people still continue to search anyway: "Maybe if I find another car, maybe if I fall in love with someone else, maybe if I eat another hamburger, maybe if I go on a diet and lose some weight…I'll be happy." But happiness cannot come from externality. There is a Kamitan Proverb hat goes: "Searching for oneself in the world is a pursuit of an illusion." So, what should you be searching for in life? What is worth searching for?

A Kamitan Proverb brings the answer. *"Grief is natural to the mortal world and is always about you; pleasure is guest and visiteth by thy invitation; use well thy mind and sorrow shall be passed behind you; be prudent and the visits of joy shall remain long with you."*

"Use well thy mind;" this is the key. I am sure that you know many people…you have heard of them in Hollywood or people in your town… people who have money, people who have nice cars, people who have a good job, who have a family… and they are miserable. Or something happened and they have a fight with their spouse or their child is running away, doing drugs or something else happens…there is always some trouble. How do you get into these things? Because everybody does it, and you think you should do it too. Because when you watch people on television, they are always smiling. Halle Berry is always smiling. Oprah is always smiling. Everyone on TV and in the movies is always wonderful. And they are always made up and always looking good, but it isn't true in real life, is it? Not every woman can be in a size 2 dress, can they? Then we will find out that through all the smiles and winning Oscars, that a particular TV or movie star was going through a divorce and the most miserable time of their life, or some other personal difficulty. Yet, the show must go on, right? But it appears that they are always happy, and they would like you to think so. It's all an illusion, and following that means that the mind has been led down a road of ignorance. Religion is supposed to be a means to lead to you away from ignorance, and to enlightenment. If your religion is not leading you to enlightenment, then you are not practicing correct religion… it is as simple as that. Therefore religion cannot always be laughs and screaming halleluiah all the time. There must be some suffering, some sacrifice, like a baby being born. There is some pain indeed, and then there is a birth. On the path there will be pain and sorrow, but if approached correctly, that pain and sorrow turns into a divine sacrifice and not a torture as it is for most people. That sacrifice is giving up the ego, the childish spirituality, and growing up to receive the throne of immortality and enlightenment. Then deep introspection is possible and peace and abiding happiness come. This is true religion. If you are not growing more relaxed and more peaceful, abiding more in higher consciousness, in the higher faith, even when adversity strikes in life, then you know your religion is not working.

"Self sacrifice annihilates the personality."

"To suffer, is a necessity entailed upon your nature. Would you prefer that miracles should protect you from its lessons or shalt you repine, because it happened unto you, when lo it happened unto all? Suffering is the golden cross upon which the rose of the Soul unfolds."

-Ancient Egyptian Proverbs

Forgiveness, Hope, Redemption and Healing the Errors of the Past To Become Free from the Past

Most people think of spirituality and of God in terms of sectarian forms traditionally passed on by religious organizations. The Supreme Divinity is often seen in those traditions as a powerful yet fearsome being that sends people to eternal damnation for their sins. However, in the light of Yoga philosophy and through the various disciplines developed by the yogic masters over the last 12,000 years, the Supreme Divinity is to be understood in a much more universal way. We not only discover the infinite compassion and love of the Self (Supreme Divinity) but through the various practices of the Mystery System, which have been tailored for the various levels of human spiritual development and different personalities, it is also possible to partake in the glory of Divinity. This is the goal of the Neterian Mystery System.

No matter how low a human being goes in his/her existence, the practice of The Mystery System, with the correct understanding, supplies a sure way to overcome any and all human ills, frailties and failings. This is true because all individuals are essentially one with the Divine Self. Through a process of ignorance they have forgotten their true identity and have turned to negativity. Through the process of The Mystery System, you may discover your true essence, thereby unleashing the gifts and infinite power of the soul.

With this inner power which comes from wisdom and self effort toward cleansing the heart from its negative emotions, feelings and thoughts, anyone can overcome incredible obstacles. This is the power that made it possible for the Ancient Egyptians to create the massive pyramids and temples out of stone without machinery. They were able to accomplish feats of engineering which modern society cannot duplicate. Even more importantly, they developed a science of spiritual development which has influenced all world religions and in the Neterian Book Series we show how the Ancient Egyptian elements are still present in Judaism, Christianity, Islam, Hinduism, Buddhism and Taoism.

The heart of this science of self improvement is known to the world as *Sema* (*Yoga*). In recent times Yoga has been made popular by the Indian practitioners. Many people have been introduced to yoga as a practice of physical exercise for health and relaxation, but in reality, Yoga is much more than that. Physical health and relaxation are only the beginning stages of yoga, which are necessary in order to make it possible for a practitioner to understand and practice the higher teachings of self-development. Sema (Yoga) is a vast science of self-development that has proven its effectiveness over the last 7,000 years.

Many people, however, are interested in yoga philosophy from the ancient point of view. This is the perspective which we take in all of our books and literature. While here we relate the teachings and show how other religions are all in reality aiming for the same goal, the upliftment of every human being, it must be understood that though they are in a general sense seeking the same goal, the limitations in dogmatic, orthodox religions prevent that from happening. So in principle yes, they are moving towards the same goal, however in practice that is not so. In practice there is much contradiction in the teaching and exclusivist philosophies in those religions that cause them to be hostile to others. Since they do not include mysticism, the third level of religious practice (see *The Stages of African Religion*), the spiritual development of their adherents is limited. Consequently, their followers are unable to realize the higher goals because of the dogmatic or biased and limited perspectives of many religious or spiritual traditions. This Neterian path is based on the Ancient Egyptian myths, symbols, and practices for attaining

Egyptian Mysteries Volume 1: Principles of Shetaut Neter

the highest spiritual evolution and does incorporate all the levels of spiritual practice.

Usually when we (at Sema) are contacted by someone it is because they are searching for answers to long held spiritual questions. Life has not produced happy circumstances, and there is an interest in anything that will alleviate the miseries and sorrows of life. They are looking for a way out. Our goal is to teach the ancient wisdom of true happiness and prosperity which has remained dormant or become distorted in the teachings of common religion. These inner teachings and practices can be followed by anyone who possesses maturity, sincerity and an honest desire to work toward self-improvement.

Happiness can be yours on the condition that you are willing to work for it by practicing the art of self-development. It does not matter what crime or what sin you have committed. The light of wisdom and the practices of purification can bring about a transformation in the consciousness of any human being. This is called bathing in the liquor of Maat. From the lower self you can move up to the Higher Self. This science begins with your understanding and forgiveness of yourself, and then the intensive process of introspection and realization of the truth through building a life based on order, truth and justice.

Misery in life stems from ignorance of one's true nature. Human beings are like kings or queens who wander around the countryside as beggars, not knowing their true identity. They act as beggars, treat others unkindly, indulge in hatred and anger of others; they are frustrated due to their condition and don't know what to do about it so they go on from day to day wasting their lives. You may be unaware of your talents and of your capacity to love yourself and others. You have come to a state which has led you to experience the degradation and loss of spiritual and physical freedom. You search for excitement and fulfillment of your desires through your worldly relationships, by entertaining yourself with the media, or and drugs, or and alcohol, or and by acquiring objects (cars, clothes, etc.) that you think will make you happy. You do these things because you have been taught that this is the way to pursue happiness. But have any of these things ever brought you true and lasting happiness and peace? In order to be truly happy you must unleash your Spirit. You are the one responsible for your condition because of your past actions based on ignorance of Self. Therefore, do not waste any more time by blaming others or by seeking to find explanations in society or other external causes. <u>The wonderful thing is that you are also the one who by your actions illumined by the light of wisdom in action (Maat), can change your life.</u>

The Ancient Egyptians prescribed one solution to all of the problems of life and they built an entire country based on this precept and the legacy lives on up to this day. The solution is *Know Thyself*. Through self-knowledge, all of the misconceptions of the mind which have led to degraded states, erroneous thoughts, conflict and misunderstanding are washed away. Through self-knowledge one discovers the supreme happiness which comes from inner contentment and peace which cannot come from external objects or relationships in the world.

Your interest (reading this volume) indicates that you have begun to recognize that there is a higher goal in life for you other than your current experience. This is a blessing because most people are not able to see the misery of their own condition and then choose to do something about it. Most people are caught in the web of illusion and negativity they have woven in their minds and go on like robots from one miserable situation to another. Your task is to follow up on this book, study the teachings and begin practicing them in your life right now. Develop a relationship with your inner Higher Self and discover the strength to overcome your failings. Everyone is a child of the Divine; as such everyone is capable of supreme good according to their level of awareness of their true Self.

There is no fanatical or magical way to self-development except to learn the science of self-knowledge and to then apply the teachings and practice the exercises for spiritual development by gradually incorporating them into your life. Spiritual evolution is not a continuous upward movement. You will have many ups and downs when you begin to practice. Sometimes you will not be able to follow the teachings because you are overcome by your established negative ways. But if you sincerely press on, in time you will discover the source of inner strength within you. Self-development is an inner attainment. It is revealed in your level of peace and oneness with the universe, and your level of joy and love for humanity – not in the level of callousness, egoistic selfishness or apathy toward others or the possessions you seem to own, or the status accorded by others. Many people confuse apathy or being uncaring towards others as peace, but these are intense forms of selfishness and hard-heartedness that masquerade as peace, and are in reality a form of unrest and inner pain which reaches to the very soul.

Have you committed crimes? Do you feel guilt? Do you feel suffering is your lot in life? Do you feel like an unsavable sinner? What is a sinner? And can a sin be redeemed? Can the soul truly be born again? What is a convict? Yes, there is redemption, but not perhaps as you might think. You cannot just say you are "born again" and shout halleluiah and have all the errors of life erased, nor can the errors of life be wiped away in an instant just by being repentant. Exuberant types of religious practices, that is, practices that are full of unrestrained enthusiasm, hysterical, lavish, extravagant, etc. are like a band-aid on a wound that really needs an operation with stitches. The benefits are short term in that stress is released, but the cause of the problem, spiritual emptiness, is not resolved by such limited practice of religion. However, repentance can be the first step. Then there must be serious work on yourself to remove the error that led to the sin (turning away from God in actions). Only then can there be true redemption and forgiveness – and spiritual enlightenment, abiding happiness and immortality. The dictionary defines "convict" as a person found guilty of a crime, especially one serving a prison sentence. Is such guilt or prison sentence a part of one's eternal existence? Is it a permanent blot on one's soul which will send one to hell forever? The wisdom of Shetaut Neter and Sema Tawi has taught for thousands of years that the soul is innately divine and has a possibility to evolve, to discover its own higher reality which is eternal and pure in the Supreme Self (God). This means that it is possible to overcome and transcend any and all forms of negativity or evil actions of the past. This exalted vision of life is not merely a myth inspired by superstition or fanaticism, but was the basis of Ancient Egyptian society which allowed the construction of the most extensive and longest running civilization in history. Ancient Egyptian dynastic civilization existed for over 5,000 years. No other civilization in history can compare to that record. What made the Ancient Egyptians great? It was the spiritual basis of society which was rooted in *Shetaut Neter* (spiritual values) and *Maat* (virtue).

A person may be ordered to be obedient, to follow rules, etc. However, since there are so many laws in society why, then is it that there is increasing crime and increasing strife among people? Why is there enmity in the world? Why is there a desire to hurt others? Why is there a desire to misappropriate the property of others?

Anger and hatred cannot be stopped by simply telling someone to be good, loving, forgiving and so on. One cannot become righteous by being ordered to or forced to, no more than a plant can be forced to grow, bear fruit or flowers through a command by the farmer. One can be compelled to follow rules, but this does not mean that one is necessarily a virtuous person. Many people do not commit crimes, and yet they are not virtuous because they are harboring negative thoughts (violence, hatred, greed, lust, etc.) in their hearts. Virtue is a profound quality which every human being has a potential to manifest because it is the innate nature of the innermost reality within every human being. This is because the innermost self of every person is divine. However, the revelation of this truth requires effort on the part of the individual as well as the correct guidance. Virtue is like a flower which can grow and become beautiful for the whole world to see. However, just as a plant must receive the proper nutrients (soil, water, sunlight, etc.) so too the human heart must receive the proper caring and nurturing in the form of love, wisdom, proper diet, meditation and good will. Even if you had a troubled upbringing, maybe your parents did not love you, or were not present, or you were hurt by others, realize that those things too can be resolved and you can move forward, and you will discover compassion, love, healing and nurturance in the teaching, the family of practitioners, in God and in your own Higher Self

The Purpose of Adversity in Life

Why is there adversity in life? Wouldn't it be nice if there was no misfortune or unluckiness to hamper your movement in life? Shouldn't God have created a perfect world? Human life abounds with adversity; even the very rich experience adversity. In fact, no matter who you are you will experience adversity of one form or another as you progress through life. This is an expression of cosmic justice - Maat.

Adversity is a divine messenger. Imagine how life would be if you could do anything you wanted to do. You would indulge every desire and whim. You would only seek to satisfy your desire for pleasure and you would not accomplish any thing significant in life and you would not grow. In the end you would be frustrated and disappointed because no matter how hard you try it is not possible to ever completely satisfy your desire for the pleasures of the senses.

Adversity is a form of resistance which life places on all beings for the purpose of engendering in them a need to strive to overcome the desires of the lower nature, and thus to discover the Higher Self within. When adversity is met with the correct understanding and with the right attitude it can become a great source of strength and spiritual inspiration. However, if adversity makes you hardhearted, insensitive, selfish, cold and bitter then you will lead yourself deeper into the quagmire of negativity and pain. Adversity is God's way of calling your attention away from negative ways of life and to draw attention toward the basic mysteries of life. Often when people succeed in acquiring some object they desired they develop conceit and vanity. They look down on others and feel proud of their accomplishment, not realizing that their achievement will fulfill them only temporarily. However, when they lose what they desired, they fall into the valley of adversity, despair, violence and anger. They blame others for their misfortune and seek to hurt others for their loss.

Many of those people who have experienced the most adversity in history include Sages and Saints. Why should God allow those who are trying to be closest to the Divine be plagued with adversity? The answer lies in an Ancient Egyptian proverb:

> "Adversity is the seed of well doing; it is the nurse of heroism and boldness; who that hath enough, will endanger himself to have more? Who that is at ease, will set their life on the hazard?

Have you noticed that it seems as though the people who are most righteous and deserving of prosperity are the one's who suffer the most in life? In families, the child who is most obedient gets the most attention and disciplinary control. People who were loving and compassionate suffer illnesses and pain from others. This is because nature has been set up by God to create situations which challenge human beings so as to provide for them opportunities to discover their inner resources which give them the capacity to overcome the trouble and thereby grow in discovery of their deeper Self. Those who suffer most are in reality those who have drawn more attention from the Divine; indeed they are chosen for more intense spiritual testing and training. This testing process of nature allows every soul the opportunity to face trouble with either boldness and faith or with fear and negativity. The rewards of adversity faced well are increased strength of will and an increased feeling of discovery of the Divine within (inner peace and expansion -Heaven). When adversity is faced with negativity and ignorance it leads to pain, sorrow and more adversity (Hell).

Therefore, adversity cannot be understood and successfully faced with negativity (anger, hatred, hardheartedness, etc.). Adversity can only be overcome with wisdom and virtue, and virtue is the first and most important quality to be developed by all serious spiritual aspirants.

From a mystical spiritual point of view, what is considered to be prosperity by the masses of ignorant people is in reality adversity, and what is considered to be adversity by the masses is in reality prosperity. The masses consider that becoming rich and being able to indulge the pleasures of the senses through food, drink, drugs and sex is the ultimate goal in life, yet is there anyone who has discovered true (abiding) peace and contentment even with billions of dollars? Having the opportunity to indulge the pleasures of the senses creates an opportunity for the mind to become more dependent on the worldly pleasures. This process intensifies the egoistic feelings and draws the soul away from discovering *Hetep* (true peace) within. There is increasing agitation and worry over gaining what is desired, and then preoccupation with how to hold onto it, not realizing that all must be left behind at the time of death anyway. People keep on seeking worldly fame, fortune and glory and in the process never discover true happiness and peace. They have duped themselves into believing that material wealth brings happiness because the greedy corporations, the media and popular culture reinforce this message. In reality it is a philosophy of ignorance based on lack of reflection and spiritual insight. Adversity is a call to wake up from this delusion of pain and sorrow and those who are experiencing the worst conditions are receiving the loudest call. Therefore, adversity is in reality prosperity because it stimulates the mind through suffering so that it may look for a higher vision of life and discover the abode of true happiness, peace and contentment that transcends all worldly measures.

This exalted vision of life is the innate potential of every human being. What is necessary is the dedication and perseverance to seek a higher understanding of the divine nature of creation and the divine nature of the innermost heart. Your inner Higher Self has the power to absolve and redeem all negativity. This is the highest goal of all human beings and the most difficult one as well. However, as you gain greater understanding and greater will to act with virtue, your vision of the Divine will increase and draw you closer and closer to the Higher Self. This is the glory of virtue and its power to vanquish and eradicate vice from the human heart.

Where Does True Happiness Come From?

In reality, happiness does not and cannot come from objects that can be acquired or from activities that are performed or from people outside of you. It can only come from within. Even actions that seem to be pleasurable in life cannot be considered as a source of happiness from a philosophical point of view because all activities are relative. This means that one activity is pleasurable for one person and painful for another. The same activity is desirable to the same person at some times, and not at others. This means that such happiness is inconsistent, and therefore illusory. Also, all forms of physical pleasure are fleeting. They do not fulfill the mind for long. This leads to the realization that it is not the activity itself that holds the happiness, but the individual doer who is performing the action and assigning a societal value to it. Therefore, if it was learned that going out to a party is supposed to be fun, then that activity will be pursued as a source of happiness. Here action is performed in pursuit of the fruit (desired result) of the action in the form of happiness. However, there are several negative psychological factors which arise that will not allow true happiness to manifest. The first is that the relentless pursuit of the action renders the mind restless and agitated. This prevents inner peace from entering the mind. The second is that if the desired activity is not possible, there will be depression or animosity in the mind. If the activity is thwarted by some outside force, meaning that something or someone prevented you from achieving the object or activity you saw as the "source of happiness," you develop anger towards that person or circumstance. If by chance you succeed in achieving the object or activity, you become elated; this will cause greed and craving to develop in the mind. You will want to experience more and more of the object or activity. This makes for an agitated and distracted mind. When you are not able to once again achieve the object or activity at any particular time, you will become depressed and disappointed or frustrated. Under these conditions, a constant dependence on outside activities and worldly objects develops in the mind, which will not allow for true peace and contentment. Even though it is illogical to pursue activities that cause pain in life, people are constantly acting against their own interests as they engage in actions in an effort to gain happiness, while in reality they are enhancing the probability of encountering pain later on. For every egoistic pleasure, there is an equal measure of pain that must be experienced later. People often act and shortly regret what they have done. Sometimes people know even at the time of their actions that they are wrong, and yet they are unable to stop themselves. This is because when the mind is controlled by desires and expectations, the intellect, the light of reason, and will power are *clouded* and *dull*. One is then controlled by the ego-the lower self. However, when the mind is controlled by the purified intellect, then it is not possible to be led astray due to the *fantasies* and *illusions* of the mind which engender irrational desires. When the individual is guided by their intellect, only right actions can be performed, no matter what negative ideas arise in the mind. Such a person cannot be deluded into negative actions. And when negative actions (actions which lead to future pain and disappointments) are not performed, then unhappiness cannot exist. Thus, a person who lives according to the teachings of RIGHTEOUS ACTION (Maat) lives a life of perpetual peace and happiness in the present. This implies performing actions without desire or expectations for the future results of those actions, and striving to only do good to humanity in service of Maat (God), to discover inner satisfaction.

Thus, true peace and inner fulfillment will never come through pursuit of actions when there is an expectation or desire for the fruits of those actions based on egoistic notions and ignorance. The belief in objects or worldly activities as sources of happiness is therefore seen as a state known as *spiritual ignorance* wherein the individual is caught up in the illusions, fantasies and fanciful notions of the ignorant mind. However, happiness and peace can arise spontaneously when there is an attitude of detachment and dispassion toward objects and situations in life, and attachment to what is good, beautiful and true. If actions are performed with the idea of discovering peace within, based on the understanding of the philosophy outlined above, and for the sake of the betterment of society, then these actions will have the effect of purifying the heart of the individual. The negative desires and expectations will dwindle while the inner fulfillment and awareness of fulfillment in the present moment will increase. There will be greater and greater discovery of peace within, a discovery of what is truly stable and changeless within as opposed to the mind and outer world which are constantly changing and unpredictable.

What is The True Purpose of Life?

The Purpose of Life

I have heard these songs
which are in the ancient tombs,
which tell of the virtues of life on
earth
and make little of life in the
Neterchert (cemetery).
Why then do likewise to eternity?
It is a place of justice, without
fear,
where uproar is forbidden,
where no one attacks his fellow.
This place has no enemies;
all our relatives have lived in it
from time immemorial,
with millions more to come.
It is not possible to linger in
Egypt -
no one can escape from going
west (end of life- Netherworld).
One's acts on earth are like a
dream.
'Welcome safe and sound!'
to who ever arrives in the West.

-Ancient Egyptian
Harper's Song

(Slide #18)

What is the purpose of life? In order to tread a true and beneficial path in life it is necessary to understand what is good in life and is worth pursuing, as opposed to what is not true or worth pursuing. The philosophy provides insight. The wisdom teachings related to this important issue need to be carefully studied and diligently reflected upon until the message is understood clearly by your mind.

Kamitan Proverbs:

"The purpose of human life is to achieve a state of consciousness apart from bodily concerns"

"Men and women are to become godlike through a life of virtue and cultivation of the spirit through scientific knowledge, practice, and bodily discipline."
"Salvation is freeing of the soul from the bodily fetters. Becoming a god through knowledge and wisdom, controlling the forces of the cosmos instead of being a slave to them.
Subduing the lower nature and through awakening the higher Self, ending the cycle of rebirth and dwelling with the neters who direct and control the great plan."

What should be the purpose of life? Should the purpose of life be to get rich, to have lots of fame, or a big family? No, the purpose is to become God-like, and further, to become one with God!

Now, if you decide to adopt Shetaut Neter, and you meet, say, a Christian person on the road, how will you respond to them? Perhaps you have friends in your family who are Christians, Muslims, etc., and they may ask you what are you doing? You may answer: "I am practicing African Religion." "I am practicing Neterianism." Suppose they now ask you, "What is your goal in Neterianism?" Do not tell them you are trying to become a god or a goddess. Don't waste you time getting into that kind of conflict, because in their view only Jesus can do that. But in African Religion… everybody can do that, and not in some future time, but right now…in your lifetime.

In ancient times, there was a certain genre of literature called "The Harper's Songs." This is a special genre of ancient Egyptian literature that deals with the understanding of the meaning and purpose of life. Through the following Harper's Song, the purpose of life becomes clear. The song goes:

> "I have heard these songs, which are in the ancient tombs
> Which tell of the virtues of life on earth, and make little
>   of life in the Neterkert (cemetery).
> Why then do likewise to eternity?
> It is a place of justice, without fear,
> where an uproar is forbidden,
> where no one attacks his fellow.
> This place has no enemies;
> All our relatives have lived in it from time immemorial.
> and with millions more to come.
> I joined in?
> It is not possible to linger in Egypt
> No one can escape from going west (note: west is the land
>   to death, the land of the afterlife, the Netherworld)
> One's acts on earth are like a dream
> Welcome safe and sound,
> to whoever arises in the West"

The Harper is telling us we cannot linger on earth. We must plan for our departure, and that our acts on earth here are like a dream. If you consider what the Harper's Song is saying, it is like when you have a dream when you are asleep. Your dream appears to be very real, but when you wake up from it in the morning, then you realize that it is not real. What happens when you go to sleep? When you go to sleep you believe that dream world is real, and this waking world is unreal. Which is the reality then? Do you see the high philosophy that is going on here? It means that there is something within you that is beyond the changing realms of consciousness… the waking and the dream state.

How are you to discover that state that is beyond illusion? How are you to elevate yourself to transcend this mortal finite existence? Accomplishing this is what is referred to as becoming gods and goddesses. The question then becomes how is this to be achieved? It is wonderful for me to tell you what Shetaut Neter is all about. But it is also important that you know how this is achieved. I am sure that you have heard of that saying "many are called and few are chosen."

Those of you who are studying this now, as opposed to the millions of people who are out there in the world – you are reading this because you are ready to pursue some new path to life. You are ready to discover some insight that leads you to the answers to your questions, and most likely, as to the true purpose in life and the source of pain in life. I am mainly just confirming what you already know anyway, because you have the wisdom inside you, but you have to know how to tap into it.

The Kamitan (Neterian) philosophy of teaching:

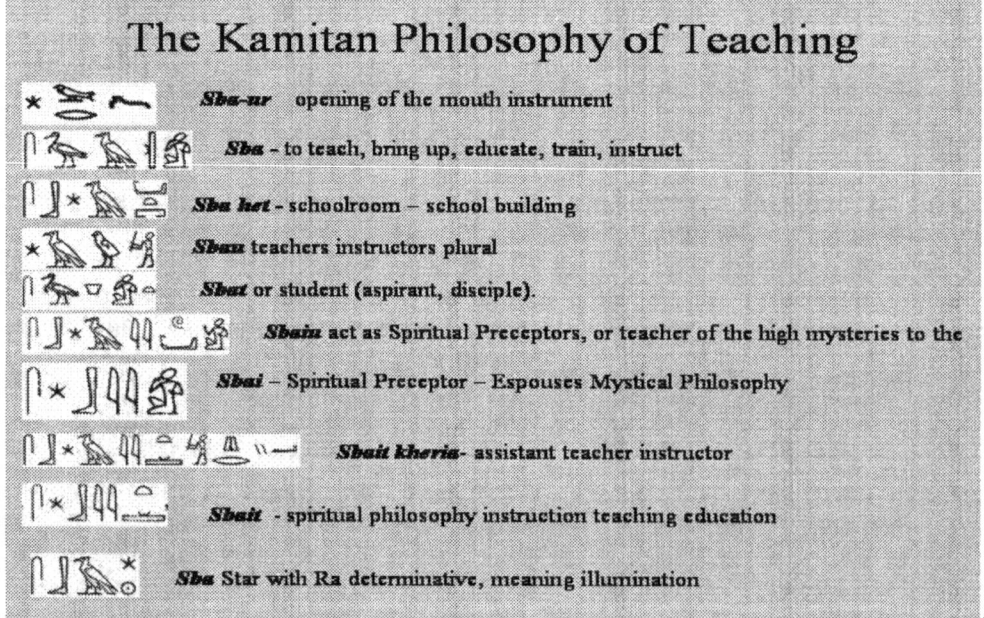

(Slide #19)

The term Seba means to teach, to bring up, to educate, to train, to instruct. Its etymology comes from Seba Ur. Seba Ur is an instrument that is held to the mouth of the initiate to open the consciousness. You have seen the pictures of the *opening of the mouth*; you have probably heard of that term.

Sba het – means "schoolroom."
Sbau means "teachers, instructors plural."
Sbat means "student" (aspirant, disciple).
Sbaiu are "those who act as spiritual preceptors."
Sbai is a single "preceptor."
Sbait kheria means "assistant teacher, or instructor or assistant to the Sbai."
Sbait means "spiritual philosophy."
Sba – is the origin for all the other terms. It means "star"(with Ra determinative means illumination)

So sba means light, to illumine, to enlighten. Sebai means star, light, illuminer, illumined, enlightened. So we have shown that the term Buddha, meaning "the enlightened one," is not the first time that such a term was used in history.

The Philosophy of the Afterlife

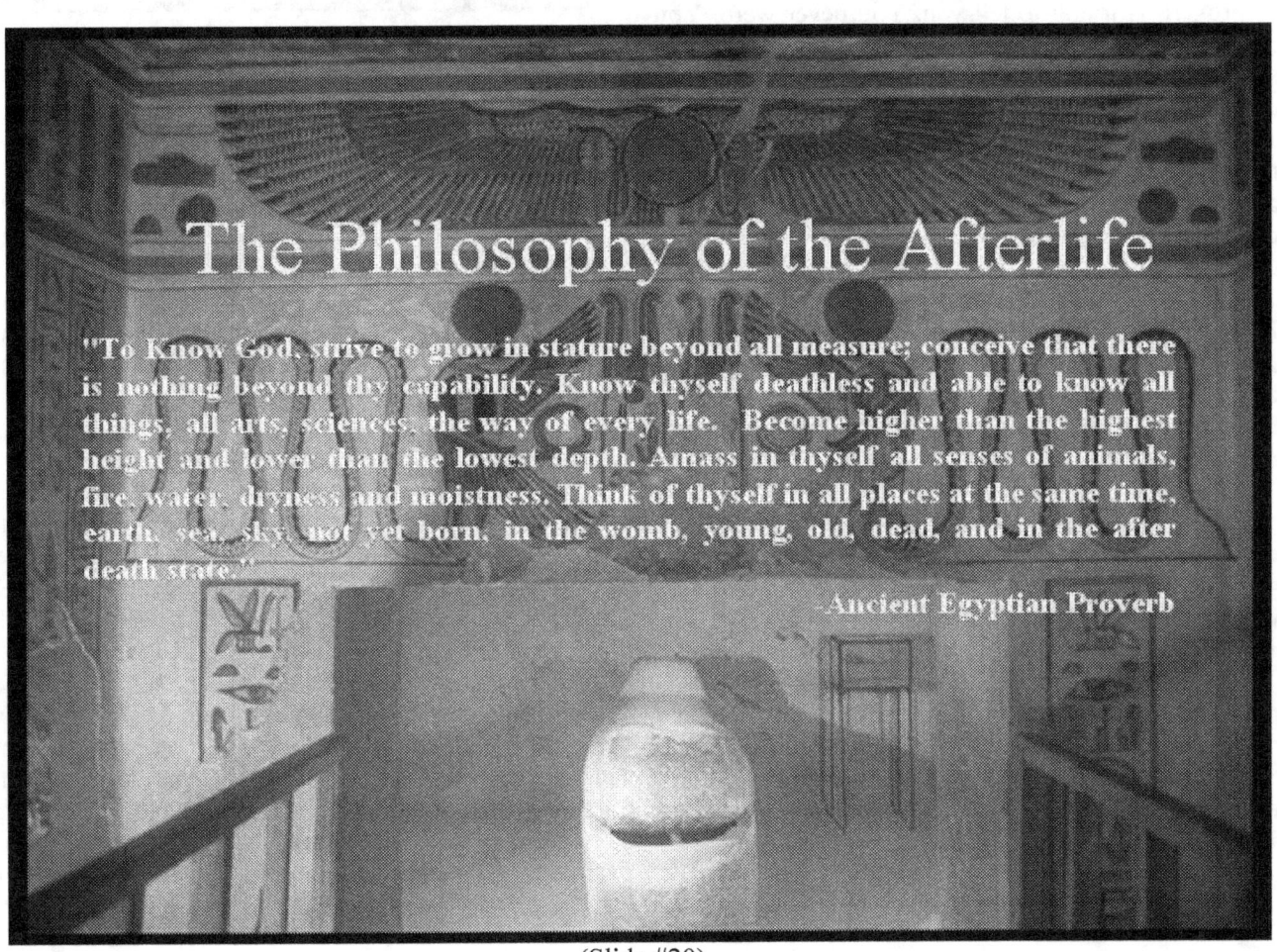

(Slide #20)

The Neterian Philosophy is dedicated to the lofty purpose in life: *to know God*. The Philosophy is extensive, and must be studied carefully and systematically with proper guidance. For more details you should read all of the books in the Neterian (Egyptian Yoga) series, but you must also realize that you cannot learn everything from the books. Ultimately, there must be personal instruction from teacher to disciple.

What is the difference between this scene (above) and any typical western cemetery that you can visit? Can you see what the difference this? Is it the hieroglyphs? Not really, because cemeteries have inscriptions on the tombs also. The answer is that here we are looking at a Temple dedicated to rebirth, whereas with sectarian cemeteries in the western culture, we are looking at dirt…dirt, that according to Christian teaching, is supposedly going to be revived at some time in the future.

Egyptian Mysteries Volume 1: Principles of Shetaut Neter

"BA AR PET SHAT AR TA"

which means:

"THE SOUL BELONGS TO HEAVEN, THE BODY BELONGS TO EARTH."

From the Prt m Hru of the *Pyramid Texts* (3,200-2,575 B.C.E.)

There is an Ancient Egyptian proverb that says "The body belongs to the earth and your soul belongs to heaven." This means that you are not the body… that is what the Ancient Egyptian proverb is trying to tell you. You never were. You have an association with typical matter, that allows you to have a typical experience, and that is the end of your association with time and space. Actually the deeper you is transcendental and immortal, but you just don't know that. Shetaut Neter or authentic religion is supposed to be helping to discover that, to realize that. That is what you are supposed to be doing. That is the purpose of life.

The purpose of life is not to get rich, not to have big families, not to have big cars, or fame and fortune; all this will wash away. Can anybody name a person, any person, who existed 500 years ago who was rich and famous? It does not matter. No one is going to care who Oprah Winfrey was 500 years from now, or about Bill Gates for that matter.

If you think that having 4 billion dollars is going to make you happier in life, think again. Money can take care of the basic necessities and that is necessary and proper. But beyond that, money is actually the source of much worry and strife. The only thing that will make you truly happy is to discover and to realize that you are immortal, and transcendental and all-encompassing. Then no matter what happens in this time and space reality, you will be above it. Then there will be no changes in yourself, whether you have gas in your car or don't have gas in your car, whether you have a sports car or a beat-up Toyota.

This is what the proverb on the previous slide is leading us to.

"To know God, strive to grow in stature beyond all measure; conceive that there is nothing beyond thy capacity. Know thyself deathless and able to know all things, all arts, sciences, the way of every life. Become higher than the highest height, and lower than the lowest depth. Amass in thyself all senses

of animal, fire, water, dryness, and moistness. Think of thyself in all places at the same times, earth, sea, sky, not yet born, in the womb, young, old, dead and in the after death state."

This teaching is magnanimous isn't it? This is a magnanimous vision of life. There is an image (above) of the god Heru holding all the animals. He is the master of nature. This is what is being described in this proverb. And this is what you are shooting for. And as this proverb indicates, you are to know yourself in this way. You are to know that this is possible for you.

We have over 30 books. But don't be overwhelmed by all the books. Don't be overwhelmed by all this knowledge that is being brought forth in this book; you are only going to retain about 25% - 40% of it anyway. You have to get the books, get the tapes, and study them, attend classes and live the teaching. That is how it works. Allow yourself to be impressed by the books however, and I want you to believe that this mystical attainment is possible for you. This has been done from time immemorial, and the loss of this is why we are in the state we are in now. You must know that this is the same teaching that was used by the ancients, and they accomplished great things. It was possible for Imhotep, 5,000 years ago, those who came before him thousands of years earlier, and it is possible for you now, as they were made out of flesh and blood, just like you. But Imhotep, Ptahotep, Hetheru, Aset, etc., minds that were trained and purified through the disciplines.

Nehast: The Great Spiritual Awakening

The Great Awakening

— Nehast —

Nehast means to "wake up," to Awaken to the higher existence. In the Prt m Hru Text it is said:

Nuk pa Neter aah Neter Zfah asha ren
"I am that same God, the Supreme One, who has myriad of mysterious names."

The end of all the Neterian disciplines is to discover the meaning of "Who am I", to unravel the mysteries of life and to fathom the depths of eternity and infinity. This is the task of all human beings and it is to be accomplished in this very lifetime.

This can be done by learning the ways of the Neteru, emulating them and finally becoming like them, Akhus, (enlightened beings), walking the earth as giants and accomplishing great deeds such as the creation of the universe!

(Slide #21)

The ultimate goal of life is *Nehast*. Nehast means "Spiritual Awakening." It is the spiritual awakening that leads one to discover the glory of life beyond death, discovering immortality, eternity and supreme peace. This is the coveted goal of all spiritual aspirants in all religions of the world, past or present. This is the goal that is to be striven for in life. It is the most worthy goal because all else will fade away one day. All else is perishable, fleeting and illusory. And this is what is called the Great Awakening, Nehast, the Awakening to spiritual consciousness. In the upper left hand corner of the slide you can see Asar Awakening from the tomb being assisted by the four sons of Heru. These four sons are also the first Shemsu, the Shemsu Heru. They are the ones who follow Asar, and they help to resurrect him. Nehast means to wake-up, to awaken to the higher existence.

The question is how to attain that lofty goal (Nehast). Just because all religions are striving for that does not mean they are engaging the correct methods to achieve that goal. They may have the dogma, the idea, but that does not mean that they have the how. One cannot attain resurrection, the spiritual awakening, just by faith. Faith must be followed by action, living in accordance with the teachings. That leads to growing understanding of and finally experience of the Divine. The end of all of the Neterian disciplines is to discover the meaning of "Who am I?," to unravel the mysteries of life, and to fathom the depths of eternity and infinity. This is the task of all human beings, and it is to be accomplished in this very lifetime. This can be done by learning the ways of the Neteru and emulating them, and finally becoming like them, Akhus walking the earth as giants and accomplishing great deeds.

Akhu is a term that we use in Neterian Theology that means "enlightened beings." Akhu is a person who has achieved Nehast, who has achieved awakening…the great Enlightenment.

Six Main Traditions of *Shetaut Neter*

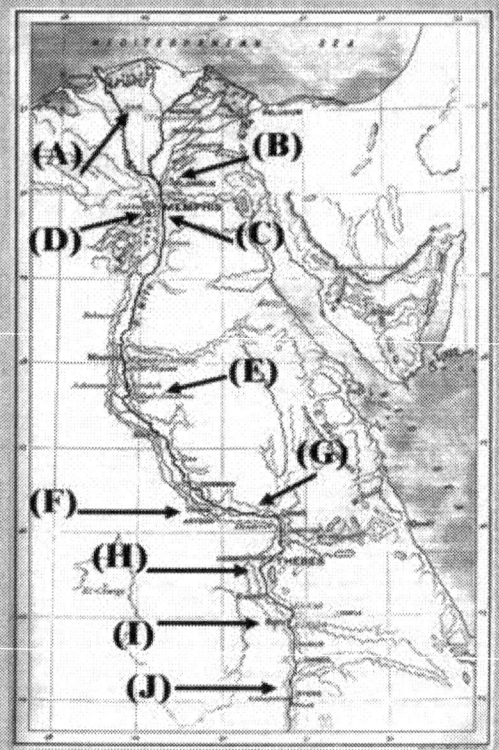

(Slide #22)

There are six main traditions of Shetaut Neter. Shetaut Neter is the all-encompassing national name to refer to the religious program of life of Ancient Kamit. It is a general term. Within that general reference meaning "Ancient Egyptian Religion" there are six main traditions of spirituality. They are all related. So there is no conflict between them. In fact all of them emerge from a single one, which is Anunian Theology, Shetaut Anu.

All the other ones emanate from this one. You should not think of them as sects in the context of Christian sects, like Presbyterians versus Pentecostals, or the Pentecostals versus the Catholics or something like that. This would be more like branches within one spiritual tradition.

These traditions relate to different forms of spiritual practice; that is why they were devised. Some are more psychologically oriented, some more ritualistic, and some deal more with the wisdom aspect, and so on and so forth, to accommodate the different inclinations of different personality types. And they were spread out throughout the different main cities of Ancient Kamit, to serve the need of the different parts of the population.

Within those six traditions there are three main theologies. These are based on the Great Trinity of Amun, Ra, and Ptah, which is also the basis of the chant that we use: *Om, Amun-Ra-Ptah.*

Egyptian Mysteries Volume 1: Principles of Shetaut Neter

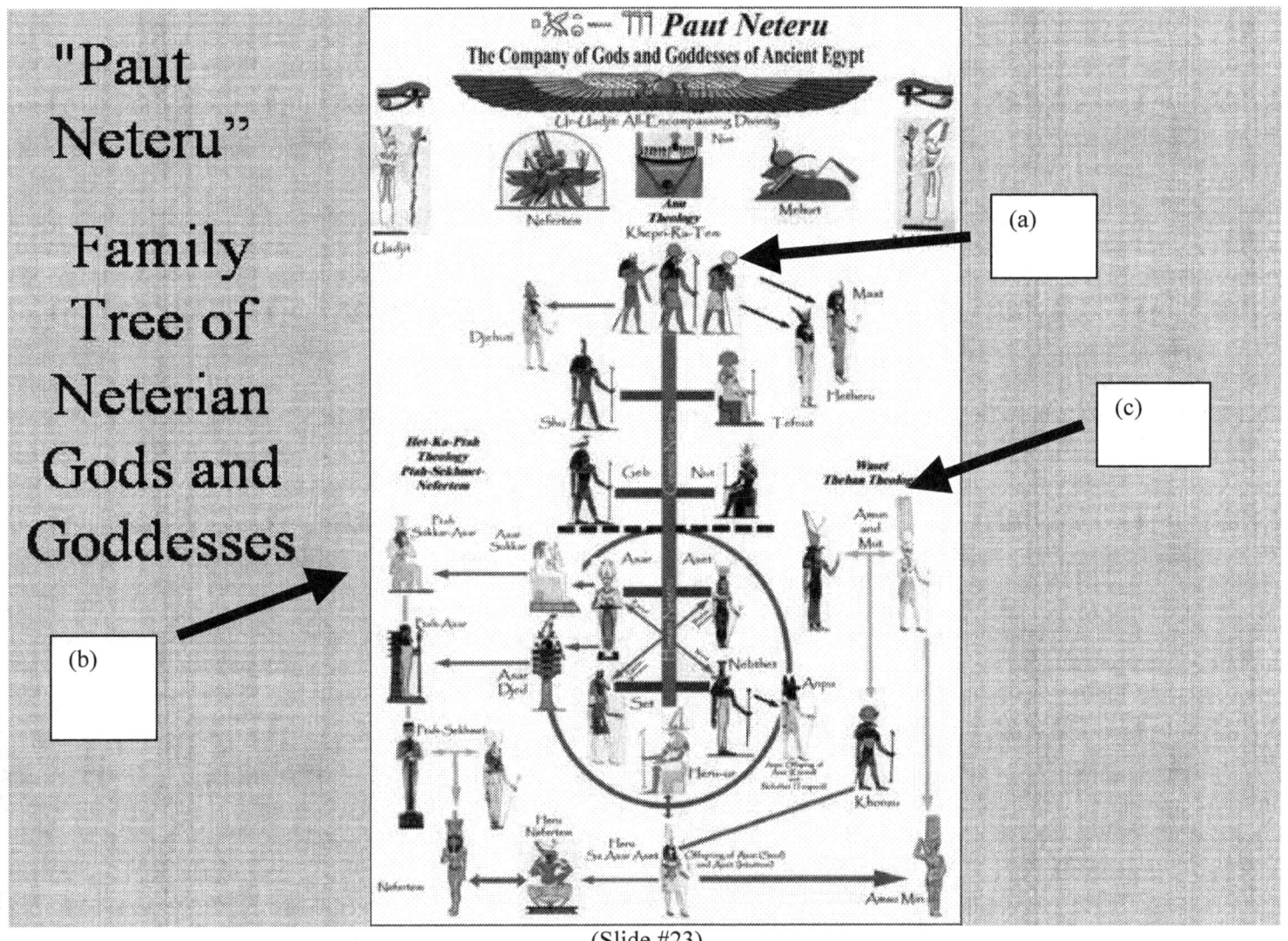

(Slide #23)

The branches of Neterian theologies:

In the center of the slide (above) you can see the Ra tradition, the Anunian Theology or tradition (a). The Ptah Theology or tradition is identified by (b), and the Amun Theology or tradition by (c). This slide illustrates that the Anunian Theology gave rise to the Divinities in both of the branches (Wasetian {Theban} and Menefer {Memphite}). Thus, the Divinities from the Ptah Theology arise from the Anunian Theology and the Divinities from the Amun Theology also emerge from the Anunian Theology. The Asarian Tradition is another branch which also emerges from Anunian Theology. The Asarian Tradition is based on the divinities Asar, Aset, and Heru, (Osiris, Isis, and Horus). It is from this tradition that the Christian myth develops.

This slide illustrates that though there are many gods and goddesses in the Neterian Theology, called Neteru, they all emanate from the single Supreme Being. The group of gods and goddesses are called Paut (group of gods and goddesses) or Pautti (groups of gods and goddesses). All the gods and goddesses emanate from the single One.

So if anyone refers to Ancient Egyptian or African Religion as polytheistic, that is an incorrect assessment. Such persons did not study ancient African Religion; it may be that they are ignorant or did not care to study, or to understand. If they understood this, then they would have to give Ancient Egyptian (African) Religion its due respect. With respect to those in other religions who propagate this erroneous idea (of polytheism), their acknowledgement of this truth would require that they admit that they are not the only ones with a so called elevated (monotheistic) notion or advanced conception of religion. It would mean that someone else is as civilized as they are, and maybe even more advanced. This realization is hard for degraded, egoistic personalities to accept. So their reaction is often to denigrate, disparage, marginalize and ridicule anything contrary to their own beliefs, ideas and concepts, so that they may continue to feel good about themselves. They need that form of egoistic notion of superiority in order to compensate for the low self-esteem and low culture of human development that is based on material accomplishments. So it is fitting that western religions should be so based in the historicity of the myths of the western religions. That is a reflection of the materialistic nature of those societies. In other words, those types of religions are materialistic and consequently idolatrous. Yes, contrary to their own beliefs, western religions practice idolatry because they tend to concretize the Divine into one image, one proprietary culture, one sacred scripture, etc. This act of confining God into a materialistic concept is idolatry. Further, these religions/cultures support the worship of objects not as expressions of the Divine as in African and Eastern religions, but as worthy objects that can bring happiness, even to the point of killing to preserve or acquire them. In African and Eastern religions, objects and images are not absolutes; however they are infused with Divinity, since Divinity is everywhere and in all things. They are used as objects to focus or concentrate the mind. They are not viewed as The God, but rather, as a lesser manifestation that can be used to gain entry into the transcendental plane of consciousness. This view is sometimes referred to as animism, and what I have just explained is the correct philosophy of the animistic practice. In materialistic type of societies, money, power, image, etc. become the gods and goddesses that people worship, and therefore, they are leading themselves down the road of pain and frustration. Those objects can never bring abiding happiness as they are evanescent, limited objects. Worshipping such objects is actually a very degraded form of human culture. Therefore, western civilization cannot be considered advanced. Rather it is devolution from the heights of ancient African culture and philosophy.

This Neterian-African notion of religion is actually superior because it actually divinizes the entire creation. All of these gods and goddesses of Anunian Theology represent the elements of Creation. Earth is Geb. The sky, the heavens is Nut. Water is Tefnut, and air and space is Shu.

With this kind of a notion, you cannot take a step outside of creation, outside of the Divinity. I am walking on Geb, I am breathing in Shu, I look up at the sky I see Nut. Where is Divinity not present? The entire Creation is the Temple then.

What is not readily visible is the Shetaut, "The hidden Divine Self." What we see here is called Bes. Bes means "outer image." We cannot see the hidden, because the hidden Divinity is transcendental, and we cannot see that with mortal eyes. Yet it sustains that which is visible in this time and space reality.

This is the same philosophy that occurs throughout African Religion, generally. This is what western scholars called "lesser beings." Those lesser beings in African religion are the lower gods and goddesses. These "lesser beings" are to be propitiated, so they can lead the aspirant or initiate to understand the highest Supreme Being, who is the source of all.

In western culture you do not have lesser beings or gods and goddesses per se. You are supposed to revere God or Jesus directly. But you cannot be as good as Jesus; there is really no one who can be as perfect as Christians would like to achieve communion with Jesus. Consequently, everything is a guilt trip. As a Christian, seemingly everything you do is wrong, everything you do is upsetting… everything you do is a problem from the beginning – thus the concept of being born in sin. So consequently, Christians have to be seeking forgiveness all the time. In this way one cannot have a full communion with the Divine and discover true purity of heart that brings virtue. There is always that separation, that beholding nature, that inferiority complex that never seems to go away. But western religions do have intermediaries, saints and angels, which are essentially the same as gods and goddesses, even though they are not referred to in the same way. It is therefore hypocritical for proponents of western religions to look down on non-western religions when they doing the same thing.

So in the Kamitan system everything is divine. You understand everything as spiritual energy, a spiritual cosmic force that you are living in and working through, and trying to master. In mastering these forces, then you transcend their influences. Therefore you are not innately controlled by nature; you are potentially a master of nature.

These systems of divinities give us easier entry into spirituality, because we could start with a turtle god of the river or Hapi, the Nile, and then that leads us to his relatives, and ultimately to the Supreme Being, Her/Himself.

Furthermore, the divinities represent principles in nature and in our personalities that we need to control. Their propitiation removes egoism and ignorance, making it easier for the aspirant to grasp, and therefore understand and control the personality, so as to purify and realize the higher essence within. So the worship and study of those divinities is actually a study of our own constitution, our own psychological makeup (psyche) and our own spiritual architecture and the architecture of the universe. And this is why Neterian religion has many gods and goddesses. It is a scientific approach to allow a person to propitiate the Divine, leading them in an elevating process, to discover the Supreme Being. So this is not degraded religion at all; actually it is advanced religion.

Anthropomorphic and Zoomorphic iconography in Neterian Religion

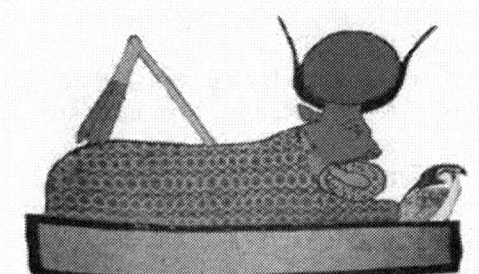

(Slide #24)

Many people ask the question, "Why are the Neterus (gods and goddesses) depicted in anthropomorphic forms or zoomorphic forms?" The Neteru may be depicted anthropomorphically or zoomorphically in accordance with the teachings being conveyed through them.

Here we have pictures of Amun seated (right side) in his full anthropomorphic (human) form, goddess Hetheru in her full zoomorphic (animal) form (cow-lower left), and the god Heru in a composite (part animal, part human) form (far left). Heru is in a composite form, with a human male body and the head of a hawk. This depiction of Heru is imparting that this divinity, Heru, holds the keys to the hawk-like energy. He represents the teaching that a human being has a Heru-like aspect, which, if discovered, leads to lordship, kingship, and rulership over Creation, becoming, like Heru, an enlightened master of time and space. Of course this means attaining Nehast, the great goal of life, self-mastery and spiritual enlightenment.

Amun is shown in a full anthropomorphic form, having blue skin. In the book *African Origins*, I show that the blue-black skin relates to higher consciousness. Amun means the hidden consciousness. You can find the same kind of iconography in the pre-Hindu concept of the god Vishnu in India. This is because the Kamitan and Hindu cultures are directly related. Here we have goddess Aset (Isis) in the center of the slide, in another composite form. Aset has three forms. She has a form as a cow, a kite (hawk), and a form as a physical woman. The above depiction is of her composite form with wings. Aset is the mother of Heru, and like Heru, she has a hawk form. She is the consort of Asar. She is the goddess of intuitional wisdom and has the power to resurrect souls, symbolizing that it is intuitional wisdom that allows one to resurrect their Higher Self.

Egyptian Mysteries Volume 1: Principles of Shetaut Neter

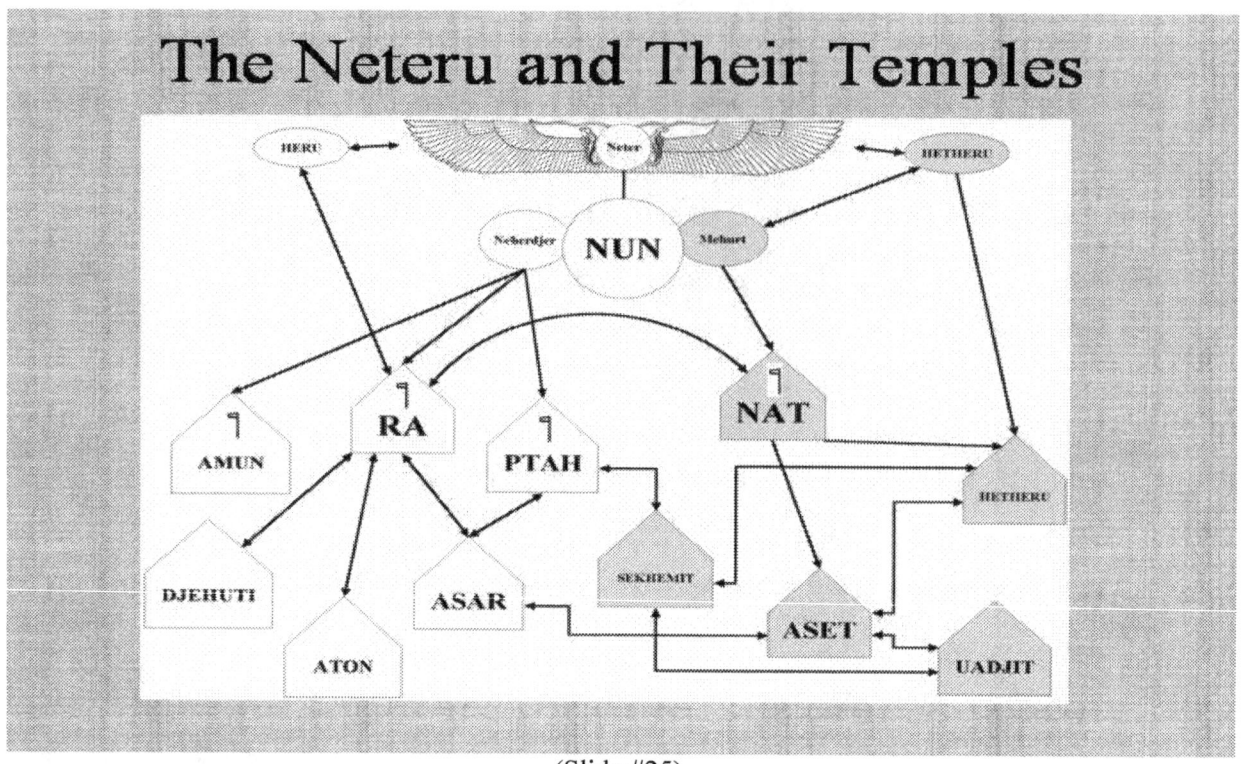

(Slide #25)

This is a physical depiction, which I explained in more detail in the *African Origins* book, of the system of Temples. Remember the cities that I showed you in the map of Kamit (Slide #3), and the Nile (Hapi); these are the different gods and goddesses, and their temples that were worship in the different cities.

The above slide (slide #25) depicts the system of Temples of Ancient Egypt. The arrows represent the filial interrelationships between the Temples and the gods and goddesses themselves. In other words, the gods and goddesses are all related, i.e., family. And they all emanate from the same one Supreme Being. There is a male aspect and female aspect in the Neterian divinities, and so certain Temples are dedicated to female divinities, and some to the males. There is a balance between the male and the female principles in Neterian spirituality; this is reflected in the system of Temples. You don't only have God has being 'male.' God is male or female, or both together. This is a very important point to understand about Neterian spirituality in particular, and African religion in general. This is I may refer to God and then use the pronoun "She."

The sages of Kamit instituted a system by which the teachings of spirituality were espoused through a Temple organization. The major divinities were assigned to a particular city. That divinity or group of divinities became the "patron" divinity or divinities of that city. Also, the priests and priestesses of that Temple were in charge of seeing to the welfare of the people in that district as well as maintaining the traditions and disciplines of the tradition based on the particular divinity or divinities being worshipped. So the original concept of "Neter" became elaborated through the "theologies" of the various traditions. A dynamic expression of the teachings emerged, which though maintaining the integrity of the teachings, expressed nuances of variation in perspective on the teachings to suit the needs of varying kinds of personalities of the people of different locales through the different stages of the long Kamitan history.

In the diagram above, the primary or main divinities are denoted by the Neter symbol ( ). The house structure represents the Temple for that particular divinity. The interconnections with the other Temples are based on original scriptural statements, espoused by the Temples themselves, which linked the divinities of their Temple with the other divinities. So this means that the divinities should be viewed not as separate entities operating independently, but rather as family members who are in the same "business" together, i.e., the enlightenment of society, albeit through variations in form of worship, name, form (expression of the Divinity), etc. Ultimately, all the divinities are referred to as Neteru and they are all said to be emanations from the ultimate and Supreme Being, Neter. Thus, the teaching from any of the Temples leads to an understanding of the others, and these all lead back to the source, the highest Divinity. Therefore, the teaching within any of the Temple systems would lead to the attainment of spiritual enlightenment, Nehast, the Great Spiritual Awakening. Now we will look at the temple itself, as its architecture holds special teachings for the beginning initiate of The Mysteries.

Egyptian Mysteries Volume 1: Principles of Shetaut Neter

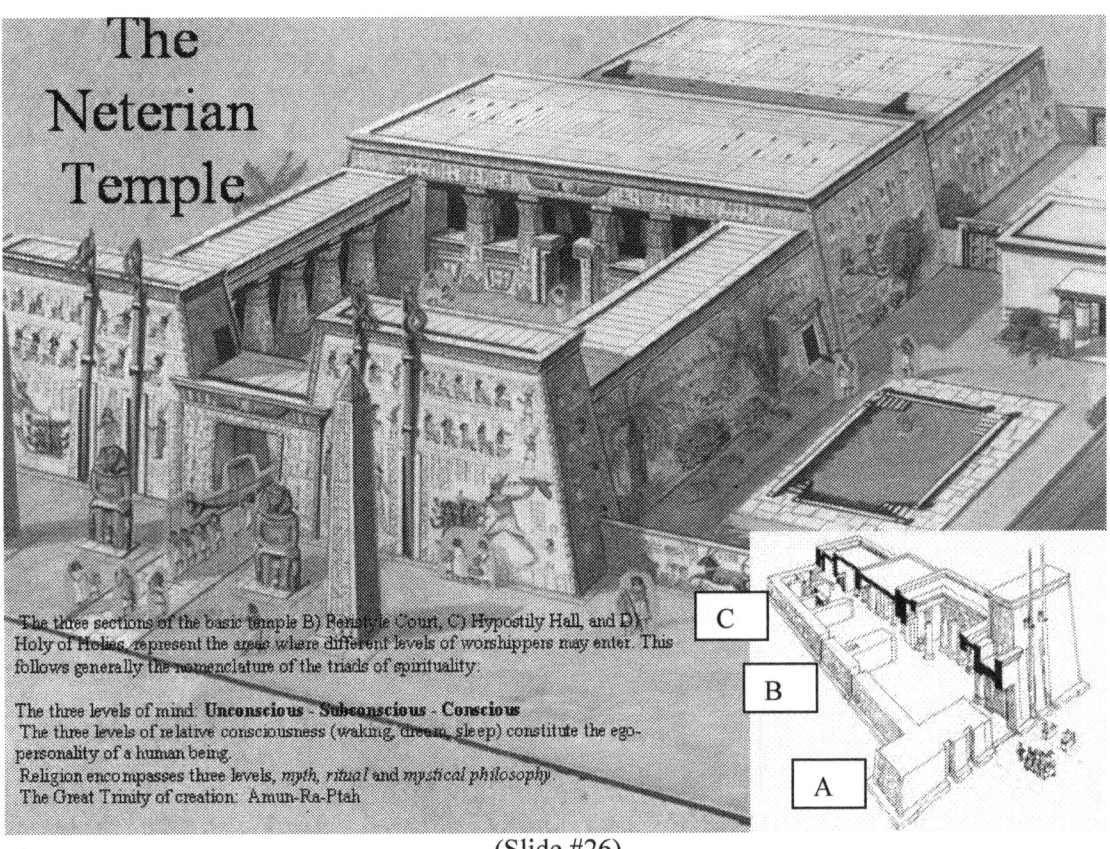

(Slide #26)

This is a New Kingdom Temple, which can still be seen on a trip to Egypt today. This is one of the later period Temples, from around 1800BCE - 2000BCE. The inscriptions on the outer Temple walls are still visible, although most of the color has faded. Some of the colors do remain however. With the use of special instruments, it has been possible to detect the original colors, and create accurate reproductions that show how the temple looked in ancient times. Some of the scenes on the outer Temple walls show the king worshipping the gods and goddesses, and different scenes of the Neterian myths. The purpose of this is for expressing and promoting the outer expression of the teaching through the Temple; this is for people outside the Temple to see. This is an outer teaching, an exoteric teaching. 'Exo' means "outer." Esoteric means inner. The esoteric teaching is reserved for the interior portion of the Temple.

The first section of the temple is the peristyle court or hall (A). It is called the peristyle court or hall because of the way the columns are placed. These columns are placed in the periphery, on the outside edge, allowing the court to be open to the sky. The next hall, moving towards the interior portion of the temple is called the hypostyle hall (B). "Hypostyle" means that there are many columns. Hypo means many. What this Temple is trying to re-create is the original mound of creation. The teaching is that creation occurred when God came into the primeval ocean. He said His name, and the water started vibrating. Then out of those waters emerged a mound, a little point where God was able to sit. And that mound is in the Holy of Holies (C), all the way in the back of the Temple. The columns are reproductions of papyrus plants and palms. So the temple is a reproduction in stone of what exists in nature as plants and wood. If you walk in the Temple, you will see that the peristyle court is one step up, then the hypostyle hall is one more step up, and the holy of holies is one more step up. The roof of the temple comes down and floor goes up.

The floor in the Holy of Holies is the highest point in terms of floor area elevation, in the Temple complex. This is where the divine image is placed. What we have discussed so far has been the outer, the exoteric portion of the Temple. Now you have an idea about what goes on there, but I haven't yet discussed the specifics about the disciplines that are to be practiced, and the metaphysics that are to be enjoined in order to achieve the high consciousness; these were practiced in the inner part of the Temple in ancient times.

Ordinary followers (the masses) worship and give their offerings to the Temple outside the Temple. They are not permitted to enter the Temple. They are not purified enough or ready to understand the depth of the mystical spiritual teaching. So this more advanced teaching cannot be given to them. It will not be useful to them… it will be a waste of time for them until there is purity of mind and body. They have to do work in purification and qualification as spiritual aspirants. This means study of the teaching, living by righteousness, order and truth, and the practice of devotion to the Divine and meditation on the Divine.

This outer peristyle area (A) is the first area where aspirants are allowed. There are three levels of aspiration. First of all is aspiration, where you make propitiation and say, "I would like to become a spiritual aspirant." Here an ordinary person has experienced a desire for spiritual awakening. There is a conscious desire, "may I turn towards spirituality instead of just towards worldliness."

Otherwise if you are out in the world, and you want to be in business, to have fun, to party, or to "enjoy things in life," and you want to have a little spirituality, that is fine. In this case, you worship on the outside of the Temple. You come to the Temple, make your offering and then go home. But if you come into the outer court area with the peristyle hall, this means that you aspire to something more than the ordinary masses of people. What is it that to which you are aspiring? You are aspiring to go into higher levels of the teaching.

There are certain disciplines for the aspirant and certain disciplines for those who are striving, which is the next level after aspiration. The number three is prominent in this study. The three levels of aspiration are: aspiration, striving and established. There are also three levels of religion: myth, ritual and mysticism.

The outer peristyle court correlates with the levels of myth and aspiration. The inner court with the hypostyle hall correlates to the ritual aspect of religion and the striving level of aspiration. And the Holy of Holies correlates to the mysticism as level of religion and the established level of aspiration. Also, the trinity Amun-Ra-Ptah correlates to that same scheme.

The Stages of African Religion

The Three Stages of African Religion		
Program of Religion (Universal Religion) 3-Stages	**African Religion**	**Sema (Smai) Tawi (Egyptian Yoga) Based on the teachings of the Temple of Aset (Aswan, Egypt)**
Myth	Storytelling (myths – proverbs)	Listening (to spiritual scriptures, teachings)
Ritual	Ritual (ceremony – Virtuous living)	Reflection (on & practice of the teachings)
Mysticism/Metaphysics	Ecstasy (Transcendental experience)	Meditation (on the teachings)

The complete program of religion has three steps, which are necessary to achieve the goal of religion, to discover and experience Neter (God). Any spiritual movement that includes these steps can be called authentic "religion" regardless of the name that it may be given by the culture that practices them. These steps include *Myth, Ritual* and *Mysticism* or *Metaphysics*. The table above shows how these three steps or stages manifest in African Religion (2nd column) and also how this same program is enjoined in the practice of Egyptian Yoga (3rd column). Egyptian Yoga (Sema Tawi)[xli] may be thought of as the advanced disciplines to be practiced in order to promote the highest goal of the religious movement.

In African Religion, storytelling achieves the purpose of transmitting myths, which contain the basic concepts of human identity as part of a culture, and offers insight into the nature of the universe. Myths also contain a special language of self-knowledge and also proverbs that provide moral education for an ethical society. Rituals are formal (ceremony) and informal (virtuous living) practices which allow a human being to come into harmony within themselves, the environment and the Spirit. This movement eventually leads to an ecstatic experience, which transcends time and space and allows a human being to discover and experience the Divine.

- Unlike a modern Church, Mosque or Synagoge, The Neterian Temple is not fully open to the public. There are sections reserved for different levels of spiritual practice and attainment.

- The Neterian Temple is the House of the particular Divinity being worshipped. The work of the outer areas of the temple is more devotional while the work of the inner areas is more metaphysical.

- The priests and priestesses of the inner hall carry out the daily, monthly and annual rituals that regenerate the power of life in Creation, through service and maintenance of the sacred shrines.

- Those same rituals also have the effect of linking the practitioner in a mystical way, to the Divinity, leading that practitioner to direct illumination, the experience of oneness with that Divinity

The Temple is the House of Life (hospital) and University where the whole town gathers, for instruction, healing and worship of the Divine.

(Slide 27)

It is important to understand that unlike a modern day church, mosque or synagogue, the Neterian Temple is not fully open to the public. There are sections reserved for different levels of spiritual practice and attainment.

The Neterian Temple is considered as the house of the particular divinity being worshipped. The work of the outer areas of the Temple is more devotional (peristyle court), while the work of the inner temple areas is more philosophical (hypostyle hall) and metaphysical (inner shrine). The priests and priestesses of the inner hall carry out the daily, monthly, and annual rituals that regenerate the power of life and creation in the universe, through service and maintenance of the sacred shrine and by uttering the special words of power that carry the wisdom teaching of Shetaut Neter and other special rituals. These same rituals also have the effect of linking the practitioner, in a mystical way, to the divinity, leading that practitioner to direct illumination, the experience of oneness with that Divinity.

Egyptian Mysteries Volume 1: Principles of Shetaut Neter

 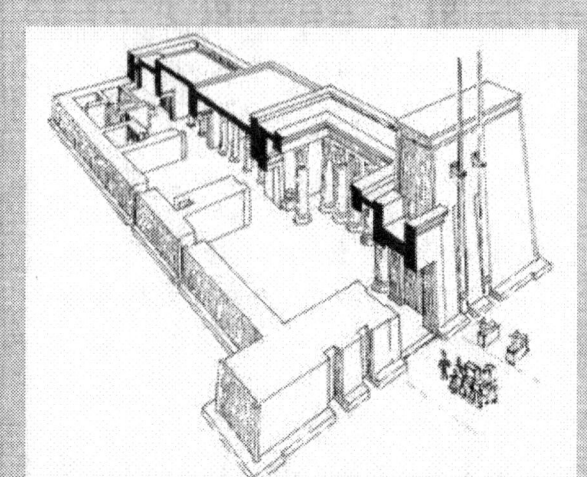

The Three sections also represent the three levels of aspiration:

- **1- The Mortals**: Students who were being instructed on a probationary status, but had not experienced inner vision.
- **2- The Intelligences**: Students who had attained inner vision and had received a glimpse of cosmic consciousness.
- **3- The Creators or Beings of Light**: Students who had become IDENTIFIED with or UNITED with the light (GOD).

• Thus, the outer court is open to the lowest ranking practitioners to the temple, the middle hall is open to more advanced practitioners and the innermost hall is open only to the most advanced aspirants. The innermost shrine is reserved for those who are ready to have union with the Divine.

There are three forms of actions: Thought, Word and Deed The outer court is the place for deeds, work to propitiate the divinity i.e. lower worship; physical rituals, offerings to the divine and prayers to the divine.

The middle hall is the section of the temple for words. In this section the wisdom teaching is espoused.

The inner hall court is the section of the temple for advanced ritual and metaphysics, meditations and mystical exercises that sustain creation and unite one to the Divine.

(Slide #28) **Cross section of that Temple.**

One important thing for you to understand about the New Kingdom Temple is that it has two pylons, and these two pylons symbolize the duality of life and Creation. Thus, if you go through the door of the Temple, it means that you are seeking oneness; you are seeking to unite the duality of life.

What is the duality of life? The duality of life means the idea that there is "self" and other. It means that you believe that you are separate from the universe and separate from the Divine. This is a dual state of consciousness. If you discover oneness, that consciousness of duality dissolves, and all you see is Divinity. You see God/The Goddess everywhere. So together with the door, the pylons represent a trinity, the trinity of Creation and of human consciousness.

There is often a row of Sphinxes in front of the opening of the temple, outside the Temple. The pathway is straight all the way through to the back of the Temple. There are doors blocking all the entrances to the different sections of the Temple, as these areas are only open to the higher initiates.

Above is another cross section or diagram of the Temple. You can see it showing: the Peristyle court, the Hypostyle hall, and Holy of Holies. The two rooms off to the side of the Holy of Holies are known as "the rooms of fire and water." They are the rooms of duality. They are the rooms of the Serpent Power. Refer to the *Serpent Power* book for more about this.

So the three sections of the basic Temple, the Peristyle court, the Hypostyle hall, and Holy of Holies represent the areas where different levels of worshipers may enter, and follows, generally, the nomenclature of the triads of spirituality: The three levels of mind - unconscious, subconscious and conscious; the three levels of relative consciousness - waking, dream and deep sleep; the three levels of religion: myth, ritual, and mystical, and the great trinity; the three levels of aspiration – aspiration, striving and established. The three sections of the Temple also represent the three levels of human existence: Mortals, Intelligences and Creators or Beings of Light.

Thus, the outer court is open to the lowest ranking practitioners of the Temple, the middle is open to the more advanced, and the innermost is open to the most advanced. The innermost is reserved for those who are ready to have union with the divine and experience transcendental consciousness and become established in that higher consciousness, leaving the lower (egoistic consciousness) behind. They are ready to let go of the world and all that is temporary, fleeting and evanescent in life.

There are three modes of actions: thought, words and deed. The outer most court is the place for deeds...work to propitiate the divinity...lower worship. Lower worship means physical rituals, making offerings to the divine, offering prayers to the divine, and chanting, self-purification, etc.

The middle hall is the section of the temple for words. This section is reserved for the wisdom teachings, and this is where classes would be held and spiritual wisdom imparted.

The inner hall court is the section of the Temple for advanced rituals, metaphysics, meditations and mystical exercises that sustain creation and unite one to the Divine. So there is an alchemy that goes on in the inner court – a transformation of mortal consciousness to immortal, from worldly to spiritual, from mundane to cosmic, from physical body to the body of light, called *Akh*.

The Temple complex houses different buildings where various services are provided to the community. There is the House of Life (hospital), a school for children, and university rooms for instruction of varied disciplines, where the whole town gathers for instruction, healing and worship of the Divine. Again, the hospital is not located inside the Temple itself; it is a building within the Temple complex. There would be special buildings in the Temple complex that would serve as the schoolrooms for disciplines other than spirituality.

(Slide #29) Ritual you might see at Temple

The above picture is to give you an idea of a ritual that you might see at the Temple. This is a reenactment, to give you an understanding of what that might have looked like in ancient times. It shows the ritual of the procession of the Divine Boat being conducted by the priests. The procession is part of the metaphysics of the Temple.

Firstly, The temple is created on an axis; all temples are created on an axis. The axis may be related to a particular spiritual teaching, the cardinal points, or to the path of a celestial body, like the sun.

The procession proceeds from outside, all the way to the inner court (see arrows), for those aspirants who are allowed to enter. In the picture, you can see the boat entering the temple.

Egyptian Mysteries Volume 1: Principles of Shetaut Neter

The symbol above is called "Rekhyt." The "Rekhyt" symbol means the "common folk." The rekhyt symbol is inscribed on the pillars where the common folk offer praises, adorations, and perform devotional practices to the Divine. The term "common folk" here means ordinary people who are not priests and priestesses or people. However, this should not be taken to mean that non-devotional people, i.e., non-believers, are allowed to enter. This is meant for followers of the tradition who are also laypersons and not professional clergy or initiates. The upraised arms of the rekhyt bird symbolize the "Dua" posture.

Above: an Ancient Egyptian woman and man in the "dua" posture

The Dua posture is performed with upraised hands, and palms facing outwards, towards the image of the divinity being worshipped, and it means "adorations."

(Slide #30) **Temple of Aset (Isis)**

You can go to Egypt even now and visit an actual Temple, such as the Temple of Aset (Isis)-pictured above. the two pylons (A), (B) of the Temple of Aset represent the two dual goddesses, the Maati Goddesses who are also Aset and Nebthet, and the doorway entrance represents Asar. If you go through that door, you go to the inside Peristyle court area, with the columns on the periphery of the court, and the center area opened to the sky.

Unlike what you sometimes hear on some television shows, such as the nature channel or other educational channels and programs, the king and queen are actually considered as spiritual as well as secular leaders, and not just as political or royal leaders. They were not considered as gods and goddesses in the context of Supreme Beings. The reason for those kinds of conclusions is that most western authorities view the African culture in terms of European social organizational forms. Since they do not know any better or have no interest or ability to understand a culture other than their own, they simply label other societies in terms that they already know.

(Slide #31)

Egyptian Mysteries Volume 1: Principles of Shetaut Neter

The king and queen were considered as divinities to the extent that they are placed (chosen by divine agency) in a position of power to minister to the people on behalf of the Supreme Being, just as the gods and goddesses, like Asar and Aset, did in the beginning of the Pharaonic history. That is how it should be viewed. They are leaders of the secular and non-secular aspects of the culture, which means that they are leaders of the religion, army, bureaucracy, government, etc.

Heka means Prince or Ruler, and *Hekat* means the people who are ruled. There is a linguistic sexual relationship in the terms because one is a male term (*Heka*) and the other is a female term (*Hekat*). The same is true in the terms for teaching; *Seba* is the male term, meaning teacher, and *Sebat* is the female term, meaning student. In that relationship there is an exchange that goes on, so the metaphor is a sexual metaphor, a metaphor that plays on the duality of life, the duality of the universe, the dynamic force in creation that makes everything change and progress. The teacher and the student come together to produce knowledge and produce a knowledgeable person. Similarly, Heka and Hetat, relates to the king and queen who come together to preside over their family, the people, for their spiritual welfare and their physical well-being. This is one of the important factors that allowed Kamit to be great and to be able to sustain itself for thousands of years. It was that kind of order, high culture, high vision of life, and glory of spirituality, which was inculcated with Maat philosophy (righteousness, order and truth), that was the basis of society.

Sacred Scriptures of Shetaut Neter

MYTHIC SCRIPTURES Literature	Mystical (Ritual) Philosophy Literature	Wisdom Texts Literature
SHETAUT ASAR-ASET-HERU The Myth of Asar, Aset and Heru (Asarian Resurrection Theology) - Predynastic **SHETAUT ATUM-RA** Anunian Theology Predynastic **Shetaut Net/Aset/Hetheru** Saitian Theology – Goddess Spirituality Predynastic **SHETAUT PTAH** Memphite Theology Predynastic **Shetaut Amun** Theban Theology Predynastic	**Coffin Texts** (c. 2040 B.C.E.-1786 B.C.E.) **Papyrus Texts** (c. 1580 B.C.E.-Roman Period)[1] Books of Coming Forth By Day Example of famous papyri: Papyrus of Any Papyrus of Hunefer Papyrus of Kenna Greenfield Papyrus, Etc.	**Wisdom Texts** (c. 3,000 B.C.E. – PTOLEMAIC PERIOD) Precepts of Ptahotep Instructions of Any Instructions of Amenemope Etc. Maat Declarations Literature (All Periods) Harer's Songs

(Slide #32)

There are three kinds of scriptures in Kamitan culture. We have Mythic scriptures, Mystical scriptures, and Wisdom Text scriptures. In addition to these, there is also the genre of the Harper's songs. Though belonging in the category of music, they are also to be considered as part of the wisdom literature. All the books that I have written are based on these scriptures.

Some of you have been amazed by the extensive writings that I have brought forth in reference to the Neterian teachings. Well, I have not invented them; they are not fabricated.

This is what I have discovered through my researches and meditations and from the past masters. We have reconstructed the teachings based on our own scriptures, our own traditions, and our own ancestry. So I believe we do not have to look beyond the original scriptures for records of the teachings. We don't have to invent them, and we don't have to speculate about them. We can confirm this because you can see the tradition being practiced by other African cultures. What I mean is that they are practicing the rituals and customs, but not necessarily understanding the meaning. If they were to study the true depth of the Neterian Spirituality, they would realize the deeper meaning of the rituals and traditions they have kept for so long.

You see parts of Neterianism being practiced in the Western religions, and also in Asia, in Hinduism and Buddhism, which have their origins in Neterian theology. This is partly how the teaching has been reconstructed and confirmed. For more on this see the book *African Origins*.

Part 2: The 4 Neterian Principles: Introduction to Neterian Spirituality

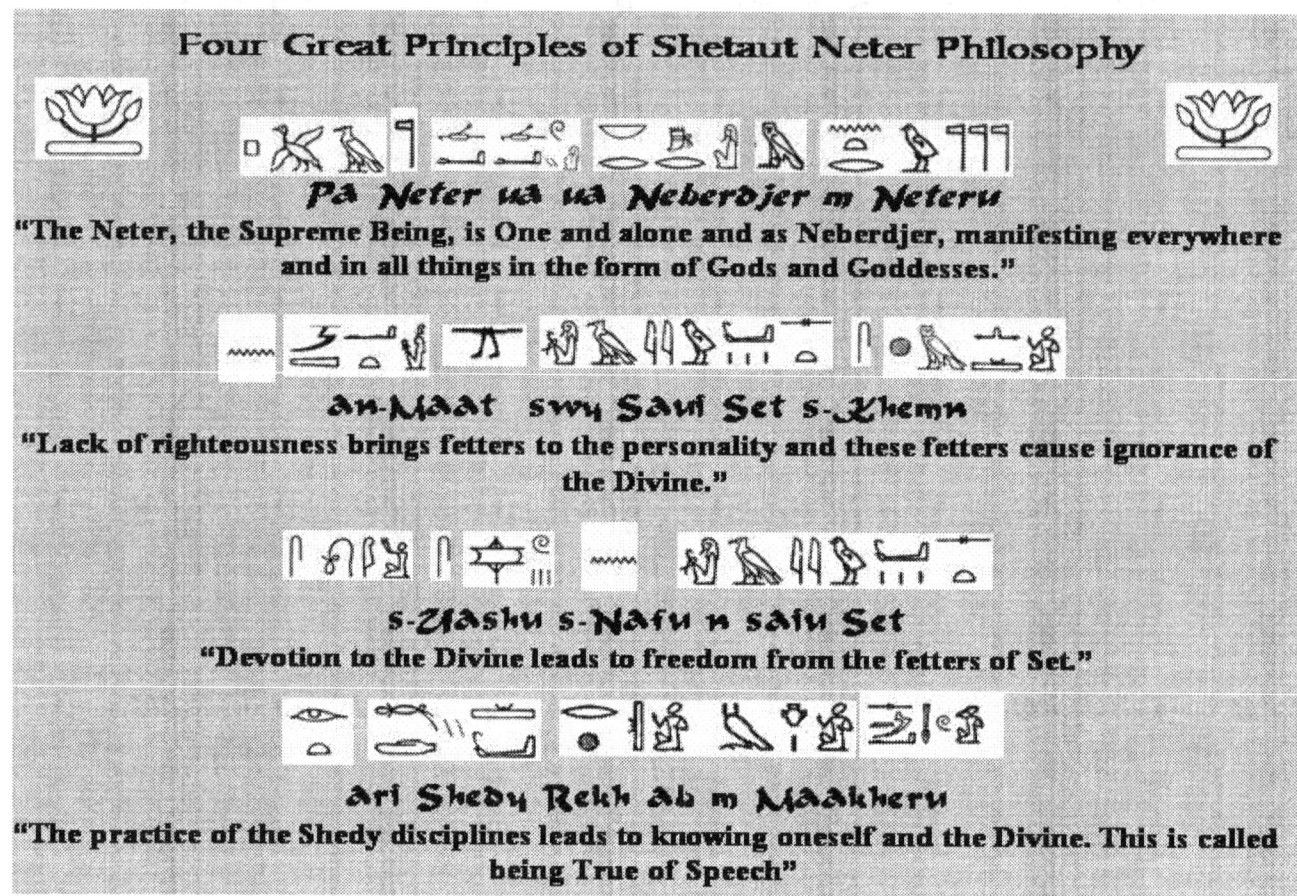

(Slide #33) **The 4 Neterian Principles**

Part 1 was an introduction, and now in Part 2, we are going to get into a more detailed description of the basic teachings of Shetaut Neter.

Shetaut Neter can be summarized in many ways, but perhaps most succinctly it may be condensed into four teachings. These four teachings are called *"Maa Ur n Shetaut Neter"* – "Great Truths of Shetaut Neter." These four great principles of Shetaut Neter Philosophy are like formulas. In chemistry, when you have a formula, it is a code. If you mix certain elements in a particular way, you will get certain elements or certain compounds to come out of it. In essence you can build something great out of a very small and condensed piece of information; the Four Neterian Principles are like that. They are a blueprint for the entire Neterian teaching.

These four principles condense the entire teaching of Shetaut Neter; they encapsulate the entire teaching. If you were to know these four teachings, that would give you the keys to understand the entire philosophy of Shetaut Neter.

However, only knowing the keys to the philosophy does not lead you to enlightenment. In order to have enlightenment, you must understand the philosophy and practice the disciplines. Information plus experience equals wisdom. Information with no action cannot equal anything; it equals zero. It equals ignorance. It equals more information, but you still have ignorance. Take this society for example. We still have so much more technology than we have ever had before and yet the culture is more degraded, and it continues to degrade more and more every day.

Egyptian Mysteries Volume 1: Principles of Shetaut Neter

Great Truth #1:

The first Great Truth is "*Pa Neter ua ua Neberdjer m Neteru,*" which means, "The Neter, the Supreme Being, is one and alone and as Neberdjer, manifesting everywhere and in all things in the form of Gods and goddesses."

So, the first point to understand is that the philosophy holds that there is one Supreme Being. This is the first key to understanding the philosophy. And that philosophy manifests as Neberdjer. Neberdjer is the Kamitan term that means all-encompassing Divinity, the All. There is one Supreme Being manifesting as everything. That is the first key to understand. This is important because if you miss this first key, the rest of it does not fall into place.

This is not a spiritual tradition about many spirits or different gods and goddesses at one end of the spectrum, and God at the other end, nor do we have God in one place and the devil in another, and whatever God does, the devil goes and messes it up. "The devil made me do it"....remember the comedian Flip Wilson who made that saying popular years ago? That is the teaching of western culture and the western religions. In Neterian philosophy there are only order and chaos, truth and error. If a person acts in unrighteous ways, they are being controlled by the forces of entropy (egoism and ignorance). If they act righteously they are controlled by Maat.

The Forces of Entropy

- In Neterian religion, there is no concept of "evil" as is conceptualized in Western Culture. Rather, it is understood that the forces of entropy are constantly working in nature to bring that which has been constructed by human hands to their original natural state. The serpent Apep (Apophis), who daily tries to stop Ra's boat of creation, is the symbol of entropy. This concept of entropy has been referred to as "chaos" by Western Egyptologists.

(slide #34)

There is no devil in Shetaut Neter, rather, there is ignorance in Shetaut Neter. You are either ignorant of your true essence (Self) or you have wisdom of your true essence (Self). If you are ignorant, then you act in demoniac ways; that does not make you a demon. There is no devil in Shetaut Neter; there is only the Supreme Divinity, and those who are ignorant about that Supreme Divinity are capable of error, unspeakable acts of cruelty, selfishness and violence. The task of religion is to make you knowledgeable and wise about the true source of strife in life, and then to bring you in harmony with creation. If you are in harmony with creation then there is no conflict. Conflict comes when you are out of harmony with creation – when there is self and other. Disharmony comes when one falls away from truth and Neter (God) is the ultimate truth.

In the slide above, at the bottom right, there is a picture of the God Ra who is sitting in his boat In his boat, Ra sails on the primeval ocean, which is inhabited by the serpent Apep. Apep is a demon of chaos who is trying to stop the creative movement of the boat. Set, who was previously a negative personality, was redeemed and now stands at the bow (front) of the boat to protect it from the giant serpent; in other words, Set is serving Ra, the good. So having turned away from evil Set is no longer demonic. Thus, Nehast is attained when the ego (Set) is purified and placed in the service of the Higher Self (Ra).. This is the heart of the great teachings:

Egyptian Mysteries Volume 1: Principles of Shetaut Neter

"Men and women are to become God-like through a life of virtue and the cultivation of the spirit through scientific knowledge, practice and bodily discipline."

"Salvation is the freeing of the soul from its bodily fetters; becoming a God through knowledge and wisdom; controlling the forces of the cosmos instead of being a slave to them; subduing the lower nature and through awakening the higher self, ending the cycle of rebirth and dwelling with the Neters who direct and control the Great Plan."

Neterianism is an African religion. Like other African religions, it espouses the teaching that there is One Supreme Being manifesting in the form of lesser beings, with lesser powers; they do the work of sustaining Creation. The concept that African religion is polytheistic is a falsehood, a misunderstanding, and a fabrication by people who don't understand what they are talking about. This goes for the Yoruba religion, Dogon spirituality, and other similar African systems of religions where practitioners propitiate the lesser divinities to lead themselves up to the higher Supreme Being, who is abstract, and cannot be touched with thought. You first need to have something you can touch with thought, and with your eyes, your senses, to purify you, to help you grow in devotion and knowledge about Spirit; this then prepares you to experience the higher (mystical). However, realize that in African, as well as Eastern religions, when situations occur that cause a disruption of the culture and create conditions that prevent the native tradition from being practiced, such as wars, the destruction of their society, the removal of the religious authority, and the imposition of new religions, practitioners often let go of the higher principles and practices, and these can become forgotten after a long period. Then the original teachings become lost, while the rituals are still practiced. This can be seen throughout areas where the orthodox western religions have sought to force people to adopt the western religions.

Great Truth I: The Supreme Being is One

Neberdjer means "all-encompassing divinity," the all-inclusive, all-embracing spirit which pervades all and who is the ultimate essence of all.

Neberdjer is closely associated with the divinity Khepri. Khepri is the Creator, the morning sun and the first aspect of Ra. Thus we are to understand that from the all-encompassing Divinity, there arises a creative principle and that principle is the divine will, who is Khepri, the scarab-beetle who brings itself and Creation into being.

The great divinity who brought its own forms into being

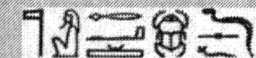

Neter Aah kheperi djesef
The Supreme Being Is One

(Slide #35)

Neberdjer means all- encompassing Divinity. Neberdjer is closely associated with the divinity Khepri. Khepri is the creator of the morning and the first aspect of Ra (Creator-Sustainer-Dissolver). There is an Anunian trinity, which will be discussed shortly. Khepri is the creator aspect of the Divine. He is the one who creates the day, and creates the cycle of time. The scripture says, *"Neter Aah Khepri djesef:"* "The Supreme Being creates Himself." Thus, Khepri is one. No one created Him. He emerged on His own from the spiritual oceans, from the Nun. Because if we say that Khepri was created, then we have to ask who created Khepri, and who created the god who created Khepri, and who created the god who created the god who created Khepri, etc. And this will not lead you to an endpoint. You don't find the Absolute, the Ultimate, in that way. The philosophy gives a definitive answer, an absolute answer. The one Supreme Being brought Himself into existence out of that same primeval ocean, manifesting as the universe we see today. God is not very far then, now is she?

You must understand then, that you are wearing God right now. Those of you who are holding something, you are holding God right now. If you are sitting, you are sitting on God. If you are walking, you are walking on God. If you are wearing shoes, you are wearing God's shoes. If you are breathing, you are breathing God. If your heart is beating it is God's heart that is beating, etc. You see the glory of this philosophy if it is correctly understood? And the loss of this is just a sorry affair for those who miss out.

Egyptian Mysteries Volume 1: Principles of Shetaut Neter

The teaching goes:

> "God is the father of Beings. God is the eternal one, and infinite and endures forever. God is hidden, and no man knows God's forms. No man has been able to seek out God's likeness. God is hidden to gods and to men alike. God's name remains hidden. It is a mystery to his children, men and women and the gods. God's names are innumerable, manifold and no one knows their number. Though God can be seen in form and observations of God can be made at God's appearance, God cannot be understood. God cannot be seen with mortal eyes. God is invisible and inscrutable to gods as well as men."

The writings above are portions from the *Egyptian Book of Coming Forth by Day* (*Pert m Heru*) text of Nesi Khonsu.

What this is saying is that there is a Supreme "Shetaut Neter" (hidden Divinity) and even the gods and goddesses, meaning those beings that are in the next realm above ours, even they cannot fathom the essence of that Supreme Being. So even the gods and goddesses, the lesser beings we were talking about, the ones that are below the Supreme Being, even they don't have full knowledge, full enlightenment. They have to do the same thing human beings have to do. They have to practice Uashu (devotion) – they also have to practice the disciplines in order to enlighten themselves.

Gods and goddesses are beings that are more elevated than us, but not the Supreme Being. The scripture makes it particularly clear that men, women, and gods are in the dark about this highest mystery, so they have to discover this mystery.

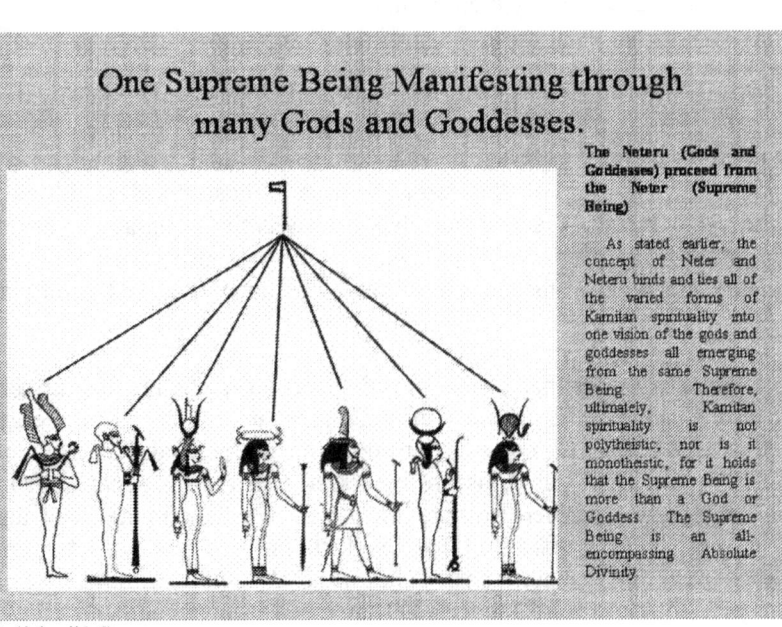
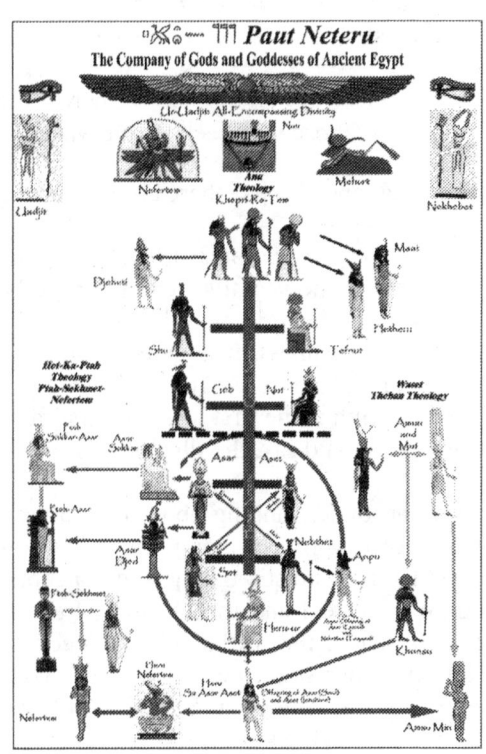

(slide #36)

The Neteru (above left), gods and goddesses, proceed from the one Supreme Neter and this is a graphic depiction for you to understand. One Supreme Being gives rise to all the other beings, the divinities, gods and goddesses, and to human beings, and to nature, the planets, the stars, etc. This is what the philosophy says. This is what "ua ua" means: one one (one and alone).

Diagram (above right): The Primary Kamitan Neteru and their Interrelationships

The same Supreme Being, Neter, is the winged all-encompassing transcendental Divinity who, earlier in history, was called "Heru." The physical universe in which Heru lives is called "Hetheru" or the "House of Heru." This divinity (Heru) is also the Nun or primeval substratum from which all matter is composed. The various divinities and the material universe are comprised of this primeval substratum. Neter is actually androgynous, and Heru, the Spirit, is related as a male aspect of that androgyny. However, Heru in the androgynous aspect gives rise to the solar principle, and this is observable of in both the male and female divinities.

Egyptian Mysteries Volume 1: Principles of Shetaut Neter

The image above (right) provides an idea of the relationships between the divinities of the three main Neterian spiritual systems (traditions): Anunian (Heliopolitan) Theology, Wasetian (Theban) Theology and Het-Ka-Ptah or Menefer (Memphite) Theology. The traditions are composed of companies or groups of gods and goddesses. Their actions, teachings and interactions with each other and with human beings provide insight into their nature as well as that of human existence and Creation itself. The lines indicate direct scriptural relationships and the labels also indicate that some divinities from one system are the same as others in other systems, with only a name change. Again, this is attested to by the scriptures themselves in direct statements, like those found in the **Prt m Hru** text Chapter 4 (17).[xlii] Thus, all the divinities emanate from one divinity: *Khepri*. He manifests as Neberdjer, and Neberdjer manifests as *Amun-Ra-Ptah three in one"* (see image at left of the Great Trinity.) (at left, the glyphs Amun-Ra-Ptah)

Great truth #2:

The second Great Truth is *"An-Maat swy Saui Set s-khemn"* which means: "Lack of righteousness brings fetters to the personality, and these fetters cause ignorance of the Divine." This teaching is reflected in the Neterian proverb:

"There are two roads traveled by humankind,
those who seek to live MAAT and those who seek to satisfy their animal passions."

In a higher, more advanced sense there are only two groups of people, the *Nehastu* -"spiritually awakened" and the *kmn* {ignorant} "worldly." While there are generally good people in the world, actually all people who are not enlightened have some negative Ariu (Karmic basis). One day, that negativity will lead them to pain and suffering (error). So in the end, worldliness is unrighteousness in a broad understanding of the term, from a philosophical standpoint. Unrighteousness is selfishness. It is greed, lust, jealousy, and envy, but the greatest unrighteousness is the unrighteousness of ignorance. The Kamitan proverb goes, *"There is no darkness like the darkness of ignorance."* Unrighteousness leads one to untruth, and this untruth is the first loss, the first fall in humanity; this is what makes it possible for human beings to fall into, as the Kamitan Harper would say, the illusion of life.

Just to give you an understanding about the nature of the Divine, consider that in the twentieth century, science has already confirmed the fact (has proven) that all matter is composed of the same elements, and those elements are composed of energy. That fact supports the animistic-pantheistic concepts of non-western religions. Yet we continue to have it pushed that orthodox western religion is correct and that African, Eastern and Native American religions are incorrect, that God is separate from Creation, and so on. This means that all the objects that you see in the room where you are, the plastic, the tiles on the floor, this mat, your clothing, your skin, the sound of my voice, the writing on this book, the book itself, the air that you are breathing …they are all composed of the same "stuff." In Neterian philosophy, this is what is called the *Nun* or *Paut*, the primeval ocean. When this primeval ocean takes on forms – that constitutes creation. How was/is that done? By the word. Remember we have discussed this before…the teaching of the word of God coming into the waters, vibrating it and causing it to take forms. This teaching does not only occur in Christianity; it is also found in the religions of Africa, India, and also the Americas, and in fact, much earlier than in Christianity. It is important for you to have a different outlook than what is presented to you in a more limited or lesser-advanced system of spirituality. You must begin to open up to the true grandeur of creation, otherwise the mysteries of life will elude you, and you will be fit only to be a lowly follower of some dogmatic religious faith that will offer many platitudes, the same old slogans, dogmatic statements and clichés, but will limit your spiritual growth.

Unrighteousness leads us to *khemn*, ignorance, and therefore the converse is true, righteousness leads us to *ab*, purity and *rekh*, wisdom.

Thus it is said: *an gereh gereh khemn-* "there is no darkness like the darkness of ignorance"
—Ancient Egyptian proverb

Egyptian Mysteries Volume 1: Principles of Shetaut Neter

Ignorance is insidious because the ignorant mind, being deluded, believes it is following the right path when actually it is following a path of its own design. Even when errors and contradictions are pointed out to such a person, his/her mind develops rationalizations to justify the *an-maat-* "unrighteous actions." Such a person has not purified his/her mind, and is led by ignorance and egoism. Ignorance leads to *techatecha-mit* – "confused, haphazard, disarranged, incorrect manner-order-procedure, sequence, progression" and *techatecha* – "confused, haphazard, disarranged movements and actions" as well as *techatecha medu–* "confused speech." Only through humility and subjecting the ego to a higher authority, listening to and heeding the teachings and practicing the disciplines of *Shedy* {"to study profoundly-penetrate the mysteries"} can it be conquered, and the highest goal of life, *Nehast*, be attained.

Great Truth # 3

The third Great Truth is "S-Uashu s-Nafu n saiu Set." "Devotion to the Divine leads to freedom from the fetters of Set." Saui Set relates to the fetters. As spiritual enlightenment dawns, there will be many new feelings that arise, because a new world heretofore unknown by the mind has been accessed. Devotion purifies the personality by dissolving the ego. Then you begin to discover the world in which enlightened sages live. Along with devotion, your actions must be pure. When your actions are unrighteous, you are fettering your consciousness; you are fettering your personality. The unrighteous act itself is a fetter of the personality. Why? Because it causes you to be conscious of your ego, of yourself as an individual, of yourself as a mortal being, separate from the Divine. If you act magnanimously, with purity, with righteousness, the burden of your personality is lifted, and you start coming into harmony with the cosmic order. Then you will be lifted from this *Saui Set*. Devotion and right action remove the fetters of the personality and one's mind becomes unlimited. Then it is possible to fathom the depths of Creation and the infinity of the Spirit. The mummies that are wrapped all have a special bandage that is placed over their mouth. Symbolically it is called *saiu set*. When saiu set is there, you cannot touch the mummy with the seba-ur instrument. Recall the Seba glyphs discussed previously, about the teachings sba, sbai, etc. Seba-ur is the great Seba. Seba-ur also relates to the great star in the sky that illumines, the great enlightenment. This instrument is a metaphor of the great Sba, the star that illumines perennially *"Akhemu Urdu"* in the North Pole – it never fades. So, one who is touched by that great star is fully illumined (enlightened), and not like ordinary people who are only partially enlightened. People who acquire some knowledge but who do not achieve the highest attainment, full enlightenment, can be likened to someone waking up, but then going back to sleep.

So saui set must be lifted from the mouth, to uncover the mouth, so the mouth can be opened. The mouth is the instrument of creation from which the word comes. Through the mouth we express thought. Thought takes the form of ideas and desires. Thus, we talk our way into the situations we finds ourselves in. We can create bad situations or good ones. This is why it is admonished in the teachings that we must become "Maakheru," "true of speech." If *Medu-Neter* (hieroglyphic texts containing the philosophy of Ancient Egypt) is mastered, then the spiritual aspirant becomes *Maakheru* or true of thought, word and deed, that is, purified in body, mind and soul. These Shetaut (mysteries- rituals, wisdom, philosophy) about the Neter (Supreme Being) are related in the *Shetitu* or writings related to the hidden teachings. And those writings are referred to as *Medu Neter* or "Divine Speech," the writings of the god Djehuti (Ancient Egyptian god of the divine word) – it also refers to any Kamitan hieroglyphic texts or inscriptions generally.

So words and right speech are extremely important in Neterian spirituality. If you speak wrongly you are creating negative *ariu-* (ctions, deeds, unconscious mental impressions that impel the desires of the mind-the karmic basis) accumulated over previous years. That negativity leads to dullness of mind and ignorance, as well as the inability to understand the teaching and avoid the complications and miseries of life. If your mouth is covered, if it is fettered. You cannot speak, and you cannot

Egyptian Mysteries Volume 1: Principles of Shetaut Neter

express your consciousness. You cannot live properly, so you cannot work out the mysteries of life. To open the mouth, you must have purity of heart. You must have righteousness, and that process begins with *Uashu* or *Ushet* – faith-devotion.

Uashu or *Ushet* means devotion. I told you previously about the philosophy of the culture – of a civilization. We can have devotion, but what is the devotion being directed to? Remember the ancient Egyptian ritual of the boat being practiced by the modern day Muslims. What are they devoting that ritual to? Can you say that they are practicing the ancient Egyptian ritual? No, because they are devoting it to a Muslim saint and not to the Supreme Divinity. They are practicing the ritual, the tradition, but the original meaning was lost and the new tradition co-opted it. You must be devoted to the Divine in the proper way, not fanatically, not following dogmatic leaders, not just ritualistically, but with understanding and with the idea of discovering the Divine as the very essence of oneself, here and now, and not waiting for some future heaven. This is what Neterianism is all about, *Nehast*, the Resurrection, the spiritual awakening.

So *Uashu* (devotion) leads to *Nafu*, which is freedom, …freedom from *saiu set*, freedom from the fetters of set, which is your own egoism. Devotion leads you to freedom from your own egoism, your desires, and individuality, because if you are devoting yourself to the Divine, this opens your heart so you cannot be egoistic, because there is something more magnanimous than you (the ego personality). Those who are egoistic, selfish, and greedy do not worship anyone besides themselves, the objects they desire, and others who are more egoistic, greedier and richer than they are. That is true idolatry. Those lower objects become the "gods and goddesses" of the ignorant and the unrighteous. More accurately, those objects of lower worship are the demons, because they lead to pain and suffering afterwards.

Great Truth #4:

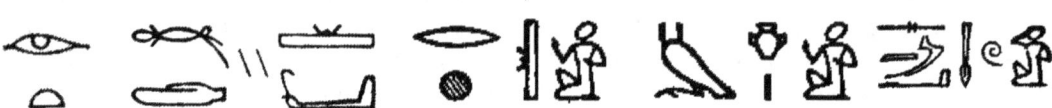

The fourth Great Truth is "Ari Shedy Rekh ab m Maakheru" which means "Doing Shedy leads to knowledge of oneself, of knowing one's heart, and this is called being True of Speech."

"True of speech" means established in truth. One who is established in truth is an *Akh*. Recall that the Akhu are awakened ones, enlightened persons. In the Neterian scripture known as the *Ru Pert Em Heru* or "*Book of Enlightenment*" (also known as *Book of Coming Forth by Day* and incorrectly known as the *Book of the Dead*), it is explained that there will be a judgment of the soul. This judgment is based on its Ariu (deeds). That judgment determines where the soul goes after death. This means that God (The Divine) does not judge anyone because we are all essentially gods and goddesses, sparks of the same Divinity. So, God within us judges us. This is an objective judgment for which only the individual is responsible. It occurs at the unconscious level of the mind, beyond any interference from the person, personality or ego consciousness which is on the surface level of the mind. Therefore, one's conscious desire to go to heaven at the time of one's death or one's conscious repentance at the time of death for misdeeds in life cannot overcome the weight of the unrighteous *ariu* – (actions, things done, make something, deeds; *Ari* -Karma) one has set up during a lifetime. Therefore, one cannot repent on one's death bed after a life of unrighteousness- after filling the heart and mind with unrighteous feelings, thoughts, words and deeds. So it is important to begin now to purify the heart and cleanse the soul so as to become or *Maakheru* (true of speech-pure of heart) at the time of the judgment.

So, to summarize the teachings of the Great Truths, we have "Pa Neter ua ua Neberdjer n Neteru," which means the God is one, one. "Ua Ua" is a particular term, a special term that is found in the Medu Neter -hieroglyphic text scriptures. It means "One-One", literally "one-one," or "One without second," or "One and alone," because think about it. If you have a Supreme Being, but then you have another god there also, not necessarily a devil, then you have to wonder if there is yet another Supreme Being above that one, and then if you have yet another Supreme Being above that one, and on and on, at infinitum. Ua Ua means "Absolute." Another term we have is *Tem*. *Tem* means completion, fullness, and completeness. That is the name of the third aspect of the Anunian Trinity of Khepri-Ra-Tem. So God is from Beginning to End. This teaching is the progenitor of the Alpha and Omega concept of Christianity.

Egyptian Mysteries Volume 1: Principles of Shetaut Neter

The philosophy is showing us that there is a highly evolved concept of One Supreme Being that manifests as all. There is one Source, one Ultimate Reality, one Spirit. So from the perspective of Shetaut Neter, the Supreme Being, Neberdjer, is the same one that the Christians call God the Father, the same one that the Muslims call Allah, the same one that the Hindus call Krishna or Vishnu, and the same one that the Buddhists call Buddha. This is what the Ancient Egyptian King-Sage Akhnaton said in the Hymns to Aton. This is a non-dual, pantheistic (God manifests as Creation), ecumenical and non-orthodox vision of religion and Spirit. But if you were to ask an orthodox Christian if they agree with this, they will not agree with it, because they believe that their God is the only one, and "He" does not operate in any other religions, and all other names are blasphemy. Orthodox Muslims also will not agree with this for the same reasons. Orthodox Jews also will not agree with it. Orthodox followers of these three traditions all believe they and their traditions are different, special and true, and that all others are false. Thus, Orthodox western religions will not agree with any of this, because orthodox western religions are exclusive, not inclusive. For these reasons, the orthodox (adhering to the accepted or traditional and established concepts of their faith alone) religions come into conflict with each other and with other religions of Africa, the East and the Americas.

Orthodox philosophies do not comprehend or allow the concept of pantheism or what is called monism (there is only God, there is not Creation). These mystical, pantheistic concepts are referring to an understanding that God, the Supreme, manifests as all. He-She manifests as me and manifests as you. In fact, we are all neterus, gods and goddesses. Some people have more awareness of this, some have less, and some have none. The person living on the park bench, or under the overpass, they have the least, but in many ways the rich people, the worldly ones, the Hollywood crowd, have even less because they may have more egoistic entanglements that take their minds away from truth of the Spirit and mire them in the tangled web of the world process and materialism. The person in the park may be more elevated than a lot of other people because he or she may be less egoistically involved in the world.

The following terms are extremely important in Shetaut Neter, and you should remember them. You should remember the terms 'ua ua' meaning 'one one,' and Neberdjer, meaning all-encompassing divinity. 'Saiu Set' is another important term to remember, meaning the fetters of the mouth and also, 'khemn,' meaning ignorance. Khemn comes from the root word kam (as in Kamit), which means black. This is the negative aspect of blackness, not black people, but darkness, as in philosophy, i.e, that darkness that shrouds and blocks intelligence. The positive aspect of blackness is Asar, the Lord of the Perfect Black, the Blackness of consciousness, the blackness of the primeval ocean. Another important word is 'Maat' meaning truth and righteousness. Maat is also the name of the goddess who symbolizes truth, harmony, balance, justice and righteousness.

In the third principal, 'Uashu' is the important term, the key term in that statement. Uashu is devotion. There is an Ancient Egyptian proverb that says "The path to the Divine is one, with two parts, wisdom and devotion." Devotion without wisdom is "blind faith." Wisdom without devotion is "dry intellectualism." Neither blind faith nor dry intellectualism can lead to enlightenment. Blind faith leads to fanaticism and hysteria. Dry intellectualism leads to cold indifference and callousness, which will destroy virtue and spiritual sensitivity. Cold indifference is a kind of dull detachment wherein a person does not care for others or about anything. That is not the ideal of Maat. Those kinds of people cannot help humanity in the four important ways espoused by the Maatian teachings (give food to the hungry, drink to the thirsty, clothes to the clotheless, boat to the boatless {shelter, opportunity and means to sustain oneself}. If you cannot help humanity you will not be able to help yourself. Social service is the path to purify the personality. Don't be fooled by people who are highly intellectual, who can quote all the scriptures, and can say many things that sound very good, theatrically jump up and down and shout halleluiah. This does not mean anything if they do not have experience of the Divine, or if they do not have the mystical philosophy. You will know those who have the true attainment if you see a grasp of the philosophy and its expression in their lives; they will act with righteousness and truth. They will not lead double lives or be caught up in the illusoriness of life, or its desires and sorrows.

In our tradition, the philosophers write, and it is the same in the eastern tradition. There are very few spiritual scholars who have written one book… you should wonder about that. They can talk extensively, they can impress you with their theatrics, they may drive fancy cars, but all these won't help you. Sages may have a fancy car, but they do not live for it, and if it were taken away for some reason, they would not care. What makes sages happy is extolling the teaching. They are happier than you could ever imagine, writing the books and extolling the wisdom of the Divine; that is what they are about. What are you about? What is your purpose in life and do you want to be a true aspirant or a mindless follower of orthodox religion? The orthodox are interested in imparting dogmas and demanding obedience to those blindly following. Mystical religion is interested in making you free, making you an enlightened being, and not a slave to ignorance and illusion.

"Shedy" is the important principle in the fourth teaching. "Shedy" or "Sheti" means the spiritual disciplines. The disciplines are what we refer to as the yogic disciplines. There are four basic yogic disciplines that we will discuss shortly. These are to be practiced so that you can reach knowledge and purity of heart. Purity of heart leads to 'Maakheru,' which is "truth of speech," "truth of the mouth," "opening of the mouth," "awakening of the Spirit."

Egyptian Mysteries Volume 1: Principles of Shetaut Neter

What are you supposed to be devoting yourself to? The Divine. What are you supposed to be studying to get the knowledge of? The wisdom philosophy. These are the keys. We will go into a little more detail now based directly on the Medu Neter.

The disciplines of *Shedy* are: *Maat Shedy*, study and practice of virtuous living to purify the heart so that one becomes one with the cosmic ordering power of the universe- i.e. become one with God. *Uash Shedy*, practice of rituals, study of myths of the gods and goddesses, chanting the Divine Names and developing *Neter Merri*, Divine Love – universal and transcendental love in which the personality melts into all existence- becomes one with it. *Rekh Shedy*, listening to, study of, and meditation on the wisdom teaching so as to understand the nature of the Divine, Creation, and thereby realize the intrinsic oneness with the Divine. *Uaah Shedy*, formal practice of meditation on the Divine to discover the innermost reality within, thus discovering *Sema-Aton* –"Cosmic Union with the Divine (Aton)" or *Sema-Asar-* "Cosmic Union with the Divine (Asar)."

This state of consciousness, *Nehast*, can only be accomplished by *uaa*, "Meditation." All of the disciplines of shedy lead to a meditative experience; they act to attenuate the personality and allow it to be purified. Then the mind can enter into extended concentration and super-consciousness, deeper levels of awareness.

What is needed to overcome these fetters or obstacles is *Shemsu udja shedy* –"real and powerful, burning following and practice of the disciplines of the spiritual teaching." This implies constant and not intermittent contact with the temple, the teaching, the *Sbai* – {wise person, teacher, instructor, sage, spiritual preceptor}, regular practice of the disciplines, studies and rituals. It also implies a movement in which *Uash* – "praise worship, devotion" and desire to be involved with and experiencing the teaching, rituals and mysteries of the temple increase rather than decrease. Otherwise, if *Shemsu udja* is not present, the higher purpose of *Shems* will not be realized. Instead a different movement is present: *tenem*- "losing the way, wandering, lost, turned away from." The small bird symbol, , indicates reduction, contraction, or negativity in the movement. The knife with legs, , symbolizes the cutting off with that which was followed before. The legs, , face in the opposite direction to the rest of the glyphs. This indicates opposite (backwards-away) movement. Devotion to the Divine should increase and there should be increasing turning away from worldly egoistic ideals and desires.

"It is very hard, to leave the things we have grown used to, which meet our gaze on every side. Appearances delight us, whereas things which appear not, make their believing hard. Evils are the more apparent things, whereas the Good can never show Itself unto the eyes, for It hath neither form nor figure."
–Ancient Egyptian Proverb

The final objective of the Mysteries is to be able to say: *Nuk pu Nuk Asar Neter* – "I am that I am" (Asar the Divinity).

This is recognition of one's identity as one with the Divine Self. Also, *tf pu nuk tjsy wdjb* - he is me tied to each other- *"He is I and I am he"* This is recognition of one's unbreakable connection to the Divine.

The following are categorizations of our books of the Shetaut Neter Theologies. The other books in the series augment the different sections or topics of the teachings. The book *Anunian Theology* details the theology of Ra. *Egyptian Yoga Volume 2* details the mysteries of Amun and Theban theology. *The Mysteries of Mind and Memphite Theology* book has the teachings related to Ptah Theology, and the *Resurrecting Osiris* book has the teachings related to the Asarian Tradition. Anunian Theology is the source for all of these as I have said before. The Asarian tradition was the most popular national religion of Kamit in ancient times. It was practiced generally throughout the entire country, but recall that all these existed side by side without conflict. We might find a person going to the Ra Temple in the morning and to the Asar Temple in the evening. There is also the Goddess Path. In African tradition, and particularly in the Kamitan tradition, the Goddess has a special place especially in the forms of Goddess Aset (Isis), Goddess Net, Goddess Hetheru and Goddess Sekhmet. These are some of the main forms of the Goddess.

The Creation of The Universe

Above: The papyrus containing the ancient Egyptian myth of the History of Creation.

The process of creation of the universe is explained in the form of a cosmological system for better understanding. Cosmology is a branch of philosophy dealing with the origin, processes, and structure of the universe. Cosmogony is the astrophysical study of the creation and evolution of the universe. Both of these disciplines are inherent facets of Ancient Egyptian philosophy through the main religious systems or Companies of the gods and goddesses. A Company of gods and goddesses is a group of deities, which symbolize particular cosmic forces or principles that emanate from the all-encompassing Supreme Being from which they have all emerged. The Self or Supreme Being manifests creation through the properties and principles represented by the *Pautti* Company of gods and goddesses - cosmic laws of nature. The system or Company of gods and goddesses of Anu is regarded as the oldest, and also forms the basis of the Asarian Trinity. It is expressed in the diagram of the ***Pautti of Anunian Cosmology*** or Company of Gods and Goddesses who formed the creation of the universe based on the creation story of the theological teaching that was developed by the priests and priestesses of the Ancient Egyptian city of Anu (also known to the Greeks as "Heliopolis.")

GOD IS CREATION

The *Pau*  - self existent spirit, God, created all things out of *Paut*  the stuff or matter or substance or material out of which all is made (food-objects-people-gods-planets-stars-etc.) Thus, came into being the *Pauti*  company of gods and goddesses, and God is also known as Pauti because Creation is made of God stuff.

Egyptian Mysteries Volume 1: Principles of Shetaut Neter
The Pautti Of Anunian Cosmology (The Ra Tradition)

```
Khepr-Ra-Tem        ⇨⇨⇨⇨⇨
                         ⇩
         ⇩              Hetheru
         ⇩              Djehuti (Thoth)
         ⇩              Maat
      Shu ⇔ Tefnut
         ⇩
      Geb ⇔ Nut
      ⇙  ⇩  ⇘
Set (Seth)  Asar (Osiris)⇔ Aset (Isis)  Asar⇔ Nebthet (Nebethet,
                                                    Nepthys)
                ⇩                          ⇩
             Heru (Horus)              Anpu (Anubis)
```

The Mystery Teachings of the Anunian Tradition are related to the Divinity Ra and his company of Gods and Goddesses.[1] This Temple and its related Temples espouse the teachings of Creation, human origins and the path to spiritual enlightenment by means of the Supreme Being in the form of the god Ra. It tells of how Ra emerged from a primeval ocean and how human beings were created from his tears. The gods and goddesses, who are his children, go to form the elements of nature and the cosmic forces that maintain nature.

Shetaut Anu

Top: Ra. From left to right, starting at the bottom level- The Gods and Goddesses of Anunian Theology: Shu, Tefnut, Nut, Geb, Aset, Asar, Set, Nebthet and Heru-Ur

The diagram above shows that the *Psedjet* (Ennead), or the creative principles which are embodied in the primordial gods and goddesses of creation, emanated from the Supreme Being. Ra or Ra-Tem arose out of the *"Nu,"* the primeval waters, the hidden essence, and began sailing the *"Boat of Millions of Years"* which included the Company of gods and goddesses. On his boat emerged the "neters" or cosmic principles of creation. The neters of the Pautti (Ennead) are Khepri-Ra-Atum, Shu, Tefnut, Geb, Nut, Asar, Aset, Set, and Nebethet. Hetheru (Life Force), Djehuti (mind) and Maat (order-truth) represent attributes of the Supreme Being as the very *stuff* or *substratum* which makes up creation. Shu, Tefnut, Geb, Nut, Asar, Aset, Set, and Nebethet represent the principles upon which creation manifests. Anpu is a son of Asar and is not part of the Ennead. He represents the feature of intellectual discrimination in the Asarian myth. "Sailing" signifies the beginning of motion in creation. Motion implies that events occur in the realm of time and space, thus, the phenomenal universe comes into existence as a mass of moving essence we call the elements. Prior to this motion, there was the primeval state of being without any form and without existence in time or space.

After being separated, Geb and Nut formed our planet and the heavens. Geb (the earth) rests under Nut (the sky), as Ra traverses the heavens in his Divine Boat and with him is Maat, who establishes order in the vibrations of time and space formed by the movement of the boat so that Creation may exist. See the book Anunian Theology

Egyptian Mysteries Volume 1: Principles of Shetaut Neter

The Memphite Tradition

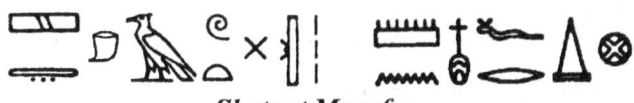

Shetaut Menefer

Below: The Memphite Cosmogony.

The city of Hetkaptah (Ptah)

The Mystery Teachings of the Menefer (Memphite) Tradition are related to the neterus known as Ptah, Sekhmit, and Nefertem. The myths and philosophy of these divinities constitutes Memphite Theology.[xliii] This Temple and its related Temples espoused the teachings of Creation, human origins and the path to spiritual enlightenment by means of the Supreme Being in the form of the god Ptah and his family, who compose the Memphite Trinity. It tells of how Ptah emerged from a primeval ocean and how he created the universe by his will and the power of thought (mind). The gods and goddesses, who are his thoughts, go to form the elements of nature and the cosmic forces that maintain nature. His spouse, Sekhmit, has a powerful Temple system of her own that is related to the Memphite teaching. The same is true for his son, Nefertem.

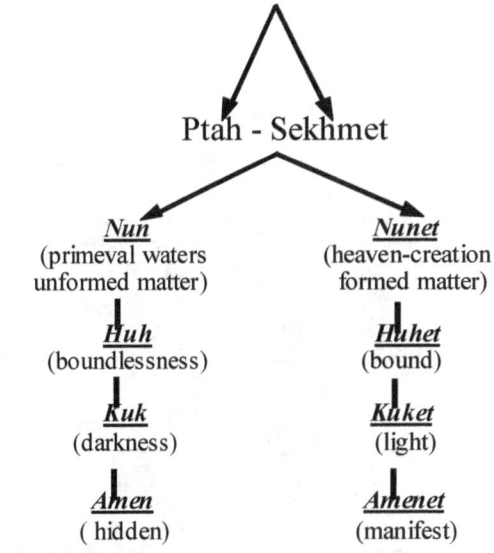

The Neters of Creation -
The Company of the Gods and Goddesses.
Neter Neteru
Nebertcher - Amun (unseen, hidden, ever present, Supreme Being, beyond duality and description)

Ptah - Sekhmet

Nun (primeval waters unformed matter) — *Nunet* (heaven-creation formed matter)

Huh (boundlessness) — *Huhet* (bound)

Kuk (darkness) — *Kuket* (light)

Amen (hidden) — *Amenet* (manifest)

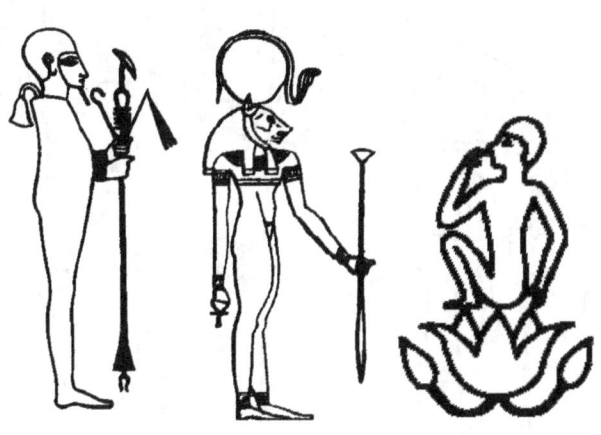

Ptah, Sekhmit and Nefertem

Egyptian Mysteries Volume 1: Principles of Shetaut Neter

The Theban Tradition

Shetaut Amun

The Mystery Teachings of the Wasetian Tradition are related to the neterus known as Amun, Mut and Khonsu. This Temple and its related Temples espoused the teachings of Creation, human origins and the path to spiritual enlightenment by means of the Supreme Being in the form of the god Amun or Amun-Ra. It tells of how Amun and his family, the Trinity of Amun, Mut and Khonsu, manage the Universe along with his Company of Gods and Goddesses. The Amun Temple became very important in the early part of the New Kingdom Era. The Hymns of Amun are an extremely important aspect of Shetaut Neter, on a par with the Pert m Hru texts and other main texts of Shetaut Neter. (For the Hymns of Amun, see our book *Egyptian Yoga Volume 2*.

Above left: Amun with Mut and Khonsu. Right: Amun in Ram form with Maat and Uadjit

Below: The Trinity of Amun and the Company of Gods and Goddesses of Amun

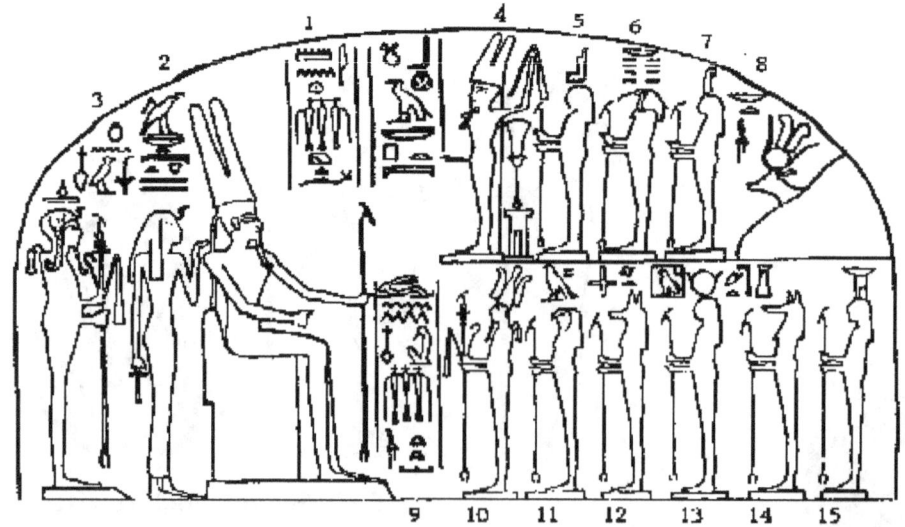

See the Book *Egyptian Yoga Vol. 2* for more on Amun, Mut and Khonsu by Muata Ashby

The Goddess Tradition

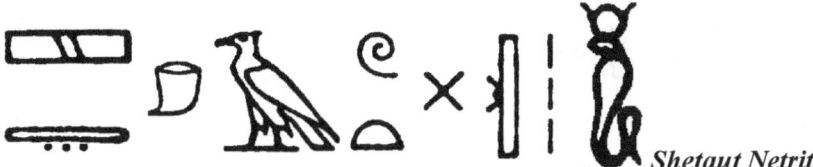

"Arat"   *Shetaut Netrit*

The hieroglyphic sign Arat means "Goddess." Goddess worship was general throughout ancient Kamit. The Mystery Teachings of the Goddess Tradition are related to the Divinity in the form of the Goddess. The Goddess was an integral part of all the Neterian traditions, and special Temples also developed around the worship of certain particular Goddesses who were also regarded as Supreme Beings in their own right. Thus, as in other African religions, the goddess as well as the female gender were respected and elevated just as the male divinities. The Goddess was also the author of Creation, giving birth to it as a great Cow. The following are the most important forms of the goddess.[xliv]

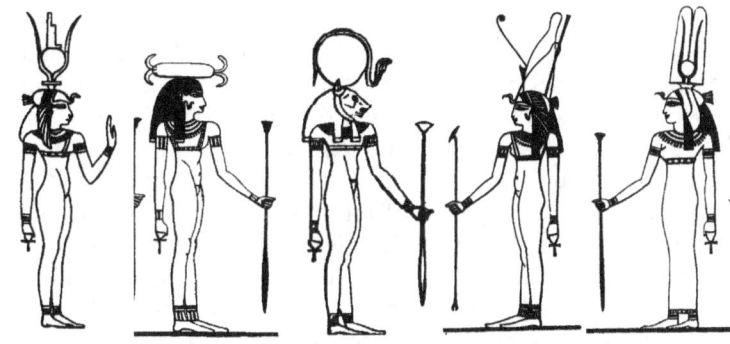

Aset, Net, Sekhmit, Mut, Hetheru

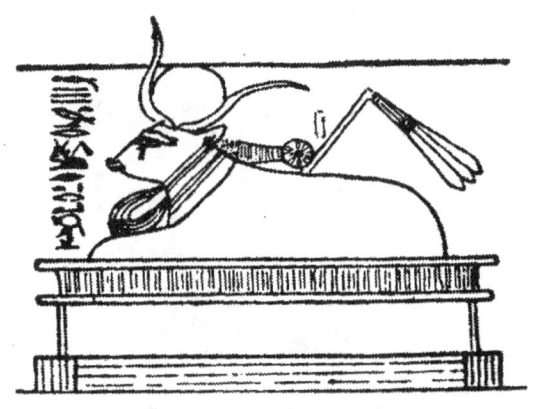

Mehurt ("The Mighty Full One")

Egyptian Mysteries Volume 1: Principles of Shetaut Neter

The Asarian Tradition

Shetaut Asar

The temple of Asar is located in the ancient city, Abdu; its ruins still remain today. It was built by Seti I and his son Rameses II (1300 BCE) on top of another Temple that was at least 2,000 years older. This Temple and its related Temples espoused the teachings of Creation, human origins and the path to spiritual enlightenment by means of the Supreme Being in the form of the god Asar. It tells of how Asar and his family, the Trinity of Asar, Aset and Heru, manage the universe and lead human beings to spiritual enlightenment and the resurrection of the soul. This Temple and its teaching were very important from the Pre-Dynastic era down to the Christian period. The Mystery Teachings of the Asarian Tradition are related to the neterus known as: Asar, Aset, Heru (Osiris, Isis and Horus, respectively)

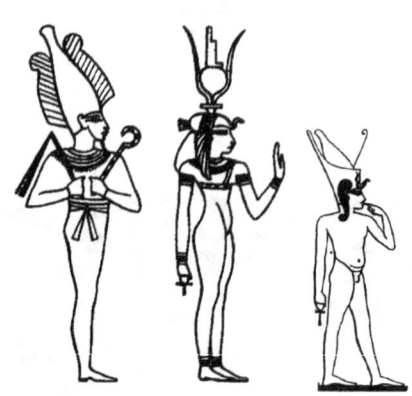

THE FIRST KING AND QUEEN OF KAMIT AND THE ASARIAN RESURRECTION MYTH TO BE KNOWN BY ALL NETERIAN FOLLOWERS

In order to better understand the culture and fundamental teaching of Neterianism, it is important to know the Creation Myth (presented earlier) and the following Myth of Asar, Aset and Heru. The tradition of Asar, Aset and Heru was practiced generally throughout the land of ancient Kamit and was the most popular. The centers of this tradition were the city of Abdu containing the Great Temple of Asar, the city of Pilak containing the Great Temple of Aset[xlv] and Edfu containing the Great Temple of Heru. Asar and Aset were two souls who were sent to earth by Ra, the Supreme Being, to incarnate (be made flesh, become embodied) on earth in human form to help humanity.

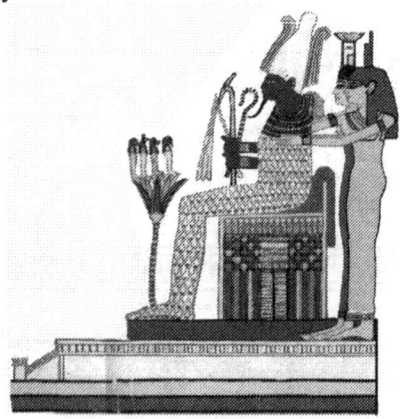

Above: Asar, Aset and Nebethet hold Royal Court in the city of Abdu, the city of Asar

Asar and Aset dedicated themselves to the welfare of humanity and sought to spread civilization throughout Africa and the earth, even as far as Europe, India and China. Aset became the custodian of the wisdom teachings and Asar founded the religious practices, he instituted the rituals and built the first temples where the teaching was practiced. So Lord Khepri is the founder of Shetaut Neter Philosophy and Asar is recognized as the founder of the religious practices of Shetaut Neter. Asar brought the teaching to a practical level for people to adopt, with the assistance of Lord Djehuti and Lady Aset. Lady Nebethet also assisted her brother (Asar) and sister (Aset) to lead the country. Set was jealous and he stayed away.

During the absence of Asar from his kingdom, his brother Set had no opportunity to make innovations in the state because Aset was extremely vigilant in governing the country, and always upon her guard and watchful for any irregularity or unrighteousness.

Asar (right) holds the crook and the flail. The crook symbolizes royalty and also the capacity to lead, to be a guide, to be a shepherd for humanity. Righteous men and women are the flock who follow Asar.[xlvi] The flail symbolizes the power of mastery over the three worlds (Physical, Astral, Causal) and the capacity to discipline. Upon Asar's return from touring the world and carrying the teachings of wisdom abroad there was merriment and rejoicing throughout the land. However, one day after Asar's return, through his lack of vigilance, he became intoxicated and slept with Set's wife,

Nebethet. Nebethet, as a result of the union with Asar, gave birth to Anpu.

Set, who represents the personification of evil forces, plotted in jealousy and anger (the blinding passion that prevents forgiveness) to usurp the throne and conspired to kill Asar. Set secretly got the measurements of Asar's body and constructed a coffin. Through trickery Set was able to get Asar to "try on" the coffin for size. While Asar was resting in the coffin, Set and his assistants locked it and then dumped it into Hapi, the Nile River.

The coffin made its way to the coast of Syria where it became embedded in the earth and from it grew a tree with the most pleasant aroma in the form of a Djed. The Djed is the symbol of Asar's back. It is a column made from the trunk of a tree that has four horizontal lines in relation to a firmly established, straight column. The Djed column is symbolic of the *Sefekh Ba Ra* upper energy centers (known as charkas to the Indians) that relate to the levels of consciousness of the spirit within an individual human being.

Aset received the Pillar from the King of Syria

The King of Syria was out walking and as he passed by the tree, he immediately fell in love with the pleasant aroma, so he had the tree cut down and brought to his palace. Aset (Auset, Ast), Asar's wife, the personification of the wise, life giving, mother force in creation and in all humans, went to Syria in search of Asar. Her search led her to the palace of the Syrian King where she took a job as the nurse of the King's son. Every evening Aset would put the boy into a "fire" to consume his mortal parts, thereby transforming him to immortality. Fire is symbolic of both physical and mental purification. Most importantly, fire implies wisdom, the light of truth, illumination and energy. Aset, by virtue of her qualities, has the power to bestow immortality through the transformative power of her symbolic essence, her wisdom, the Neterian philosophy. Aset then told the king that Asar, her husband, is inside the pillar he made from the tree. He graciously gave her the pillar (Djed) and she returned with it to Kamit (Egypt).

Upon her return to Kamit, Aset went to the papyrus swamps where she lay over Asar's dead body and fanned him with her wings, infusing him with new life. In this manner Aset revived Asar through her power of love and wisdom, and then they united once more. From their union was conceived a son, Heru, with the assistance of the gods Djehuti and Amun (Amon).

One evening, as Set was hunting in the papyrus swamps, he came upon Aset and Asar. In a rage of passion, he dismembered the body of Asar into 14 pieces and scattered them throughout the land. The 14 pieces symbolize the 14 days of the waxing and waning moon and the dismembered eye of awareness. According to the myth, after his resurrection and ascendance to heaven the pieces of Asar's body were buried in different parts of Kamit. Asar's head is buried somewhere near the temple at Abdu. In this way it is Set, the brute force of our bodily impulses and desires, that "dismembers" our soul consciousness. Instead of oneness and unity, we see multiplicity and separateness which give rise to egoistic (selfish) and violent behavior. The Great Mother, Aset, once again sets out to search, now for the pieces of Asar, with the help of Anpu and Nebethet.

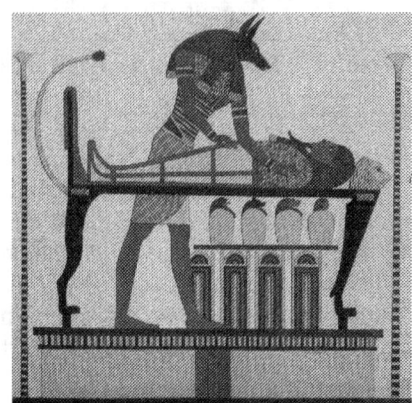

Above: Anpu assists in embalming the body of Asar

After searching all over the world they found all the pieces of Asar's body, except for his phallus which was eaten by a fish. In Ancient Egyptian and Hindu-Tantra myth, this loss represents seminal retention in order to channel the sexual energy to the higher spiritual centers, thereby transforming it into spiritual energy. Aset, Anpu and Nebethet re-membered the pieces, all except the phallus which was eaten by the fish. Asar thus regained life on earth and then later in the realm of the dead, the Duat. So he is the first dead and resurrected savior in religious history. His life and example show the way for all humanity to rise from death and discover immortality. Anpu embalmed Asar and wrapped him up in bandages, and so all who die become mummies like Asar, they are reconstituted by Anpu, Aset and Nebethet and are to become resurrected like Asar.

Asar Resurrected, rising from the tomb

Aset lay on top of Asar and blew air on him with her wings. This special air contained life force. That life force revived Asar and enabled him to impregnate her, even without the phallus that was missing.

Above: The birth of Heru. Aset is assisted by Djehuti and Amun.

Heru, therefore, was born from the union of the spirit of Asar and the life giving power of Aset (Creation). Thus, Heru represents the union of spirit and matter and the renewed life of Asar, his rebirth. When Heru became a young man, Asar returned from the realm of the dead and encouraged him to take up arms (vitality, wisdom, courage, strength of will) and establish truth, justice and righteousness in the world by challenging Set, its current ruler.[xlvii]

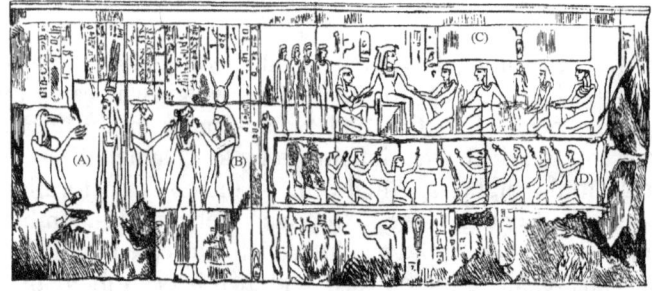

The Annunciation of The Birth of Heru

The origins of the transcendental themes of Christianity reach far into ancient Egyptian antiquity. In the New Testament Book of Matthew 1:20-23, the story of the Annunciation, Conception, Birth and Adoration of the child, Jesus, is presented. It tells how the "angel of the Lord" appears to Joseph, informing him that his wife Mary is pregnant by the Holy Spirit of God. The figure above is a drawing of the image engraved in the Holy of Holies or *Mesken,* in the ancient Egyptian Temple of Luxor (5,500-1,700 BCE). In the first scene (A) at left, the god Djehuti, the transmitter of the *word* (logos), is depicted in the act of announcing to queen Mut-em-Ua (who has assumed the role of Aset) that she will give birth to the child who will be the righteous, divine heir (Heru). In the next scene (B) Knum (Kneph), the ram headed god (also associated with Amun), along with Hetheru, provide her with the Life Force (spirit) through two Ankhs (symbols of life). In this same scene (B), the virgin is pictured as becoming pregnant (conceiving) through that spirit. In the following scene (C), the mother is being attended to while the child is being supported by nurses. The next scene (D) is the Adoration wherein the child is enthroned and adored by Amun, the hidden Holy Spirit behind all creation, and three men behind him (Amun) who offer boons or gifts with the right hand (open facing up) and eternal life with the left (holding the Ankh).

This set of scenes attests to the deeper significance of the virgin birth mystery. Every mother is a goddess and every child is a product or mixture of Creation or physical nature and the spirit of God. Through this metaphor, we are to understand that each human being has a divine origin, heritage and birthright. Therefore, it is clear to see the meaning of the Christian statements: *"I and [my] Father are one," "Jesus answered them, 'Is it not written in your law that ye are gods?'"* from John 10:30 and 34, respectively.

The Battle of Heru and Set

When Heru grew up he challenged Set for having murdered Asar and usurping the throne of Kamit as well as for being an unrighteous ruler. Set refused to relinquish the throne so a battle between him and Heru ensued. The battle between Heru and Set took many twists, sometimes one seeming to get the upper hand and sometimes the other, yet neither one gaining a clear advantage in order to decisively win. At one point Aset tried to help Heru by spearing Set, but due to the pity and compassion she felt towards him she set him free. In a passionate rage Heru cut off her head and went off by himself in a frustrated state. Even Heru was temporarily susceptible to passion which leads to performing deeds that one later regrets. Set found Heru and gouged out Heru's eyes. During this time Heru was overpowered by the evil of Set. He became blinded to truth (as signified by the loss of his eyes) and thus, was unable to do battle (act with Maat) with Set. His power of sight was later restored by Hetheru (goddess of passionate love, desire and fierce power), who also represents the left Eye of Ra. She is the fire spitting, destructive power of light which dispels the darkness

(blindness) of ignorance. Djehuti imparted that teaching also to Heru. Djehuti restored Heru's Udjat (Uatchit) (left) Eye, ☥, which Set had blinded.

Heru as the Supreme warrior: Heru-khuti (left)

Heru now became a fierce warrior and Set had no quarter. When the conflict resumed, the two contendants went before the court of the Ennead gods (Company of the nine gods who ruled over creation, headed by Ra). Set, promising to end the fight and restore Heru to the throne, invited Heru to spend the night at his house, but Heru soon found out that Set had evil intentions when Set tried to have intercourse with him. The uncontrolled Set also symbolizes unrestricted sexual activity. Juxtaposed against this aspect of Set (uncontrolled sexual potency and desire) is Heru in the form of ithyphallic (erect phallus) the divinity Min, an aspect of Heru, who represents not only the control of sexual desire, but its sublimation as well. Min symbolizes the power which comes from the sublimation of the sexual energy.

Through more treachery and deceit Set attempted to destroy Heru with the help of the Ennead, by tricking them into believing that Heru was not worthy of the throne. Asar sent a letter pleading with the Ennead to do what was correct. Heru, as the son of Asar, should be the rightful heir to the throne. All but two of them (the court of gods and goddesses) agreed because Heru, they said, was too young to rule. Asar then sent them a second letter (scroll of papyrus with a message) reminding them that even they cannot escape judgment for their deeds; they too will be judged in the end when they have to finally go to the West (abode of the dead).

This signifies that even the gods cannot escape judgment for their deeds. Since all that exists is only a manifestation of the absolute reality which goes beyond time and space, and that which is in the realm of time and space (humans, spirits, gods, angels, neters) are all bound by its laws. Following the receipt of Asar's scroll (letter), Heru was crowned King of Egypt. Set accepted the decision and made peace with Heru. All the gods rejoiced. Thus ends the legend of Asar, Aset, and Heru.

The Importance of the Asarian Resurrection Myth and its Teaching

The Resurrection of Asar and his reincarnation in physical form, then as King of the dead and in the form of Heru are a symbol for the spiritual resurrection which must occur in the life of every human being. In this manner, the story of the Asarian Trinity of Asar-Aset-Heru and the Egyptian Ennead holds hidden teachings, which when understood and properly practiced, will lead to spiritual enlightenment.

Asar (center), Aset (right) and Heru (left)

It is important to understand that there are many levels of teaching contained in the myth. The myth itself has many episodes and the scripture itself is to be studied in detail line by line. The higher aspects of the scope of the myths are beyond the scope of this book; what is being presented here is just an introduction. However, the essential teaching for those new to Neterianism is as follows. The Name "Asar" and the name "Aset" are very important to the understanding of their teaching.

 Asar

The woman-goddess, who symbolizes creation itself, the physical universe, supports the incarnation of the soul (Asar). In this way, the physical (Aset) supports the spirit (Asar). This symbol of the goddess herself is the throne, and this is why the throne seat, 𓊨, is where Asar is shown seated. The name Asar is spelled with the throne symbol, 𓊨, the eye symbol, 𓁹, and the male determinative, 𓀀. The eye symbol written in this manner means "to make," "create," "to do" or "engender." Therefore, the mystical symbolism of the name Asar is the essence, which procreates or comes into existence through Aset.

Aset

The symbols of the name of Aset are the throne seat, 𓊨 "as", the phonetic sign for "t", ◯, the determinative egg, ◯, symbol of motherhood, and the female determinative, 𓁐.

86

Egyptian Mysteries Volume 1: Principles of Shetaut Neter

This manner of reading of the name of Asar is supported by the myth of Asar and Aset, as well as their epithets and iconographies. The name Asar is intimately related to the name Aset. Asar and Aset are often referred to as "brother" and "sister" and as twins. This relates to the idea that they come from the same parent, i.e. the same spiritual source. In ancient times men and women who married were also referred to as brother and sister. This had no relation to their parentage. Rather, this epithet relates to the mystical origins of all human beings. Essentially, we are all brothers and sisters, as our true nature is not man and woman, but soul, and our parent, the Universal Spirit.

Through the myth of the Asarian Resurrection, we learn that Asar and Aset are Avatars, divine incarnations, sent to earth to lead souls, incarnating as human beings, towards righteousness, prosperity and spiritual enlightenment. In a higher sense, Asar represents the soul of every human being which comes to earth and must struggle to overcome the lower nature, which is symbolized by Set.

Asar was murdered and dismembered. He suffered the fate of souls of those who incarnate on earth. But he was resurrected and he showed the way of eternal life. He showed the way to practice religion and to develop the metaphysics of rebirth. Through his own life and that of Aset and Heru, we are led to the path of truth, the path of spiritual awakening, the path of the eternal, the path of immortality.

The task of every aspirant is to study the Creation Myth and the Asarian Resurrection Myth in detail. Then the teachings are to be reflected upon and practiced in day-to-day life. Then the teaching is to be meditated upon, and the related metaphysical rituals and disciplines must be practiced and higher consciousness discovered thereby.

Then the true nature of the myth will be revealed, and it will become clear that the myths are not talking just about people who existed in ancient times, but also of the ever-present reality of the soul and the prospect of eternal life. This is the goal of Neterianism, and it should be the highest priority for every Neterian follower.

The two eyes of Heru symbolize the sun and moon, i.e., the knowledge of Spirit and matter; this is the subject of the mysteries. Having the eyes fixed by Hetheru and Djehuti means knowing and living their teaching. This is what aspirants study and practice through the disciplines of Shetaut Neter and Sema Tawi.

Heru and Set (above) are the two aspects of the human personality, aspiration and ego. These two aspects must be reconciled, balanced and transcended if there is to be enlightenment. This is what occurred in ancient times and it is what is to occur in the life of the aspirant, through the study and practice of the teachings. Just as Heru and Set reconciled and tied the unity knot, so too the aspirant is to settle the conflict of the mind and soul and reunite with the Higher Self.

After his resurrection and after begetting Heru, Asar's body died, but he went to heaven and became the king of the dead in his new name, Asar-Sokar (picture at left).

Above: After being resurrected by Aset and begetting Heru, Asar (Osiris) becomes the Life Force energy which causes all things in nature to grow. (From a Bas Relief at the Temple of Aset at Pilak {Philea}) the pieces of his body were buried all over Kamit and these made the land fertile.

Asar was so holy that his body nourished the earth, and from it grew the wheat and other plants that feed all living things on earth. For this reason there is a special association of the Eye of Heru and the Eye of Asar, with bread and wine. These are special offerings that are recognized to be the body and fluid essence of the Divine Spirit. Wine is a substance that Asar invented and he is commemorated through it, not by intoxication, but by libation and communion.[xlviii] Asar live on the blood wine made of the blood of the gods and goddesses.

The eye is the special symbol of Asar as it represents awakened consciousness, the witnessing consciousness that transcends ordinary waking and sleep, enlightenment.

Egyptian Mysteries Volume 1: Principles of Shetaut Neter

The Neterian Eucharist

Below: The ancient Egyptian Eucharist using bread, wine and incense.

The Sem Priest offers bread

The Sem priest presenting a white vessel of wine.

The Sem priest presenting a ball of incense.

"This is the Flesh itself of Asar"
From the *Egyptian Book of Coming Forth By Day*
(Book of The Dead)

The Temples of Asar

Below is a picture of the New Kingdome Era Temple of Asar built by King-Sage Seti I. It was constructed over a site of a previous Temple that was at least 2000 years older.

Below is a picture of the "Asarion" (ancient Temple of Asar) from the predynastic age. The pictured section is behind the New Kingdom Temple (above). It displays the similar architecture of the Great Pyramid Temples and the Temple of the Sphinx at Giza.

Opening the Mouth

The "Opening of the Mouth Ceremony" where the priest uses the *Sba ur* instrument is one of the most important teachings of Neterianism. It is the force of spiritual awakening that is applied to the personality that allows it to experience full and perennial awareness of higher consciousness. It is not done by magic but by leading the personality to awaken through the disciplines of *Shedy*, finally culminating in the fully illumined state. This is the task of every aspirant, to be worthy of this ritual and its psychic benefit. That awakening is the true resurrection, the rebirth into higher consciousness for which every aspirant must strive.

The Aton Tradition

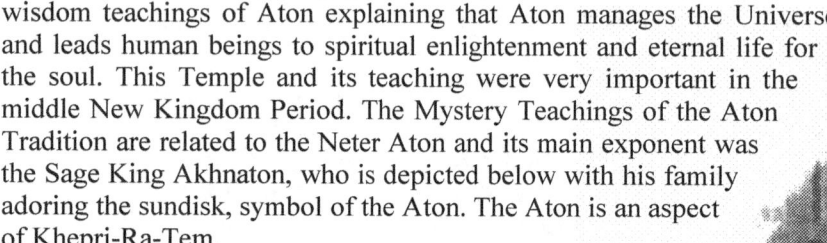 Shetaut Aton

This Temple and its related Temples espoused the teachings of Creation, human origins and the path to spiritual enlightenment by means of the Supreme Being in the form of the god Aton. It tells of how Aton with Its dynamic life force created and sustains Creation. By recognizing Aton as the very substratum of all existence, human beings engage in devotional exercises and rituals and the study of the Hymns containing the wisdom teachings of Aton explaining that Aton manages the Universe and leads human beings to spiritual enlightenment and eternal life for the soul. This Temple and its teaching were very important in the middle New Kingdom Period. The Mystery Teachings of the Aton Tradition are related to the Neter Aton and its main exponent was the Sage King Akhnaton, who is depicted below with his family adoring the sundisk, symbol of the Aton. The Aton is an aspect of Khepri-Ra-Tem.

Akhnaton, Nefertiti and their Daughters

For more on Atonism and the Aton Theology see the Essence of Atonism Lecture Series by Sebai Muata Ashby ©2001

The Fundamental Principles of Shetaut Neter
(Teachings Presented in the Kamitan scriptures)

Basic Tenets of Neterian Religion

1. The Purpose of Life is to attain the Great Awakening-Enlightenment-Know thyself.
2. SHETAUT NETER enjoins the Shedy (spiritual investigation) as the highest endeavor of life.
3. SHETAUT NETER enjoins that it is the responsibility of every human being to promote order and truth.
4. SHETAUT NETER enjoins the performance of Selfless Service to family, community and humanity.
5. SHETAUT NETER enjoins the Protection of nature.
6. SHETAUT NETER enjoins the Protection of the weak and oppressed.
7. SHETAUT NETER enjoins the Caring for hungry.
8. SHETAUT NETER enjoins the Caring for homeless.
9. SHETAUT NETER enjoins the equality for all people.
10. SHETAUT NETER enjoins the equality between men and women.
11. SHETAUT NETER enjoins the justice for all.
12. SHETAUT NETER enjoins the sharing of resources.
13. SHETAUT NETER enjoins the protection and proper raising of children.
14. SHETAUT NETER enjoins the movement towards balance and peace.

The Great Awakening of Neterian Religion

"Nehast"

Nehast means to "wake up," to Awaken to the higher consciousness. In the Prt m Hru Text it is said:

Nuk pa Neter aah Neter ZJah asha ren[xlix]

"I am that same God, the Supreme One, who has myriad of mysterious names."

The goal of all the Neterian disciplines is to discover the meaning of "Who am I?," to unravel the mysteries of life and to fathom the depths of eternity and infinity. This is the task of all human beings and it is to be accomplished in this very lifetime.

This purpose of life can be achieved by learning the ways of the Neteru, emulating them and finally becoming like them, *Akhus*, (enlightened beings), walking the earth as giants and accomplishing great deeds such as the creation of the universe!

The Oneness of Humanity

The following passages from the most important Kamitan texts directly and succinctly contradict any notion of racism, sexism and racial discrimination. Therefore, the concept that the Ancient Egyptians were racist or biased towards other groups is unfounded and misleading.

"Thou makest the color of the skin of one race to be different from that of another, but however many may be the varieties of mankind, it is thou that makes them all to live."

—Ancient Egyptian Proverb
from *The Hymns of Amun*

"Souls, Heru, son, are of the self-same nature, since they came from the same place where the Creator modeled them; nor male nor female are they. Sex is a thing of bodies not of Souls."
—Ancient Egyptian Proverb from *The teachings of Aset to Heru (Myth of Asar, Aset and Heru)*

One God for All Human Beings

"Thou settest every person in his place. Thou providest their daily food, every man having the portion allotted to him; [thou] dost compute the duration of his life. Their tongues are different in speech, their characteristics (or forms), and likewise their skins (in color), giving distinguishing marks to the dwellers in foreign lands… Thou makest the life of all remote lands."

—Ancient Egyptian
Hymns to Aton by Akhenaton

The last statement by the Sage/King Akhenaton is especially important in understanding the Kamitan view of humanity. God has created all peoples, all nations and countries and has appointed each person's country of residence, language and even their ethnicity and physical appearance (features). This statement denotes an understanding that that all people of Africa and those of foreign lands (Europe, Asia, South America, North America, etc.), have the same Creator and owe their continued existence to the same Divine Being. So there is only one human race, and all its people were created by the same Divinity and therefore, all are equal and related.

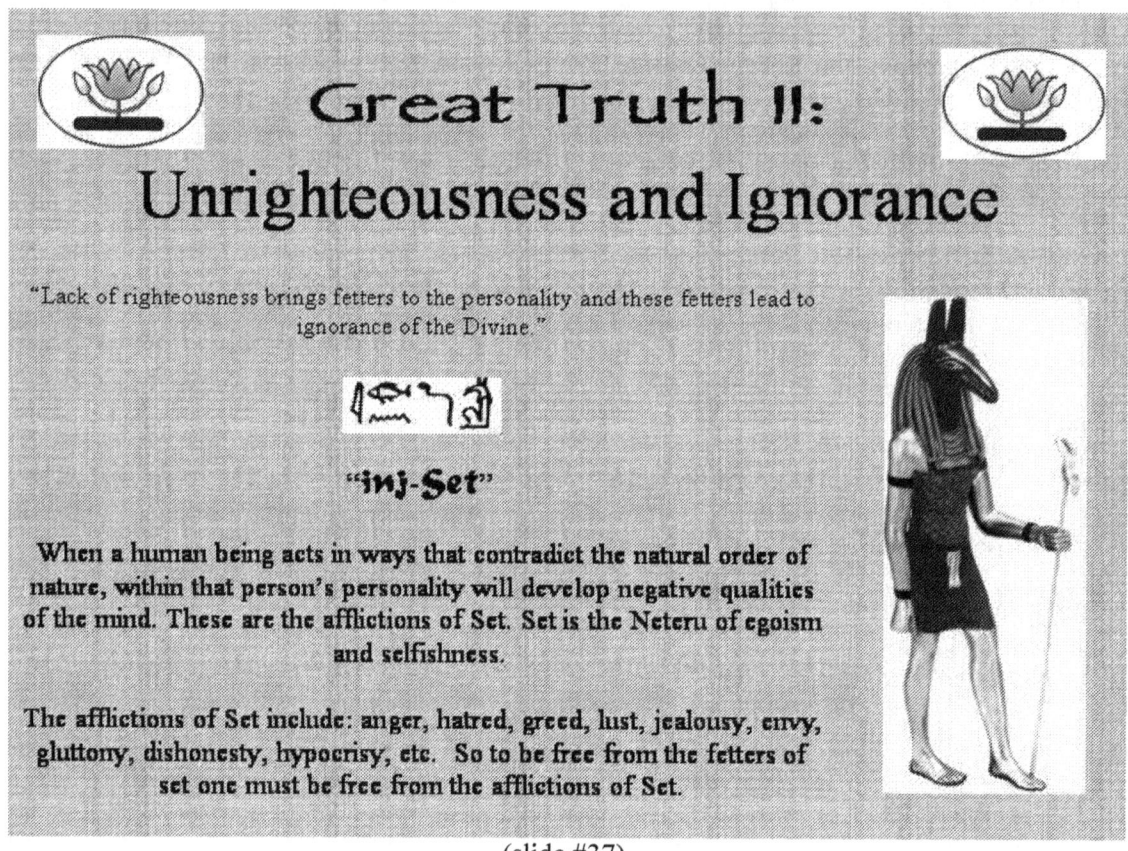

(slide #37)

Recall that Great Truth #2 is: "Lack of righteousness leads to fetters of the personality and these fetters lead to ignorance of the Divine." "*Inj-set*" refers to what happens when a human being acts in ways that constrict the natural order of nature within that person's personality. They will develop negative qualities of mind. These are the afflictions of Set, i.e., afflictions of the mind. Set is the Neteru of egoism and selfishness. Saiu Set are the fetters which cause afflictions, just like unhygienic living leads to disease, the inj-set leads to a disease of the mind, the disease of egoism, ignorance and bondage to the world of time and space. Recall that the term "*Saiu Set*" means "fetters of Set," and refers to a swathing (bandage) that is covers the mouth,, preventing one from experiencing expansion in consciousness (enlightenment). The fetters of Set as if develop into a disease, and the disease is inj-Set, which can be understood as an affliction.

In Shetaut Neter, the afflictions are anger, hatred, greed, lust, jealousy, envy, etc. These are the mental diseases, mental failings, that must be cured. Ignorance and egoism are the cause which must be removed from the personality. Aset is the Goddess that holds the cure for those ills; the cure is wisdom of Self. Those who are wise of Self cannot be ignorant, and therefore cannot be egoistic either. They cannot be selfish. They cannot be anything but helpful to humanity. The Divinity pictured above is Set. As stated previously, this is the Divinity that many scholars, including myself, believe that the early Jews confused and used to develop their concept of Satan. Recall that one of the names of *Set* is *Setek* or *Sutek*. Sutek and Satan are very similar. The Jews, we know, supposedly emerged with Moses from Ancient Egypt and the Judeo-Christian Bible says that "Moses was skilled in all the magic of the Egyptians."

Egyptian Mysteries Volume 1: Principles of Shetaut Neter

The Bible says that Moses was an Egyptian Priest, so obviously he knew the wisdom and the teachings of Kamit. So then the Jews come forth with a philosophy of a devil or a Satan. Then Christianity takes it over. You may remember a comedian by the name of Flip Wilson some years ago who took that concept and made a joke out of it … "the devil made me do it!" This concept of a devil is a big problem, because if you have a devil out there who is making you do something, and you have no control over it, then you do not have to answer to anybody, do you? You just have to say, "Oh, I could not help myself," and then you are free to be unrighteous and free to do whatever it is you want to and not be responsible, because there is some outside force controlling you, and you need to have it exorcised.

This was a new concept in spirituality that emerged with Judaism and a few other traditions, such as Zoroastrianism. The premise behind this idea is that there is some kind of evil god and there is some kind of a good god somewhere, and they are both battling, and people are caught in the middle, in a tug of war. And you have the devil on one shoulder and the angel on the other, each whispering to you…the angel telling you to be good, and the devil telling you to be bad.

Think of when you are speaking on the phone, and there is someone else in the room with you who also starts to speak to you. So you are trying to listen to the person on the phone and the person in the room at the same time. If you try this long enough, you won't get any communication done; instead you will be confused or go crazy. So this concept of a devil and an angel on one's shoulders is a concept that is driving people mad…spiritual madness. When people perceive that they are becoming insane, they push away any kind of critical thinking in order to maintain their sanity and they fall back to the dogmas, without considering the validity of these; this leads to fanaticism and the negative repercussions that fanaticism brings. Others just simply go mad… in various degrees, to the point that society has come to accept some of this spiritually abnormal behavior as normal. For example, general western society accepts that it is "normal" for people to lose their temper, to cheat on their spouses, to become depressed after some adversity, to have children even if one cannot afford to do so, to be greedy and miserly and hoard money (wealth), to be so mentally deranged that they accept the fact that movie stars can be paid one million dollars for one episode of a sit-com TV show while others in the society are existing in poverty, etc.

For those who are wiser, who do not get into religious fundamentalism, they just leave it all together, but they do not have a viable religious or spiritual process to fall back on…they just leave the church altogether. Some become atheists; they claim not believe in God or religion. Others become agnostic, believing that God cannot be known through religion or any way. Some of these people become frustrated with life later, after some time, growing older and fearing death, and they come back to religion with more intensity than before, but in a fundamentalist, fanatical way. Others retain their belief in God but not in religion; they are searching. Some make their own religion, and some try to follow their own dogmatic religion, but making changes in the way they see fit. Others are authentic mystics, those who seek the truth and are willing to go across the world if necessary, to find the true path to spiritual enlightenment.

Entropy is another major concept in Neterian theology. In Neterian theology there is really no evil. There is creation and destruction. There is creation (order) and entropy to be more precise. Consider an older building. Imagine how this building must have looked when it was first built. Now it is falling apart. That happens to everything. It will happen to the chair you are sitting in. A chair may last 500 years, but I guarantee you in 500 years you are going to find it in a dilapidated condition. Your bodies are deteriorating even as we speak; those of you who are five years old and those of you are fifty years old are all deteriorating, moving relentlessly towards dissolution.

Everything has entropy, and must be continuously maintained, and continuously worked, that is, re-ordered. Its order must be maintained so that it does not fall into chaos. So Set is not a devil because in Neterianism, we find that he is placed in the service of Ra, who represents the Supreme Being in time and space. He is depicted fighting the serpent of chaos that is trying to stop the journey of the Divine boat. Again, the boat that the priests carry into the Temple as part of their ritual (described above) is symbolic of the boat that Ra created at the beginning of time. Set is the ego, and when the ego goes the wrong way it commits evil acts, but it itself is not evil, only ignorant, ignorant of the knowledge of Self.

Egyptian Mysteries Volume 1: Principles of Shetaut Neter

Selfishness, hatred, violence, lust, jealousy, greed, etc. are all acts that seek to stop the orderly creation of the universe, the boat. Stopping that boat means that you are trying to stop creation, trying to bring creation to a halt. You are trying to stop order. You are trying to stop righteousness and truth. If that were to happen this whole world would come to an end.

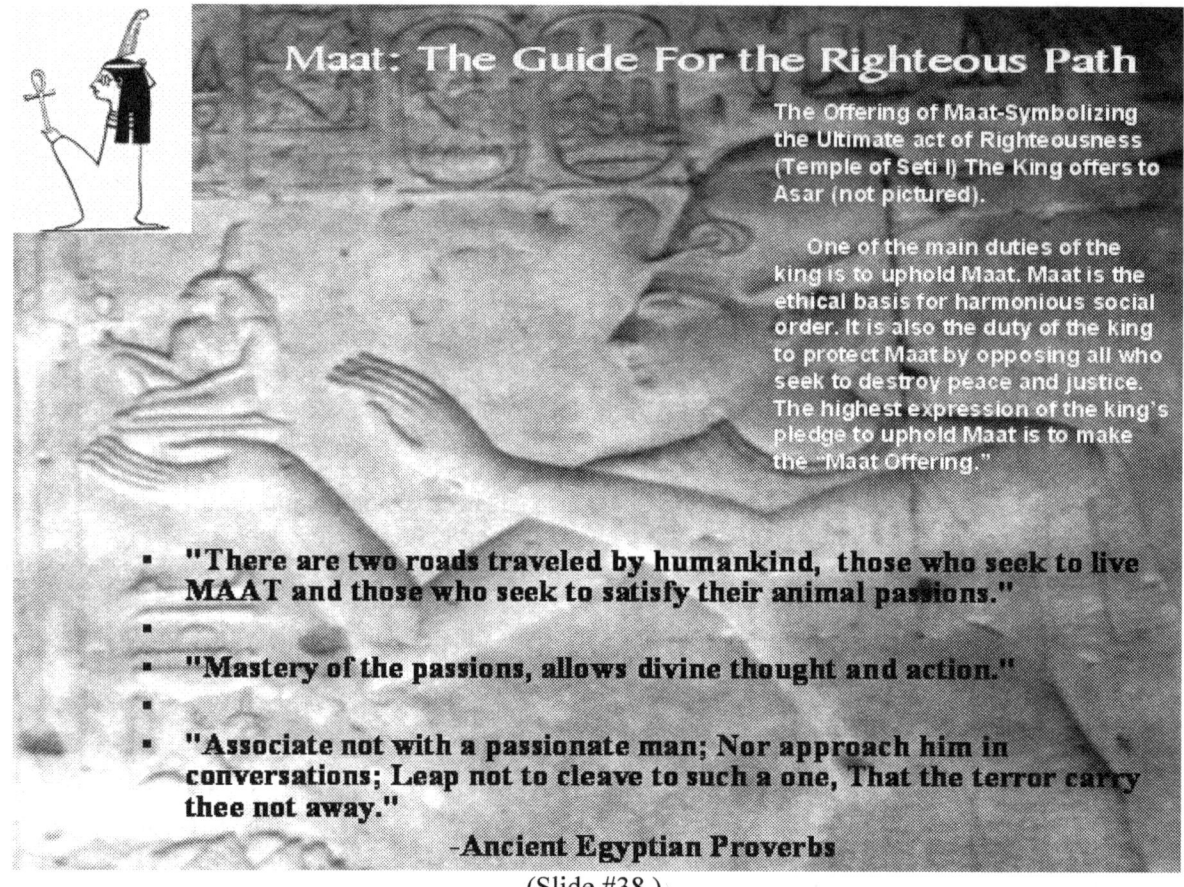

(Slide #38)

In order to uphold truth and order, all must make offerings to Maat. The highest offering is living by truth, the truth of the world and the truth of the beyond. Even the king must make offerings of Maat. One of the main duties of the king is to uphold righteousness, order, and truth. Why? So that there may be continued prosperity and peace in the land, and so there may be perpetuation of the culture and its civilization. Here Seti I is making an offering of Maat to Asar. This inscription can be seen even today in the Temple of Seti I in Abdu.

The offering of Maat is the ultimate offering that a king can make. And this is what he is expected to do; this is one of his main roles. He is to protect his people, to protect order, and to keep unrighteous people from dominating the culture.

The following Kamitan Proverbs are the injunctions of Maat:

> "There are two roads traveled by humankind, those who seek Maat and those who seek their animal passions."

> "Mastery of the passions allows Divine thought and action."

> "Associate not therefore with a passionate man or approach him in conversation, lead not to plea to such a one that the terror carry thee away."

Egyptian Mysteries Volume 1: Principles of Shetaut Neter

These are injunctions of Maat practice. These injunctions are part of the major teachings of the *Prt M Hru* text and the *Wisdom texts* of Kamit.

Slide #39 -Maat Philosophy: The Foundation of the Sebait Philosophy.

I am sure that many of you have seen this picture or a similar one since it is the most popular section of the text which contains the judgment of the soul; it is from one of the papyri called Pert m Heru, which you know as *Book of the Dead* or the *Book Of Coming Forth By Day*. This is the picture showing some of the hieroglyphic texts with the teachings that we have been discussing. This is Asar Seker, Asar in his form as King of the Netherworld, where everyone goes after death.

After the death there is a judgment that is carried out on the balance scales. On one end we have the feather of Maat and on one end we have the heart. The heart is a vessel, a container. It contains your thoughts, your feelings, your desires and residues of past actions. If the heart is heavy with worry, anxiety, unrighteousness, guilt, lies, deceit and desire, then it is going to weigh down the balance scales, and the scale with Maat goes up; this is an unrighteous soul. The balance scales can be even with Maat, or the balance scales can be uneven - the heart can be heavier or the heart can be lighter than Maat.

There are three things that can happen as a result of the balance:

1) If the heart is heavier than Maat, this means that you have been an unrighteous person and you will suffer in the Netherworld. Remember, unrighteousness here does not mean evil, but rather, ignorant, and therefore acting out of error born of egoism. When you have desires, when you have unrighteousness in your heart, you have nightmares. Nightmares are a source of your own suffering that you have brought upon yourself. If you are righteous and peaceful you cannot have nightmares. You will not have mental disease either. You will not have insanity either.

Egyptian Mysteries Volume 1: Principles of Shetaut Neter

2) If the balance scales are even, it means that you are a good soul, but you are not a perfected soul. So the decree is that you are going to be a servant of Asar. You will be able to behold Asar in his City.

3) If the heart goes up, your heart is lighter than the feather of Maat. This means that you go to actually sit in the throne. If "the heart is heavy" that means one's mind is full of desires, unresolved feelings, guilt, anger, hatred, greed, worry, anxiety, etc., due to ignorance and egoism. If "the heart is light," it has let those fetters go and has cleared the afflictions caused by them. In mystical terms, if I go sit on your lap, what happens? One of two things will happen? Either you start feeling pain and I may break your legs, or if I am so subtle and light, then I may dissolve into you. Do you follow where this is going? You become one with Asar.

That teaching about the fate of the soul after death comes from the myth of Sa Asar.

Our four main books that deal with Maat Philosophy are: *The Wisdom of Maati*, *The 42 Precepts of Maat*, *Healing the Criminal Heart*, and *The Book Of Coming Forth By Day*, the *Pert m Heru*. Actually *The Book Of Coming Forth By Day*, the *Pert m Heru*, is a higher metaphysical advancement of Maat philosophy. Maat Philosophy has a practical as well as a cosmic aspect.

The Basic Maatian Duties to Attain lightness of heart (From the Pert M Heru, Chapter 33)

> *"I have done God's Will:*
> *I have given bread to the hungry*
> *Water to the thirsty*
> *Clothes to the clotheless*
> *A Boat to the boatless, to the shipwrecked*
> *I have made the prescribed offerings to the gods and goddesses*
> *And I have also made offerings to the Temple, to the Glorious Spirits*
> *(Note: The Glorious Spirits refers to the Akhus, so the initiate made homage to those elevated souls also, the enlightened beings.)*
> *Therefore, Protect me when I go to face The God (Note: the judgment scene depicted is the showing the initiate 'facing the God.').*"

If you were to do these things, these are basic injunctions of Maat-humanism…Maat in practice in society. We are not supposed to have a society that is "I've got mine, you get yours," a society where one person/group gets all the riches and you get all the pain, or a society where one part suffers while the other part prospers." That is not Maat philosophy. Everyone should have their basic needs taken care of, and if you have the capacity, you should help give food to the hungry, water to the thirsty, clothes to the clothesless, and shelter (boat) to the shelterless.

There will be no peace in society until that is done. Everyone has an innate right to these. Why? Because everyone is essentially divine and everyone is related; we are all family, all children of spirit. If one has this understanding, one would not rest until everyone in the world has all his or her basic necessities taken care of. How can one exist in a country that is rich, and has all this food, when there are people in the world who do not have food, and therefore actually, the food is being stolen from them?

There is an injunction of Maat that states, "I have not snatched away food from the mouth of a child." And many countries are like children compared to this country. And yet, food is being stolen from them every day. The natural resources of Africa are being taken and destroyed. If Africa was strong and could control its own borders, there would be no nuclear power in the world. Do you realize that? Nuclear material or fissionable material or plutonium is mined mostly in Africa. Important components that go to create the advanced air force fighter jets are found in Africa. Important materials and minerals that are mined for this purpose come from Africa. If you control your resources, you can say no I don't want that going out, but if you are a degraded country, you cannot control your resources. Just as if you are a degraded person you cannot control your mouth, your eyes or ears. Your senses control and direct you, just as a country can be controlled by greed and lust for power over others. So the controller is just as psychologically disturbed as the one too weak to throw off the oppressor, from a spiritual standpoint.

What is going to happen? Now if people would try to stand up for themselves they will get bombed, the oppressor will get some kind of excuse, and might say "oh I think there are weapons there on your land, so that gives me the right to attack you." No one can find it, but we know it is there, right? And they give elaborate little stories to show that it is there; after the fact who is going to be worrying about that. What is done is done, right? We are all supporting this culture right? We cannot do anything about it can we? Or can't we?

- "Oh Lord Asar, Un-Nefer, Soul of Creation and foremost in Ament, the Netherworld, I am Heru, your Divine Lord"

The Pert m Hru

Slide #40

From The Pert m Heru:

O Lord Asar Un-Nefer
Soul of creation and foremost in the amit, the Netherworld
I am Heru, your son
I announced that I bring a righteous soul to see you
Oh Divine Lord

This scene is from the papyrus of Ani. It is perhaps the second most recognizable scene of the text of the *Prt m Hru*. Ani is another initiate. I want to show you this particular slide to give you an indication of what would be happening in the inner shrine. Not the specific details, but to give you an indication. This is Heru stating, "Oh Lord Un-Nefer," referring to Asar, "I am Heru." Heru is the one who leads the initiate by the hand into the inner shrine to meet Asar.

The aspirant has gone through the balance scales already and he has been judged to be righteous, therefore Heru announces him. Traditionally, a priest wearing a Heru headdress would play the part of Heru. Three personalities, a priest and two priestesses, would be in the shrine, symbolizing the Divine Trinity.
The initiate is lead in the inner shrine by Heru. In the picture above, note the differences between the depictions of Ani on the left side as compared to the right side. The hair in the picture of Ani on the left is black, whereas on the right his hair is white. What happens is that the righteous initiate is being anointed. Do you know of any other philosophy or teachings that talk about

the great anointment? Yes, Christianity, in fact 'christos' comes from the Greek term, which means, "anointed one." And there is also an Ancient Egyptian word with similar meaning, *karast*. Mind you, the Neterian anointment was recorded as early as the Pyramid texts (4,000 B.C.E.)

Here Ani is becoming an Akh, becoming enlightened, and this is the final result of Maat practice.

How to Become a Qualified Aspirant

Slide #41

How to become a qualified Aspirant therefore, means following the path of Maat philosophy. That is how the Nehast (enlightenment) is achieved. Maat philosophy teaches if you to adopt the right path that leads you to truth and you will obtain peace and prosperity. Maat teaches also that you are Divine, and that you have a divine purpose. If you study the wisdom of the Neteru you will discover your purpose of life. If you become pure of heart, righteous, you will discover God and immortality. Maat also teaches that you will succeed in life if you learn about Maat Philosophy and practice it everyday.

As I have said before, it is a perennial process. You cannot not practice Maat today and think you will become righteous tomorrow and say, "well I'll go to my spiritual preceptor and he/she'll forgive me" or at the time of your death say or think you will approach God sincerely and ask for absolution. It does not work that way. There are particular reasons why it does not work that way. When you perform an action, the residue of that action stays in your unconscious. That imprint or residue in the unconscious becomes a future impetus to perform similar actions if the act was pleasurable, or avoid similar actions if it was painful. So, if you perform good deeds or evil deeds, those good or evil memories (imprints/residues) remain in your unconscious; these lead the soul to experience heavenly or hellish situations, respectively, after death, and reincarnation.

Even after death they remain for future drive, future desires, for future reincarnation. Also unrighteous actions cause agitation in your mind. With mental agitation you cannot fathom the full spiritual teaching. That is why you need to have purity of heart.

In the slide above you can see goddess Maat and the hieroglyphic text underneath the picture means, "Rau nu prt m hru" or "The words of coming into light," or "The book of enlightenment," referring to the *Book of Coming Forth by Day*, commonly called the *Book of the Dead*.

Great Truth III:
Devotion and Freedom

"Devotion to the Divine leads to freedom from the fetters of Set."

To be liberated (Nafu - freedom - to breath) from the afflictions of Set one must be devoted to the Divine and to be devoted to the Divine means living by Maat. Maat is a way of life that is purifying to the heart and beneficial for society as it promotes virtue and order. Living by Maat means practicing Shedy.

Uashu means devotion and the classic pose of adoring the Divine is called "Dua," standing or sitting with upraised hands facing outwards towards the image of the divinity.

(Slide# 42)

Great truth number 3, "devotion and freedom." Uashu is the important concept here. With respect to Great Truth #1, we discussed that God is *ua ua* or "one-one" and the Supreme, all-encompassing Divinity. For Great Truth #2, we discussed how human beings fall away from that knowledge through *un-Maat*, which is unrighteousness, and khemn, which is ignorance.

The path of devotion (devotion to the teaching and devotion to the Divine) is a path that takes you out of ignorance and out of unrighteousness. The teaching of devotion and divine love must be studied closely, under the guidance of an authentic spiritual preceptor.

Egyptian Mysteries Volume 1: Principles of Shetaut Neter

I often say in a humorous way, you wouldn't like to go and be treated by a doctor who has learned from reading books how to be a doctor, would you? You may need to have an appendix cut out, and he has never done one before, but he reads about how to cut out an appendix. "Let me cut you open," he says! Would you prefer that doctor or would you prefer someone who has done hundreds of appendix operations? Would you prefer that doctor or would you prefer someone who has been tested and who has been taught under someone who knows. Why would you think that you can learn spiritual philosophy without having a preceptor and without practicing the teaching; it cannot work. The philosophy is actually more difficult than rocket science, engineering, and medical science. However, I am here to explain that you have the capacity to do that;

(Slide# 43)

There are two aspects of popular devotional practice for the masses in Neterianism. One is to be done in their own home, and the other is the communal practice, led by the Temple. Our book *The Path of Divine Love* deals with the Uashu (devotional) discipline. Above is an actual picture of how the Temple that you saw earlier actually looked in ancient times; it is a drawing by one of the early European explorers of the late 18th century before Arab zealot vandals and the British Aswan Dam destroyed the paint.

Egyptian Mysteries Volume 1: Principles of Shetaut Neter

The picture shows the peristyle hall, the open hall or court of the Temple. When it was first uncovered from being buried by sand, it was found to have been defaced with soot from Christian squatters and others who occupied it in ancient times, after they kicked out the original Kamitan Priests and Priestesses and vandalized the place. But that is another part of the story; go to our book *African Origins* for more on this subject.

This is how it looked, in full color, in its full glory (also see the cover of our book *The mysteries of Isis*). Then the British went in there and created the Aswan dam. The first Aswan dam backed up water which flooded the Temple and damaged it. The second one built in the 1960's created a lake, which is now called Lake Nasr, which completely submerged it. The Temple was therefore moved from its original location, but was not completely reassembled. The Temple of Aset was behind the dam. So when the Nile flooded, the waters that came up from Uganda and Sudan flowing towards the Mediterranean sea, created a lake and its water level rose up, almost completely submerging the Temple, and in the process destroyed the pa

All or most of the color faded or was lost. The picture (Slide#43) is a depiction of how the early Egyptologist found the Temple. This is how they found it two hundred years ago. You can imagine the glory of being able to walk there in ancient times; it is fantastic even today, even in the ruined state. It is my favorite Temple actually.

(Slide# 44)

This is what the Temple looks like today, devoid of it glorious color, showing the bare stone, that itself is deteriorating due to pollution, too much tourist traffic and some vandalism that still occurs.

So there are two aspects of devotional practice; one is personal practice and the other is community practice. What goes on in the interior portion of the Temple where the priests and priestesses work can be called a higher form of worship and metaphysics; I am not discussing this here. We are discussing the general classification of worship for the masses and householders. As a layperson you are to have a special room, in your home where devotion is practiced. This is how it was done in ancient times.

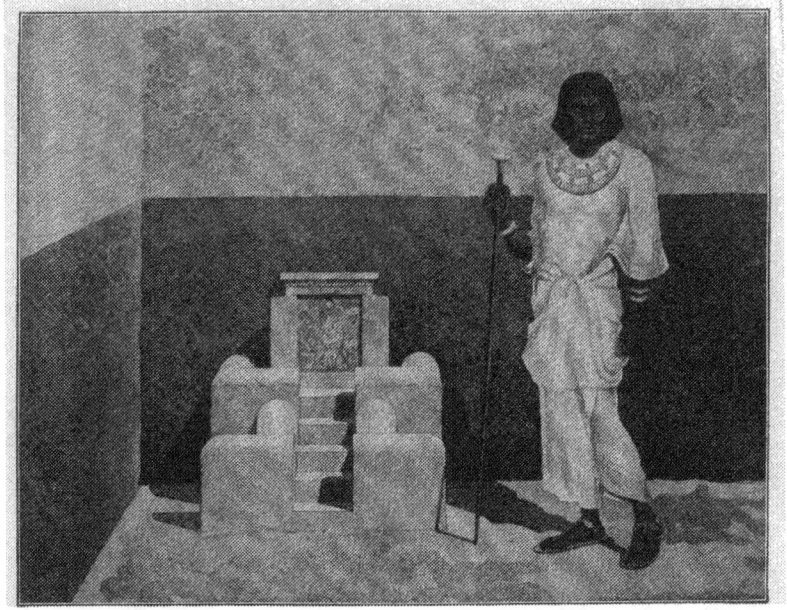

Personal private altar of Egyptian man householder 18 dyn.

The picture (left) shows a layperson who has a shrine in a room of his house which is the practice for laypersons and general aspirants. During the festival times the townspeople got together in front of the Temple and the clergy led them in ritual worship. Note the Rekhyt symbol at the bottom right hand corner of the picture above (Slide #43)

Egyptian Mysteries Volume 1: Principles of Shetaut Neter

Great Truth IIII: Shedy and Maakheru

"The practice of the Shedy disciplines leads to knowing oneself and the Divine. This is called being True of Speech"

Doing Shedy means to study profoundly, to penetrate the mysteries (Shetaut) and discover the nature of the Divine. There have been several practices designed by the sages of Ancient Kamit to facilitate the process of self-knowledge. These are the religious (Shetaut) traditions and the Sema (yogic) disciplines related to them that augment the spiritual practices.

All the traditions relate the teachings of the sages by means of myth related to particular gods or goddesses but all of these Neteru are related, like brothers and sisters, as they have all emanated from the same source, the same parent, who is neither male nor female but encompassing the totality of the two.

Becoming Maakheru means transforming one's consciousness by means of truth-living into a proper vessel for divine awareness. It is a purification of the heart which allows the aspirant to be worthy of Divine communion.

(Slide# 45)

Great Truth Number 4, "Shedy and Maakheru." Shedy is the study of the spiritual teachings. Shedy means to penetrate the mysteries, to uncover the mysteries. Shedy are the spiritual disciplines, the Sema Tawi disciplines, what we refer to in English as "Egyptian Yoga." The first aspect of Shedy is wisdom teachings, and the goddess of wisdom is goddess Aset.

On the bottom right hand corner of Slide # 46 there is a line drawing of the relief on the Temple wall, the goddess Aset giving her breast to her child Heru to nourish him. Notice that her face is damaged in the relief; this is the damage perpetrated by Christians and Muslims. This kind of damage can be seen at other Temples as well. They took out the faces so as to detract the power of the images, to destroy the "pagan" past and elevate the new orthodox traditions. This kind of damage is not the worst however. Entire Temples were dismantled and the blocks were used to build Christian churches. Later the Arabs ruined the Ancient Egyptian Temples and Christian churches to make Mosques. (See our book *African Origins of Civilization* for more details)

101

Egyptian Mysteries Volume 1: Principles of Shetaut Neter

The etymology of the term Shedy is as follows. We have the term 'shed' to dig or to excavate; that gives rise to the term 'Shedy.' Then we have 'Shedt' which means to suckle, as in a suckling child, and 'Shedy' which means to study profoundly to penetrate the mysteries. So through the image of the goddess mother and child, we are to understand that Aset is giving Heru the spiritual nectar, the nectar of the spiritual teachings that enriches the mind and the soul, and not just milk.

This is what a spiritual preceptor does. *Seba* is a male terminology and *sebat* is the female. There is giving and receiving. There is a sexual process that goes on when spiritual teachings are disseminated by a spiritual preceptor (Seba/Sebai) to aspirants (sebat). This concept applies whether you are male or female. If I were a female teacher I would still be called Sebai/ Seba in the same way. This is because the teacher is the giver, the one who is acting in the male capacity at that time. Metaphorically, the mouth is the penis, the teaching is the DNA, the seed, and the sound is the sperm that goes into the ear, which is the vagina, to fertilize the soil of the mind and to give birth to spiritual enlightenment. However, realize that you must be a willing participant in order to become pregnant with the teaching; only then will it take root in the mind. But you must first prepare the soil of your mind by clearing away the weeds and rocks, the negative thoughts and dull witted nature. Then you must introduce fertilizer, water and sun, that is, purity, wisdom and devotion. Then you will have results. Otherwise you may hear the teaching, but you will not be able to listen and heed it. It will fall on deaf ears, no matter how much you try.

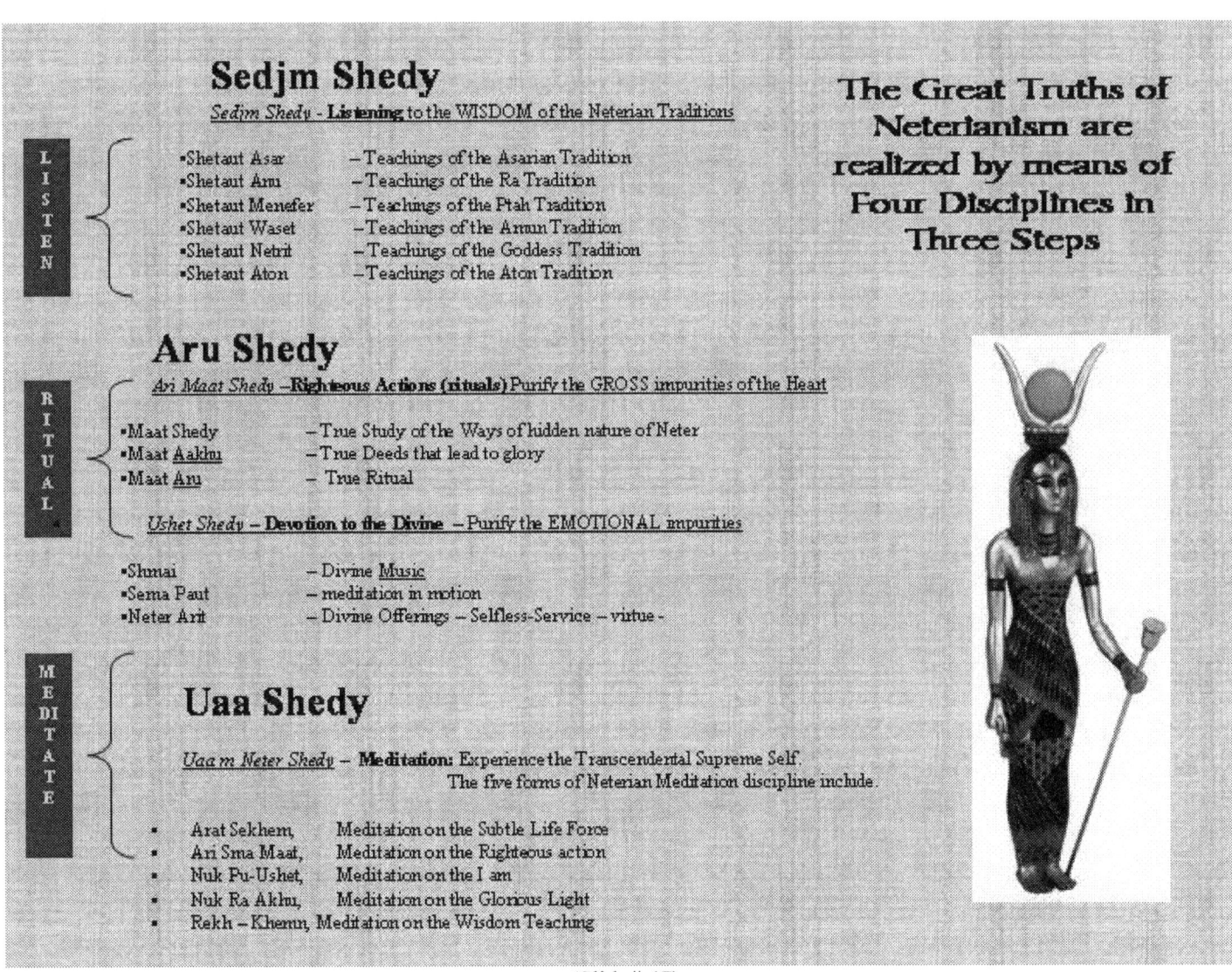

(Slide# 47)

Egyptian Mysteries Volume 1: Principles of Shetaut Neter

How does all this come together? The great truths of Neterianism are realized by means of the four disciplines in three steps. Let's try to simplify so it does not look so complicated. Listening-Reflection-and Meditation are the three basic steps of the wisdom teaching practice.

In the wisdom teaching process of the spiritual practice, you listen to the teaching, you practice the ritual relating to it, and then you meditate. Myth, ritual and metaphysics are the three steps of religion. *Sedjm* is the term that means to listen and heed. When you listen something righteous you are supposed to heed it, act in accordance with that. You are not supposed to listen to it and then forget about it, such as the way many Christians treat the Ten Commandments. They know about them but then they put the out of their minds and go ahead and do whatever they want any way.

Once you have the teachings, you listen to the teachings, and then it is time for *'aru'* which means ritual, the things that are to be done with respect to the teaching. Then it is time for *'uaah'* or meditation.

Rituals should be thought of here not as just traditional actions to do and finish up so you can get home and watch TV. Ritual here is a science of acting out the mythic teaching in order to experience its power and glory, to make it effective in your life. There are three kinds of rituals that need to be practiced: the daily rituals, monthly rituals and the annual rituals.

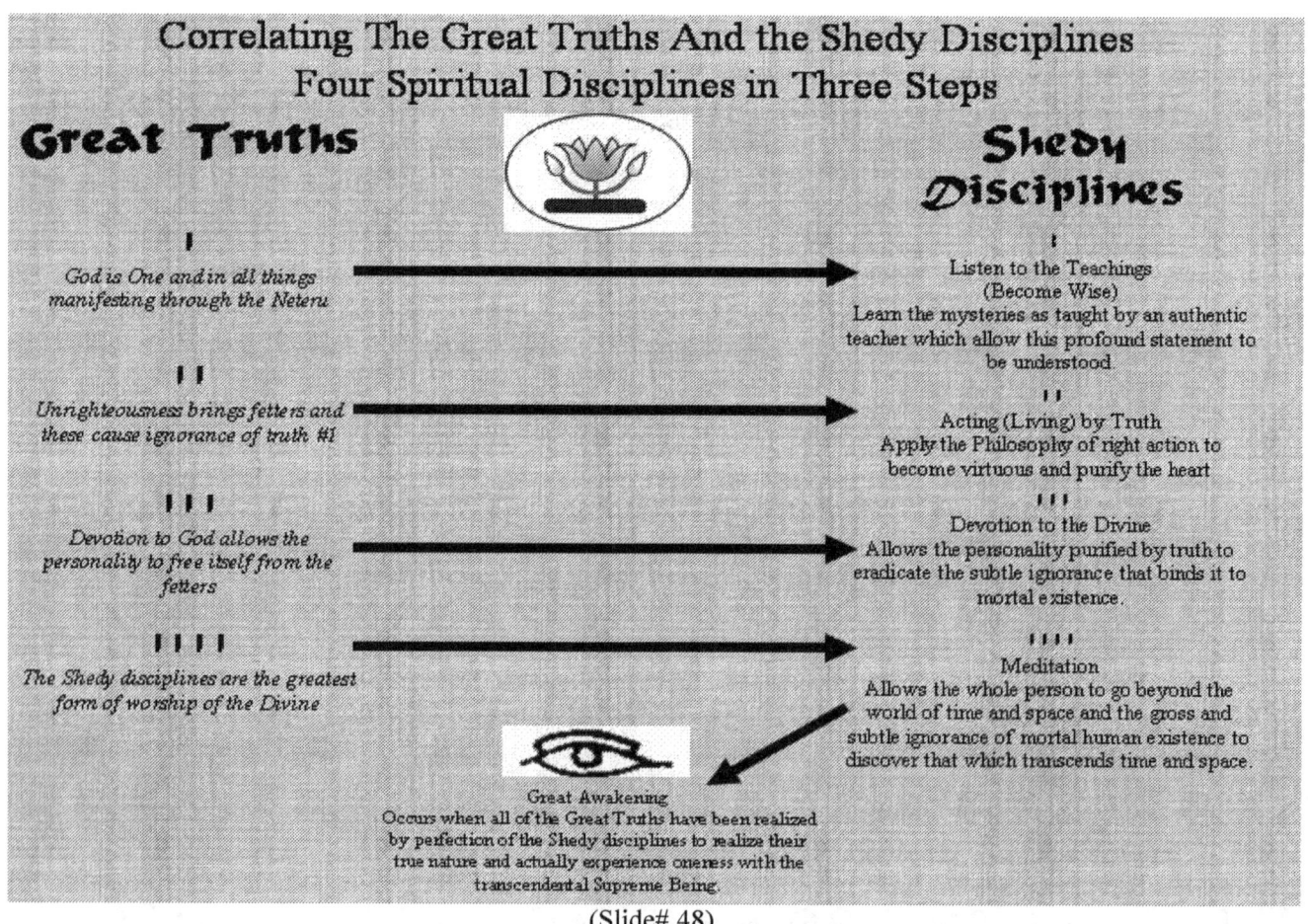

(Slide# 48)

I want you to understand that the practice of religion and the practice of Shedy, yogic disciplines, should lead to the same spiritual realization. If you go through the path of religion you have myth, ritual and mysticism, which express as devotion, action, and meditation, respectively according to the three steps discussed: aspiration, striving and established. If you go through the path of Yoga you have the Shedy disciplines: meditation, devotion, wisdom and action. Tantrism is another form of Shedy discipline also.

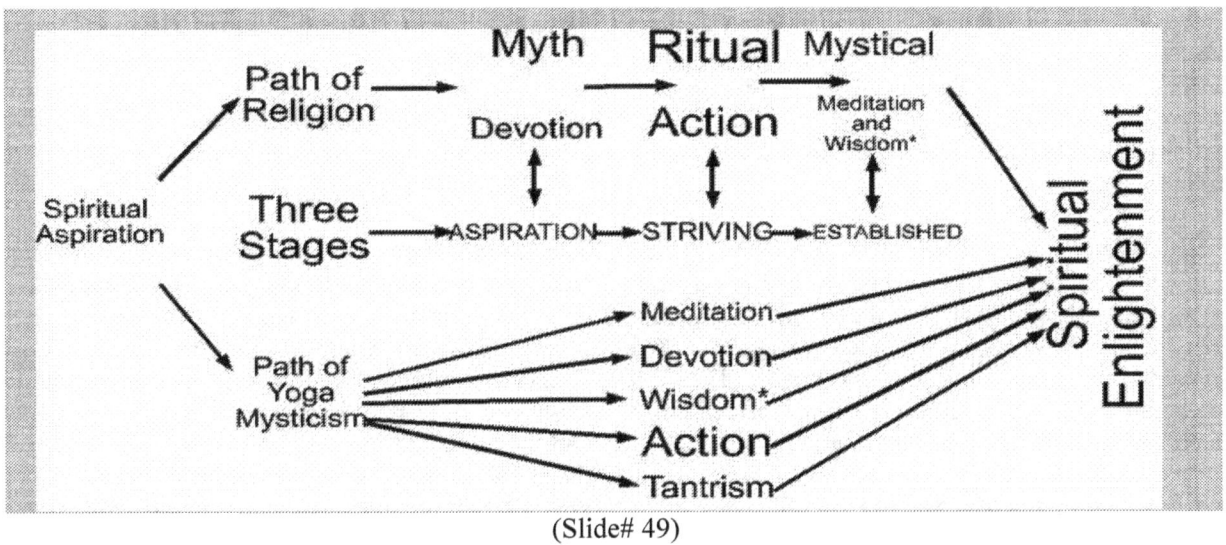
(Slide# 49)

Whether you look at Neterianism as a philosophical path, a spiritual path, or a religious path, you are leading yourself to the same result. In your religion you must practice meditation, devotion, right action and in your yogic path, your Shedy path, you practice Shedy. In religion you are moving towards the same goal, but using different terms and also using different spiritual symbols, the gods and goddesses. Needless to say, most practice of religion, especially in the western countries, does not include meditation, or study and practice of mysticism. This is why it is ultimately not effective in transforming people's lives for the better in a permanent way.

As for the basic Daily Observances of the Shemsu, if you want to consider yourself as a Shemsu, a follower of Neterianism, these are the basic requirements for what you must do, ideally. You must be able to practice the daily ritual, three times daily. You know that the Muslims practice five times a day, so three times should not be a problem for you. However, you do not have to take a bath five times a day as they did in ancient times, just one time a day; some Neterian priests and priestesses did bathe three or more times daily.

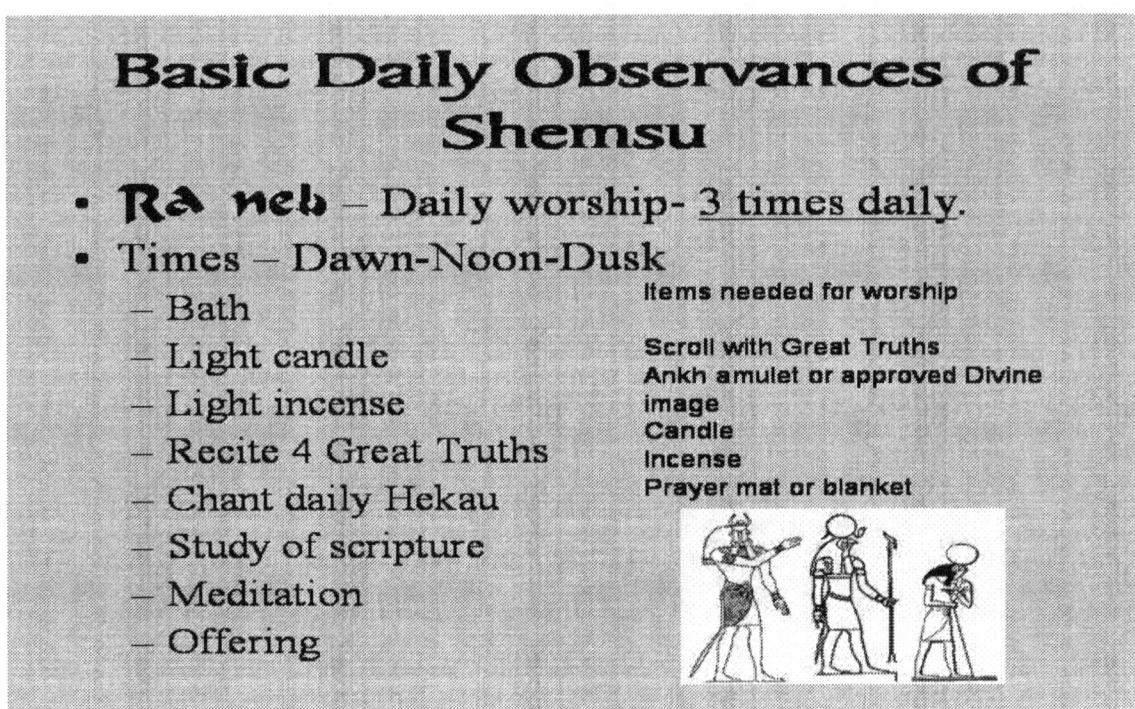
(Slide# 50)

Egyptian Mysteries Volume 1: Principles of Shetaut Neter

Daily Aru (Ritual): Light a candle, Light your incense, have your altar set-up as discussed above, in your own personal room or community room if you live in a community, or have group gatherings. Live truth, study the teachings, chant your daily hekau, and meditate daily. The instructions for the daily program are in the daily worship book.

Reading a text, listening to or watching a tape of a spiritual lecture or attending a lecture and then and reflecting on what you have read or heard may fulfill the discipline of studying the scriptures. This qualifies as a daily Shedy program. Then proceed to meditation, which can be as brief as 15 – 20 minutes to begin with. And conclude with an offering everyday, an offering to the Divine is in order.

Why should the worship be done three times per day? Three times daily comes from the understanding of the Anunian Trinity. There are three aspects of Ra (see illustration above): Khepri-Ra-Tem, the morning, noon, and evening sun, respectively. Recall that we previously discussed Khepri, the Creator. Khepri-Ra-Tem, determines the three-fold worship, dawn, noon, and dusk.

Worship is to follow the movement of the sun in the morning, and then at noontime, where the sun is at its highest and in the evening at dusk when the sun is setting. The methods that are to be used are following the instructions of the scroll of the Great Truths.

At your altar you should have the following items: an ankh amulet or an approved Divine image, a candle, incense. You should also have a blanket to sit on.

The divine image that is to be used is decided by which tradition or which divinity is most captivating to you. Whether your divinity to worship will be Aset, Heru, or some other divinity, or whether it will be a universal divinity, it all is decided in that way. You may also propitiate the ancillary lesser divinities that help remove certain obstacles (Ex. Anpu) and then worship the "High Divinity" (Ex. Asar). That is how the daily worship is organized. You must always remember that the gods and goddesses being worshipped are like doorways into the higher realm and are not worshipped as THE GOD in and of themselves. In other words this is not polytheism, but rather a highly advanced polytheistic monotheism.

This is the basic level of practice for you to consider yourself a Shemsu. What this means therefore in relation to us as a Temple is that you need to be connected to the lecture systems, the system of the teachings being disseminated and the information on how to practice them.

On a larger level all individual practitioners are connected through ritual to lead to higher realization on the spiritual goal. That is part of that oneness on the higher planes that we talked about earlier.

So, there are four Shedy disciplines and for each of those four main Shedy disciplines we have written a book to explain the detail relating to it. I am not going to go into the details of each now. I am just presenting an overview of the spiritual philosophy itself. Shetaut Neter has four disciplines: the discipline of wisdom, which is discussed in the book *Mysteries of Isis*, the discipline of Maat philosophy, which is discussed in the book *Wisdom of Maati*, the discipline of devotion to the Divine, which is discussed in the book *Path of Divine Love*, and the discipline of Meditation. There are currently three books for the discipline of meditation. The book *Meditation: The Ancient Egyptian Path to Enlightenment* is the main one. We also have *Glorious Light Meditation* System, and *The Serpent Power Meditation* System. So there are many choices, and which meditation system you use depends on which discipline is more accessible to your personality.

In order for this to work, there must be purity also – purity of the body and mind. The book Kemetic Diet was written for that particular purpose. Our own Kamitan scriptures, the *Pert m Heru*, tells us that in order to be effective you must be a vegetarian. Also, you cannot be drinking alcohol, doing drugs or leading a life of excesses; you must be a righteous personality.

You must purify your heart, so you can have subtlety of intellect. If you have disease, worry, anxiety and cancers, and you are coughing all the time, you may try to sit through meditation. You close your eyes and breathe in and breathe out, and cough, cough, cough. With that kind of health it will be more difficult. It won't work. It will be almost impossible. If you have a stroke and you are laid up in a coma, it won't work at all; there is no solution at that point, except to die and come back again. You must strive for health but health is not the ultimate goal. It is a means to an end. Health is of three types, health of the body, mind, and soul.

Sema Tawi Philosophy

SEMA PHILOSOPHY

*Sema = Yoga

Yoga Disciplines And Yoga Mystic Spirituality

Sema Tawi – Mysticism – Yoga Mystical Philosophy

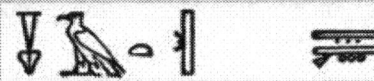

Sema (or *Smai*) *Tawi* (*Taui*)
(From Chapter 4 of the *Prt m Hru*)

What is Yoga?

Yoga is the practice of mental, physical and spiritual disciplines which lead to self-control and self-discovery by purifying the mind, body and spirit, so as to discover the deeper spiritual essence which lies within every human being and object in the universe. In essence, the goal of Yoga practice is to unite or *yoke* one's individual consciousness with Universal or Cosmic consciousness. Therefore, Ancient Egyptian religious practice, especially in terms of the rituals and other practices of the Ancient Egyptian Temple system known as *Shetaut Neter* (the way of the hidden Supreme Being), also known in Ancient times as *Smai Tawi* "Egyptian Yoga," should as well be considered as universal streams of self-knowledge philosophy which influenced and inspired the great religions and philosophers to this day. In this sense, religion, in its purest form, is also a Yoga system, as it seeks to reunite the soul with its true and original source, God. In broad terms, any spiritual movement or discipline that brings one closer to self-knowledge is a "Yogic" movement. The main recognized forms of Yoga disciplines are:

- *Yoga of Wisdom,*
- *Yoga of Devotional Love,*
- *Yoga of Meditation,*
- *Physical Postures Yoga*
- *Yoga of Selfless Action,*
- *Tantric Yoga*
- *Serpent Power Yoga*

(Slide# 52)

The health culture of body, mind and soul that we talked about is not just to a pill to heal your body. Disease comes from a deeper source, from your astral body. Your disease is created at the causal level of your mind (causal body), that is, your unconscious mind. This is the source of the disease of the Astral body, which then manifests in the physical body.

(Slide# 53) **Sunu Philosophy**

Here (above) you see a picture of massage therapy and reflexology in ancient times.

"Twain are the forms of food-for soul and body, of which all animals consist... Some are nourished with the twofold form, while others with a single... Their soul is nourished by the ever-restless motion of the Cosmos; their bodies have their growth from foods drawn up from the water and the earth of the inferior world."
—Ancient Egyptian Proverb

So therefore, this is the basis of the Kamitan Diet System. Anybody who is interested in adopting the Neterian path should begin by adopting Maat philosophy and the Kamitan Diet. Read and study the entire *Kemetic Diet* book, and also read our book *Initiation Into Egyptian Yoga*, so you can start to get into the entire process of the culture of Shetaut Neter.

We recommend the use of supplements with the diet system. These supplements are necessary because the food that we have available at the supermarket is denatured in the quality of nutrients that are necessary for human life. An important supplement is Kamut. Kamut is actually an Ancient Egyptian grain that was discovered 50 years ago and it has not been denatured or genetically engineered like most other foods on the market today.

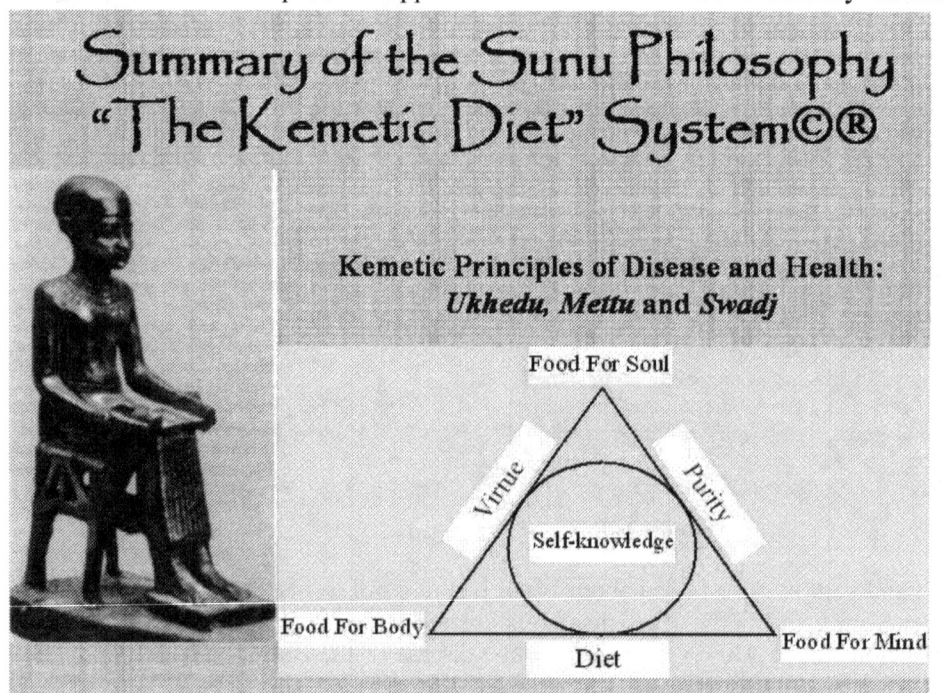

(Slide# 54)

Sunu philosophy is the foundation for the Kamitan Diet System. The sunus were the ancient Egyptian doctors who first studied the human constitution and developed an understanding of the systems of the body and how to promote health and healing. The Kamitan Diet is a way to promote health of body, mind and soul, not just of the body.

Egyptian Mysteries Volume 1: Principles of Shetaut Neter

At the lower left hand side of the slide you can see Imhotep, who was regarded as the creator of the Sunu philosophy, one of the first doctors in human history. Imhotep was a vizier, an architect, a lawyer, a doctor, and a philosopher. He wrote spiritual writings that have not been discovered yet, but are referred to by other sages. His name has been used in Hollywood to make many mummy horror films. Those films contain absolutely nothing but falsehood and false perception about Kamitan Philosophy and culture.

Tjef Neteru Sema Paut Ritual Postures of Enlightenment

The book *Egyptian Yoga: Movements of the Gods and Goddesses* discusses the discipline of ritual movements for spiritual enlightenment. This is a posture system similar to the Indian posture yoga system in some ways, although there are many differences. The Neterian system is more mythically based. The postures are directly based on the postures that were discovered in the Temple of Hetheru and other Temples, as well as papyruses, These movements (postures) were practiced by the priests and priestesses who were emulating the gods and goddesses. The priests and priestesses practiced these postures to emulate and meditatively identify with the divinities and the myth which extol their virtues and powers, thereby mastering these. So when we are speaking of Sema Philosophy we are really referring to the metaphysical disciplines that were developed in ancient Kamit that lead a human being to spiritual enlightenment.

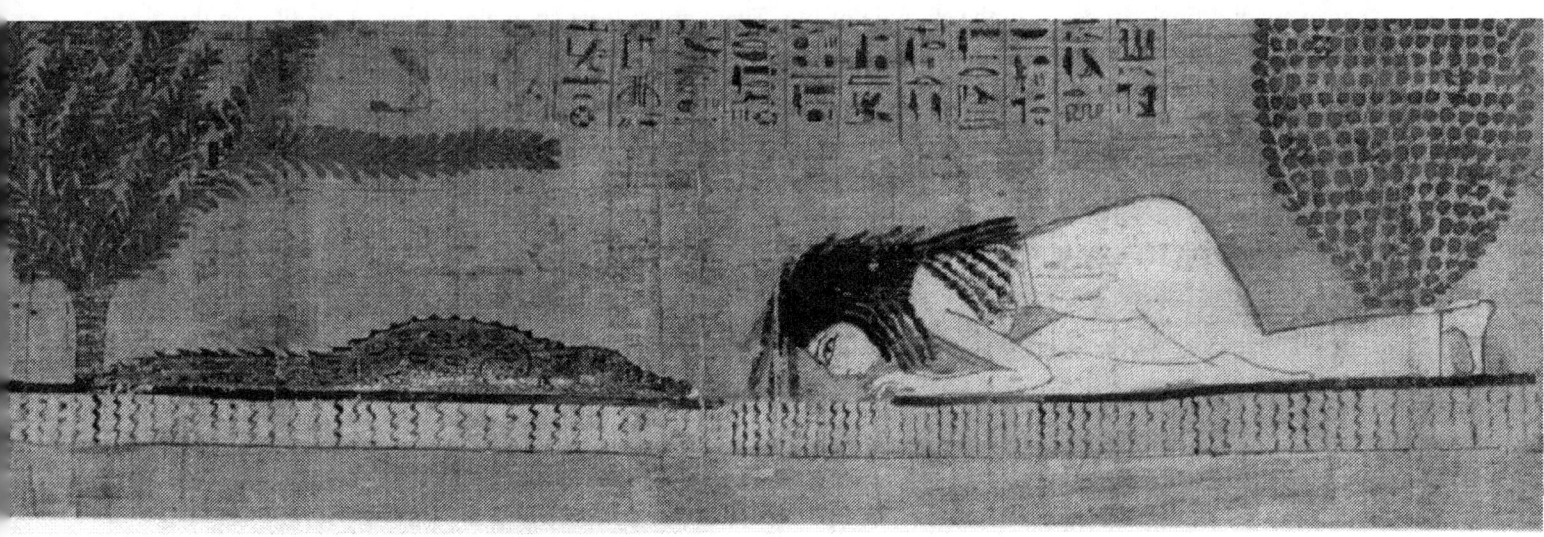

HOW IS THE HIGHER VISION ATTAINED?
Introduction to Meditation

Sage Amunhotep

Uaa Shedy

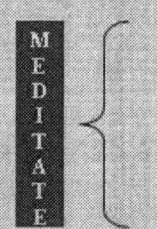

Uaa m Neter Shedy - **Meditation** Experience the Transcendental Supreme Self.

The five forms of Neterian Meditation discipline include.

- Arat Sekhem Uaa — Meditation on the Subtle Life Force
- Ari Sma Maat Uaa — Meditation on the Righteous action
- Nuk Pu-Ushet Uaa — Meditation on the I am
- Nuk Ra Akhu Uaa — Meditation on the Glorious Light
- Rekh Amun Uaa — Meditation on the Wisdom Teaching
- Khet Ankh Uaa — Meditation on the Tree of Life

(Slide# 55)

How to keep the "Higher Vision" in the midst of the challenging world? Listening to and studying the philosophy and trying to practice Maat in daily life are necessities, but meditation is the way to have the will power to sustain the spiritual disciplines. Meditation provides inner spiritual strength, the will to endure and persevere and finally succeed in the struggle of life. There are at least six major forms of meditation that were practiced in Ancient Kamit.

- Meditation on the subtle life force, the Serpent Power- what the Indians call Kundalini.
- Meditation on Righteous Action, that is, Maatian Actions in day to day life.
- Pert m Heru path, which is the "I AM" formula, or meditating on the idea "I and God are One." That teaching comes from the *Pert M Hru* text.
- "Nuk Ra Akhu," is the Glorious Light System, the oldest recorded instructions for the practice if formal meditation, in human history.
- We also have "Rekh Amun Uaa," which is the wisdom teachings, that is the teachings of the Temple of Aset.
- Ket Ankh Uaa, which is the Tree of Life System, based on the Anunian Theology.

At the top right hand corner of the slide there is a picture of Sage Amunhotep, who was 80 years old at the time; this is the Amunhotep posture for meditation. Amunhotep was regarded as one of the greatest Sages we have. In summary he was a high priest, philosopher and teacher. There was a Temple dedicated to him. He wrote on the spiritual philosophy and the practice of meditation, and obviously here he is in the meditative posture.

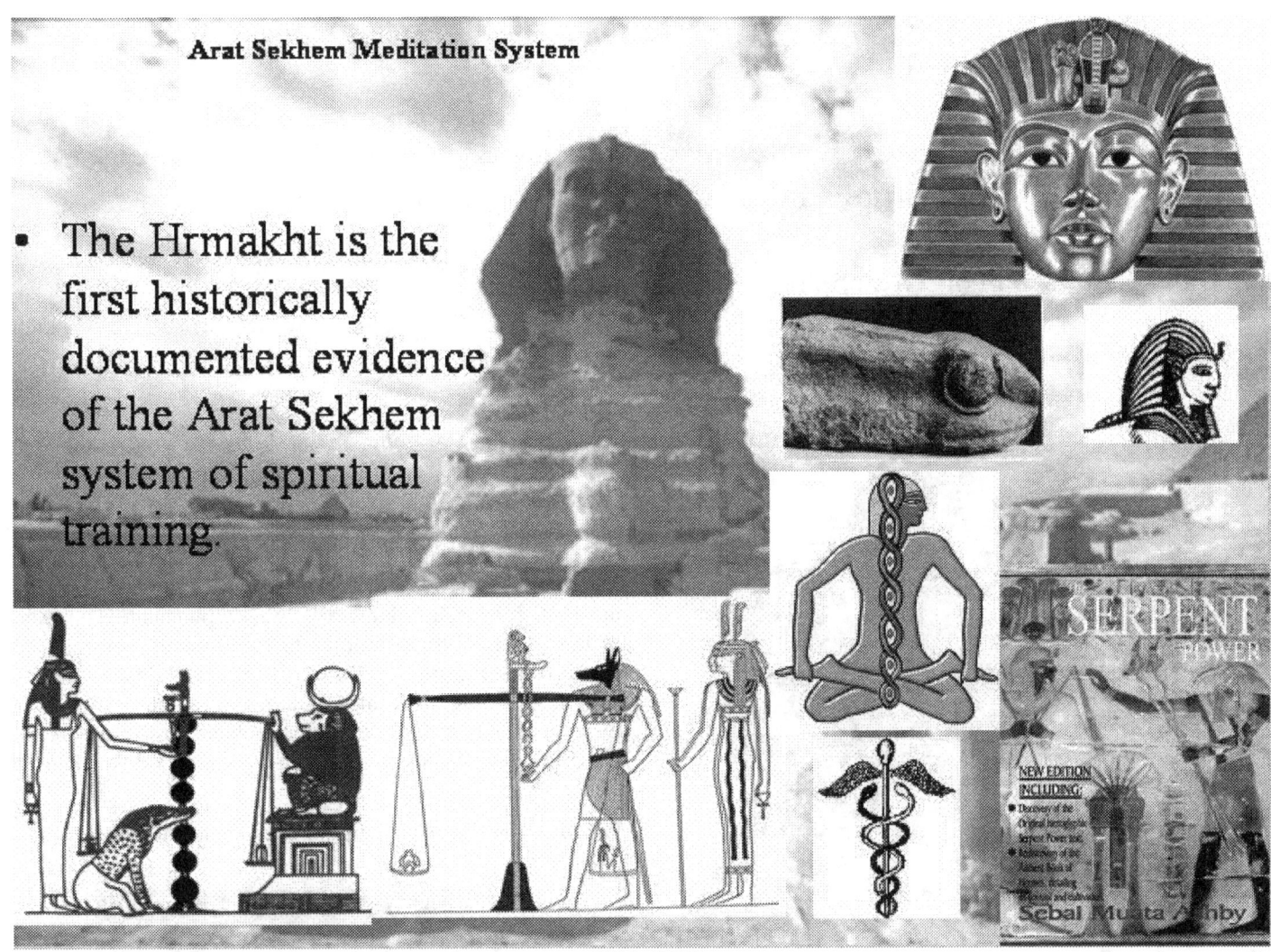
(Slide# 56)

The Arat Sekhem Meditation system is the very oldest system known. The oldest evidence of it is the Great Sphinx itself, which is dated to 10,000 B.C.E. It is also related in the Prt m Hru texts and in other texts which you can find in our book *The Serpent Power*. It is important to understand that the Serpent Power is the essence of all life and it is cultivated through all the spiritual disciplines. That means that any of the mystical, sema-yogic spiritual paths you choose will cultivate the Serpent Power. If that Serpent Power is raised, it will also lead to the cultivation and expansion of consciousness. This is one of the most powerful forms of spiritual discipline an aspirant can practice. Its philosophy is highly specialized and requires good health in order to be practiced properly. There are some specific disciplines to cultivate the life force but those are for more advanced practice which will not be discussed in this volume. The following is a brief overview of the Serpent Power in the context of history and an introduction to the mystical philosophy behind it.

Egyptian Mysteries Volume 1: Principles of Shetaut Neter

The Serpent Power: The Most Ancient Discipline

History of The Serpent Power and Yoga of Life Force Development for Spiritual Enlightenment in Ancient Egypt

Frontal Close Up View of the Great Sphinx

The Serpent Power Arat Sekhem teaching, known as Kundalini Yoga in India, was understood and practiced in Ancient Egypt. It was thrilling for me when I first discovered this so many years ago. As a scholar of African culture and spirituality as well as world religion, mysticism and yoga spirituality, I discovered correlations between Ancient Egyptian (African) and Indian culture, so many in fact that these became the subject of two books. Arat Sekhem (Kamitan Serpent Power Yoga) was one of my main disciplines of personal practice. I was surprised to discover so much documentation and scriptural discourse on the subject from the Ancient Egyptian priests and priestesses themselves. This is perhaps because the evidences, which were plain for all to see, had been misunderstood or dismissed by them. In any case, I set out to document and espouse the science, at least that part which is safe and effective, for those interested in this form of spiritual practice. The first documented evidences of the Serpent Power appear in 10,000 B.C.E. The teaching of Arat Sekhem was advanced and formed the basis of the spiritual and material culture of Kamitan society. This is all documented in the book *"The Serpent Power."* The Serpent Power is the teaching related to understanding the psychology of the human soul and personality as it relates to spiritual evolution. It is tied to the science of the Psycho-spiritual energy centers (called chakras in Kundalini system) and the three main conduits (called nadis in the Kundalini system) of the Life Force energy, known as *Sekhem* in Ancient Egypt.[1]

The origins of the Serpent Power teaching in Ancient Egypt go back to the inception of Ancient Egyptian civilization. This is proven by the fact that the oldest Ancient Egyptian monument bears the emblem of the serpent power tradition. The Ancient Egyptian Great Sphinx once had a massive head of a cobra perched on its forehead. It is now in the British Museum. However, we know that the positioning of the serpent symbol relates to the Serpent Power teaching because a scripture describing the Serpent Power movement and how it leads a human being to spiritual evolution was discovered among various papyri related to the rituals of the Temple. (Translated by Muata Ashby in our book The *Serpent Power*)

Below: Cobra of the Great Sphinx now in the British Museum

The Pharaonic headdress tradition visible in Ancient Egyptian culture from the headdress of the Sphinx in the predynastic era to the early Christian era establishes a Serpent Power tradition and the tradition of the Pharaonic system of government in Egypt of at least 10,400 years.

Below-Figure (A): The funerary mask of King Tutankhamon showing the convergence of the two goddesses (Uatchet {serpent} and Nekhebet {vulture}) at the forehead. New Kingdom Period.

Figure (B): The diadem worn by the mummy of Tutankhamun literally depicts the movement of the Serpent Power as described in the Serpent Power text. The two serpents move up the back and go to the sides of the head and then move up across the brain to meet at the point between the eyebrows.

The forehead (see images below) region is the sixth center of psycho-spiritual consciousness. The vulture and the serpent are the symbols of the serpent goddesses, one symbolizing death and the consumption of life (lower aspect-vulture) and the other symbolizing the higher aspect-(cobra).

(A)

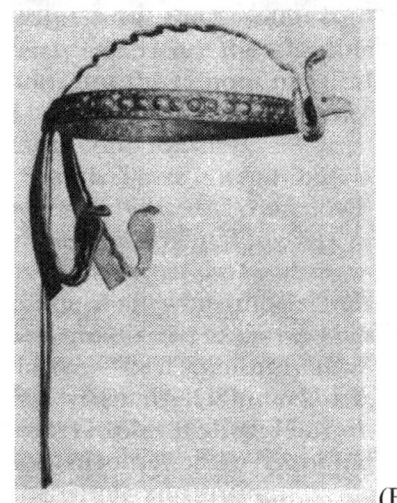
(B)

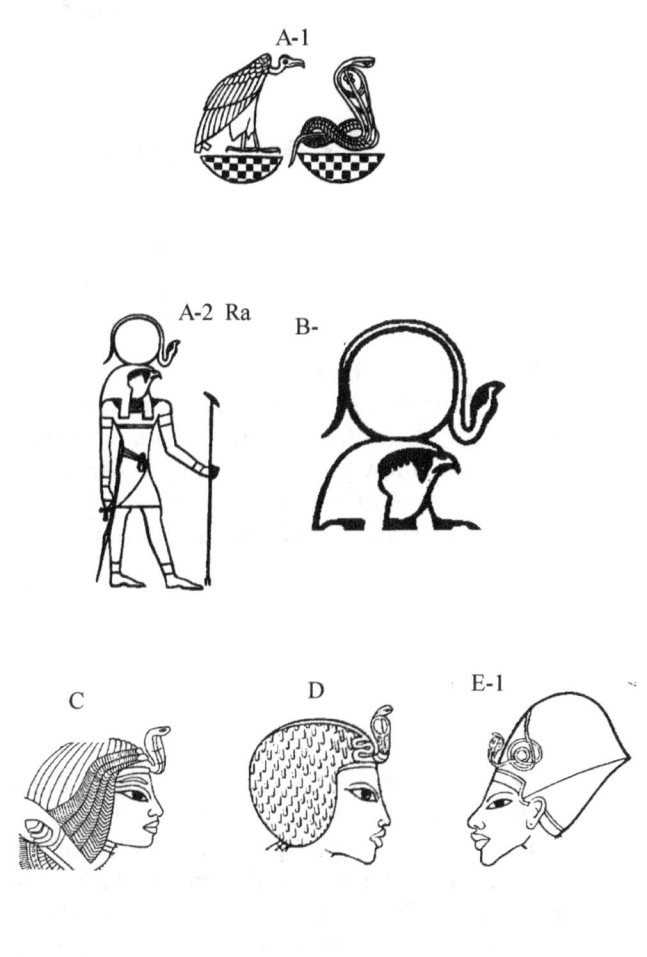

PART 3: How to Be a Disciple of Shetaut Neter: Egyptian-African Mysteries?

What Are The Disciplines of Shedy?

 "Shedy"

If you want to become a spiritual aspirant of Neterianism your first duty is to practice the disciplines of Shedy. Shedy is the means to allow the teaching of Shetaut Neter to come into your life in a real way. You cannot just study the teachings or read books. You must do certain things that will allow you to cleanse yourself and allow your personality to become a proper vessel for the teaching. Then what you learn will be useful to you and the higher mysteries will be opened to you. Every aspirant should adopt the Kamitan Diet Program of health for body, mind and soul as well as the four main disciplines of Sema Tawi.

How can religion be made effective? Religion is not simply performing rituals as an automaton or mindlessly chanting dogmatic slogans. It is a process of internal transformation through increasing virtue, self-control, wisdom and enlightenment. This cannot occur if the teachings of religion are misunderstood or not practiced. Nor can it work if there is a lack of spiritual sensitivity, cleansing of the body and heart-mind and openness to higher dimensions of being. Therefore, certain disciplines have been enjoined to promote the spiritual evolution. Those disciplines are part of Shedy. They are also known as *Sema* or Yoga disciplines.

Shedy or *Sheti* means practicing certain spiritual disciplines that will promote spiritual evolution. Those disciplines are also known as "*Sema Tawi*" or "Egyptian Yoga." Specifically, the term means "to study and penetrate the mysteries." Shedy involves everything from diet, occupation, study of scriptures, meditation, and all other aspects of life that are to be harnessed in order to promote a righteous movement towards Nehast (spiritual realization, i.e. enlightenment).

There are four main aspects of Shedy:

Sedjm / Rekh, Maat, Uash and Uaa
"Listening / Wisdom), Righteousness, Devotion and Meditation"

Each discipline is designed to inform, purify, elevate and establish the Shemsu on the path to awakening. These are the steps to the effective practice of religion that will lead a human being to maturity and spiritual realization.

Yoga in Ancient Egypt

Most people are familiar with the term Yoga from the perspective of India as that is the most popular form. In ancient times, North-East Africa and Southern Asia were populated by the same cultural and ethnic group. This was confirmed by such ancient Greek historians as Herodotus and Diodorus.

> "And upon his return to Greece, they gathered around and asked, "tell us about this great land of the Blacks called Ethiopia." And Herodotus said, "There are two great Ethiopian nations, one in Sind (India) and the other in Egypt."

Recorded by *Diodorus* (Greek historian 100 B.C.)

During this time, the myth of Heru (Horus), the Savior who was persecuted by his uncle, was also known in India in the form of Krishna, the Indian savior who was also persecuted by his uncle. In addition to this story there are other important correlations between Kamit and India with respect to the gods Osiris and Shiva, as well as ritual practices and myths along with their wisdom teachings. Some of these correlations were explored in the book *Egyptian Yoga: The Philosophy of Enlightenment*.

Indian tradition, like Kamitan tradition, encompasses many hundreds of deities and mythological stories. Perhaps the most popular deity in the Indian pantheon of Gods is Krishna. Krishna is an incarnation of the God Vishnu, who is a member of the Indian Trinity (Brahma, Vishnu, Shiva) which, like the ancient Egyptian Trinity, emerge from the Absolute transcendental Self. In India this Absolute Self is known as *Brahman*.

The first and most important teaching to understand in our study surrounds the Ancient Egyptian word "Shedy" or "Sheti." Shedy is related to the term "Sheta." The Ancient Egyptian word *Sheta* means something which is *hidden, secret, unknown,* or *cannot be seen through or understood, a secret, a mystery*. What is considered to be inert matter also possesses *Hidden Properties or Shetau Akhet*. Rituals, Words of Power (Khu-Hekau, Mantras), religious texts and pictures are S*hetaut Neter* or *Divine Mysteries*. *Shetat* or *Seshetat* are the secret rituals in the cults of the Egyptian Gods. *Shetai* is the *Hidden God, incomprehensible God, Mysterious One, Secret One*. One name of the soul of Amun is *Shet-ba* (The One whose soul is hidden). The name Amun itself signifies "The Hidden One:" *Shetai*. *Shedy* (spiritual discipline) is to go deeply into the mysteries, to study the mystery teachings and literature profoundly, to penetrate the mysteries. *Nehas-t* signifies:

"resurrection" or "spiritual awakening (enlightenment)." The body or *Shet-t* (mummy) is where a human being can focuses attention to practice spiritual disciplines. When spiritual discipline is perfected the true self or *Shti* (one who is hidden in the coffin) is revealed.

Thus, Shedy is the spiritual discipline or program to promote spiritual evolution that was practiced in Ancient Egypt. Now we can begin to discover the teachings of that spiritual program. These all fall under the broad term "Egyptian Yoga."

What is Egyptian Yoga?

Smai Tawi
(From Chapter 4 of
the *Prt m Hru*)

The Term "Egyptian Yoga" and The Philosophy Behind It

As previously discussed, Yoga in all of its forms was practiced in ancient Egypt apparently earlier than anywhere else in our history. This point of view is supported by the fact that there is documented scriptural and iconographical evidence of the disciplines of virtuous living, dietary purification, study of the wisdom teachings and their practice in daily life, psychophysical and psycho-spiritual exercises and meditation being practiced in Ancient Egypt, long before the evidence of its existence is detected in India (including the Indus Valley Civilization) or any other early civilization (Sumer, Greece, China, etc.).

The teachings of Yoga are at the heart of *Prt m Hru*. The word "Yoga" is an Indian Sanskrit term meaning to unite the individual with the Cosmic. The term has been used in certain parts of this book for ease of communication since the word "Yoga" has received wide popularity especially in western countries in recent years. The Ancient Egyptian equivalent term to the Sanskrit word yoga is: **"Sema"** or **"Smai."** *Sema (Smai)* means union, and the following determinative terms give it a spiritual significance, at once equating it with the term "Yoga" as it is used in India. When used in conjunction with the Ancient Egyptian symbol which means land, *"Ta,"* the term "union of the two lands" arises.

In Chapter 4[li] and Chapter 17[lii] of the *Prt m Hru,* a term "Smai Tawi" is used. It means "Union of the two lands of Egypt," ergo "Egyptian Yoga." The two lands refer to the two main districts of the country (North and South). In ancient times, Kamit was divided into two sections or land areas. These were known as Lower and Upper Egypt. In Ancient Egyptian mystical philosophy, the land of Upper Egypt relates to the divinity Heru (Horus), who represents the Higher Self, and the land of Lower Egypt relates to Set, the divinity of the lower self. So **Smai Taui** means "the union of the two lands" or the "Union of the lower self with the Higher Self. The lower self relates to that which is negative and uncontrolled in the human mind including worldliness, egoism, ignorance, etc. (Set), while the Higher Self relates to that which is above temptations and is good in the human heart, as well as in touch with transcendental consciousness (Heru). Thus, we also have the Ancient Egyptian term **Smai Heru-Set,** or the union of Heru and Set. So Smai Taui or Smai Heru-Set are the Ancient Egyptian words which are to be translated as "**Egyptian Yoga.**"

Above: the main symbol of Egyptian Yoga: *Sma.* The Ancient Egyptian language and symbols provide the first "historical" record of Yoga Philosophy and Religious literature. The hieroglyph Sma, "Sema," represented by the union of two lungs and the trachea, symbolizes that the union of the duality, that is, the Higher Self and lower self, leads to Non-duality, the One, and singular consciousness.

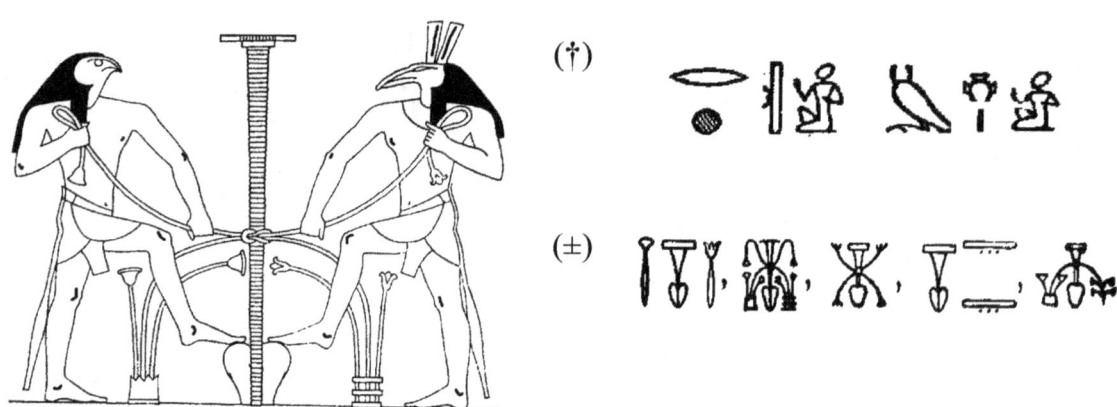

Above left: Smai Heru-Set,

Heru and Set join forces to tie up the symbol of Union (Sema –see (B) above). The Sema symbol refers to the Union of Upper Egypt (Lotus) and Lower Egypt (Papyrus) under one ruler, but also at a more subtle level, it refers to the union of one's Higher Self and lower self (Heru and Set), as well as the control of one's breath (Life Force) through the union (control) of the lungs (breathing organs). The practice is to harmonize (balance) the breath and in so doing balance the opposites of the personality. This form of breathing is to be practiced at all times. The characters of Heru and Set are an integral part of the *Pert Em Heru.*

The central and most popular character within Ancient Egyptian Religion of Asar is Heru, who is an incarnation of his father, Asar. Asar was killed by his brother Set who, out of greed and demoniac (Setian) tendency, craved to be the ruler of ancient Egypt. With the help of Djehuti, the God of wisdom, Aset, the great mother and Hetheru, his consort, Heru prevailed in the battle against Set for the rulership of Kamit (Egypt). Heru's struggle symbolizes the struggle of every human being to regain rulership of the Higher Self and to subdue the lower self.

The following are brief summaries of the Shedy disciplines.

The Discipline of Wisdom: Listening to the Teachings

"Mestchert"

"Listening, to fill the ears, listen attentively-"

What should the ears be filled with?

What should an aspirant listen to? And what should an aspirant not listen to? The sages of Shetaut Neter enjoined that a Shemsu Neter should listen to the wisdom of the Neterian Traditions. These are the myths related to the gods and goddesses containing the basic understanding of who they are, what they represent, and how they relate to human beings and the Supreme Being. The myths connect us to the Divine.

There are 6 main Neterian Traditions, and an aspirant may choose any one of these.

Shetaut Anu	– Teachings of the Ra Tradition
Shetaut Menefer	– Teachings of the Ptah Tradition
Shetaut Waset	– Teachings of the Amun Tradition
Shetaut Netrit	– Teachings of the Goddess Tradition
Shetaut Asar	– Teachings of the Asarian Tradition
Shetaut Aton	– Teachings of the Aton Tradition

The Discipline of Devotion and Love

Uash means "Worship and Devotion to the Divine." Devotional practices serve the purpose of purifying the emotional impurities of the heart and harnessing the power of the emotions, especially the emotion of love, towards the task of attaining the fulfillment of all desires and the peace of universal and unlimited love. There are three special means to practice devotion to the Divine.

God is *Neter Merri* -"God is Love" or "Beloved One"

The Neterian philosophy holds that God is Love. God created all things and in those things infused Herself. Thus all that human beings desire, though appearing to be separate and inanimate objects, or living beings, are all divine and beloved. So if egoism is left behind, the true love underlying all things can be discovered. If all things in the universe are loved then God is loved most fully. That love opens the door to spiritual enlightenment because it allows the ego and the negative mentations to subside, and the higher sense dawns in the heart, the sense of self-knowledge, universal peace, and abiding happiness. Through the disciplines of Uashu, the deviation from love is corrected and the truth is realized.

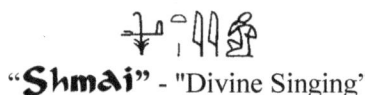

"Shmai" - "Divine Singing"

Divine singing, offering adorations to the Divine through song and chant, are special ways of practicing devotion. Music has a special way of harmonizing the human personality with the cosmic entity. When music incorporates certain qualities it becomes a vehicle to spiritual realization. Music was incorporated into the ritual and religious traditions of Kamit.

 *Hesi*- Chant Hymns to the Divine

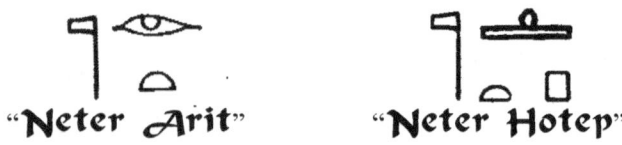

"Divine Offerings" and "Peace Offerings" Every follower of Shetaut Neter needs to make the following offerings to purify the heart and sustain the community and Temple – Selfless-Service – Virtue – Donations offerings.

Steps in the practice of Devotion Yoga:

1-MYTH: Listening to the myths and divine glories of the various forms of the divinity (god or goddess.

2- RITUAL: Effacement of the ego through cultivation of love for the Divine - Hekau (words of Power) Chanting, Praises, Hymns, Songs to the Divine

3- MYSTICISM: Mystical union with the Divine – "I Am Asar" Offering Oneself to God-Surrender to God- Become One with God

"That person is beloved by the Lord." PMH, Ch 4

The Sema (Yoga) of Devotion is the process of directing the mental energies (passion and love) to the Divine. It is a process whereby one uses one of the strongest emotions, love, to overpower mental afflictions and negative thoughts leading to union with the divine object of contemplation, one's Higher Self. In much the same manner that a person rises above his/her problems and ailments when he/she falls "in love" with another person (temporarily), so too when one directs feelings of love to the Higher Self, one is able to transcend problems and adversities in life but in a more abiding way. In addition, since human love is only a glimpse of cosmic love, imagine how much more powerful devotion to God can be in transcending the human condition. Devotion to God, also known as "Divine Love" is an effective way to produce mental health because it easily turns the mind towards the transcendental rather than towards the petty concerns of the ego. To practice Yoga of Devotion, throughout your day, feel that you are loving and serving God in others as you serve them, since all people are essentially the Self. In this way your mind does not become distracted by their personalities. When snowflakes fall, you do not become so distracted with their individual shapes that you fail to identify them as snow. Likewise, as intuitional vision of your all encompassing nature dawns in your heart, you will be able to look beyond all the different sizes, shapes, sexes and colors of people and recognize your Higher Self as the basis for their existence.

When the mind is continuously directed toward the majesty and glory of God, the Neter (its Higher Self), the mind becomes imbued with that same glory and majesty. Thus, devotion opens the way to the practice of the other spiritual disciplines (Right Action, Wisdom, Meditation), and these in turn lead to the experience of deeper devotion.

See the book *The Path of Divine Love*

The Discipline of Meditation

"Uaa m Neter"

Uaa m Neter means to meditate upon and experience the Transcendental Supreme Self. Meditation is a pathway to turn inwards to discover the ultimate reality of being. Ancient Kamit was the first known culture to practice meditation and the inscriptions show five prominent forms of meditation practice that were used by the priests and priestesses of ancient times and which are available for present day practitioners.

Arat Sekhem

Meditation on the Subtle Life Force

Ari Sma Maat

Meditation on the Righteous action

Nuk Pu Ushet

Meditation on the I am

Nuk Ra Akhu

Meditation on the Glorious Light

Rekh Maa

Meditation on the Wisdom Teaching

Meditation may be thought of or defined as the practice of mental exercises and disciplines to enable the aspirant to first achieve control over the mind, specifically, to stop the vibrations of the mind due to unwanted thoughts, imaginations, etc. Then a clear vision of self-identity emerges and the Divine becomes self-evident. Just as the sun is revealed when the clouds disperse, so the light of the Self is revealed when the mind is free of thoughts, imaginations, ideas, delusions, gross emotions, sentimental attachments, etc. In this manner the Self, your true identity, becomes visible to the conscious mind.

Below: Text from the Glorious Light Meditation instructions

Below: The Tomb of Seti I, where the text (above) is found

See the books *The Glorious Light Meditation, Meditation The Ancient Egyptian Path to Enlightenment, The Serpent Power*.

The Discipline of Righteous Action

Importance of Maat Philosophy

"Arit maatu"

Arit Maatu means to "Work rightly, lead life of integrity- actions in line with Maat."

Ari Maat also means to live and act with Righteousness. All actions should be performed in such a way that they lead to purity of the heart from the gross aspects of the fetters and afflictions of Set.

Arit Akhu

"True Deeds," "Glorious Deeds" that lead to purity of the personality and spiritual enlightenment.

Maat Aru
"True Ritual"
Rituals and ceremonies that affirm the higher reality and glory of the Divine.

A Neterian follower should learn to Act with Maat -Ethics and Law of Cause and Effect-Practice right action (working rightly, glorious deeds, true rituals) from instructors and sages.[liii] **THIS IS THE FIRST STEP** in the practice of the mysteries. In order to be successful on the path of Neterianism, an aspirant must understand the principles of Maat, and observe and practice them in day-to-day life. Maat is the original and ancient Neterian-African philosophy of purification of the heart through righteous deeds. It is the forerunner of the modern African concept known as "Ubuntu." When compared to the concept of Ubuntu, the Kamitan concept of Ari Maat (Maatian Actions) is found to be in every way compatible with this concept of humanism or social awareness and caring.

Forms of Goddess Maat

Maat is a philosophy, a spiritual symbol as well as a cosmic energy or force which pervades the entire universe. Maat is the path to promoting world order, justice, righteousness, correctness, harmony and peace. Maat is also the path that represents wisdom and spiritual awakening through balance and equanimity, as well as righteous living and selfless service or service to humanity. So Maat encompasses certain disciplines of right action which promote purity of heart and balance of mind. Maat is represented as a goddess with a feather held to the side of her head by a bandana. She is sometimes depicted with wings, and holding a papyrus scepter in one hand and an ankh (symbol of life) in the other. She is often shown kneeling with outstretched wings.

In Kamit, the judges were initiated into the teachings of MAAT, for only when there is justice and fairness in society can there be an abiding harmony and peace. Harmony and peace are necessary for the pursuit of true happiness and inner fulfillment in life. Thus, Kamitan spirituality includes a discipline for social order and harmony not unlike Confucianism of China or Dharma of India. Maat promotes social harmony and personal virtue that lead to spiritual enlightenment.

Many people are aware of the 42 Laws or Precepts of Maat. They are declarations of purity (also known as *negative confessions*), found in the *Kamitan Book of Enlightenment* (*Egyptian Book of the Dead*), which a person who has lived a life of righteousness can utter at the time of the great judgment after death. All of the precepts concern moral rectitude in all aspects of life, which leads to social order. Order leads to prosperity and harmony.

(1) "I have not done iniquity." Variant: Acting with falsehood.
(2) "I have not robbed with violence."
(3) "I have not done violence (To anyone or anything)." Variant: Rapacious (Taking by force; plundering.)
(4) "I have not committed theft." Variant: Coveted.
(5) "I have not murdered man or woman." Variant: Or ordered someone else to commit murder.
(6) "I have not defrauded offerings." Variant: or destroyed food supplies or increased or decreased the measures to profit.
(7) "I have not acted deceitfully." Variant: With crookedness.
(8) "I have not robbed the things that belong to God."
(9) "I have told no lies."
(10) "I have not snatched away food."
(11) "I have not uttered evil words." Variant: Or allowed myself to become sullen, to sulk or become depressed.
(12) "I have attacked no one."
(13) "I have not slaughtered the cattle that are set apart for the Gods." Variant: The Sacred bull – (Apis)
(14) "I have not eaten my heart" (overcome with anguish and distraught). Variant: Committed perjury.
(15) "I have not laid waste the ploughed lands."
(16) "I have not been an eavesdropper or pried into matters to make mischief." Variant: Spy.
(17) "I have not spoken against anyone." Variant: Babbled, gossiped.
(18) "I have not allowed myself to become angry without cause."
(19) "I have not committed adultery." Variant: And homosexuality.
(20) "I have not committed any sin against my own purity."
(21) "I have not violated sacred times and seasons."
(22) "I have not done that which is abominable."
(23) "I have not uttered fiery words. I have not been a man or woman of anger."
(24) "I have not stopped my ears against the words of right and wrong (Maat)."
(25) "I have not stirred up strife (disturbance)." "I have not caused terror." "I have not struck fear into any man."
(26) "I have not caused any one to weep." Variant: Hoodwinked.
(27) "I have not lusted or committed fornication nor have I lain with others of my same sex." Variant: or sex with a boy (or girl).
(28) "I have not avenged myself." Variant: Resentment.
(29) "I have not worked grief, I have not abused anyone." Variant: Quarrelsome nature.
(30) "I have not acted insolently or with violence."
(31) "I have not judged hastily." Variant: or been impatient.
(32) "I have not transgressed or angered God."
(33) "I have not multiplied my speech overmuch (talk too much).
(34) "I have not done harm or evil." Variant: Thought evil.
(35) "I have not worked treason or curses on the King."
(36) "I have never befouled the water." Variant: held back the water from flowing in its season.
(37) "I have not spoken scornfully." Variant: Or yelled unnecessarily or raised my voice.
(38) "I have not cursed The God."
(39) "I have not behaved with arrogance." Variant: Boastful.
(40) "I have not been overwhelmingly proud or sought for distinctions for myself (Selfishness)."
(41) "I have never magnified my condition beyond what was fitting or increased my wealth, except with such things as are (justly) mine own possessions by means of Maat." Variant: I have not disputed over possessions except when they concern my own rightful possessions. Variant: I have not desired more than what is rightfully mine.
(42) "I have never thought evil (blasphemed) or slighted The God in my native town."

All aspirants should work to uphold each and every precept in their day-to-day life. For a detailed study see the book *The Forty Two Precepts of Maat*, and the Audio lecture series. This is the basis for purity to attain success in the Egyptian Mysteries. As an adjunct to the 42 precepts there are other injunctions given in the Wisdom Texts. Also there are Maatian inscriptions carved into the walls of the tombs of Kamitan people who professed the philosophy of Maat. Central to the concept of order and virtue are the acts of righteousness. The highest form of right action is selfless service, service to humanity, that is, *Ari Maat*, Maat Selfless Service.

Maat Selfless Service is an important aspect of Chapter 33 of the Book of the Dead. Here the initiate states {his/her} qualifications to be allowed into the inner shrine to see and become one with Asar (The Supreme Being). The initiate states that {he/she} helped those in need in various ways. This is one of the greatest and most secure methods of purifying the heart (becoming virtuous), because it makes one humble and it effaces the ego. Selfless Service is a vast area of spiritual practice and it forms the major part of the Yogic Path of Right Action. Every human being needs to understand the profound implications of selfless service and how to practice selfless service effectively in order to attain spiritual enlightenment, social order and harmony.

First it must be understood that according to Maat Philosophy, the Supreme Spirit (God/Goddess) manifests as all Creation, and is also present in all human beings. This being so, one must realize that one is interacting in, with and through the Supreme Spirit in all actions, speech and thought. Since human interrelations have a most profound influence on the human mind, they are the most powerful means of effecting a change in the personality. However, if mishandled, they can be a most effective method of leading a human being to psychological attachment and suffering as well. A person should understand that Maat comes to {him/her} in the form of human beings in need, so as to give the aspirant an opportunity to grow spiritually through selfless service. To be successful in selfless service, the aspirant must be able to sublimate the ego through developing patience, dealing with difficult personalities without developing resentment, not taking attacks personally, and developing a keen understanding of human nature and human needs. Selfless Service allows a human being to discover sentiments of caring for something greater than the little "me." This leads to purity of heart from the gross fetters of anger, hatred, greed, lust, jealousy, envy, etc., and also the attachments based on blood relations and other filial relationships, for in order to serve in the highest order, one must serve all equally, without favorites. As a servant of humanity, one's family becomes all human beings and nature itself. Therefore, environmental well being is also a big concern of the Neterian community; this is reflected in the following injunctions of the Maat philosophy. There are two injunctions that specifically address issues of public or selfless service to the community through service to nature and the preservation of natural resources.

(15) "I have not laid waste the ploughed lands."

(36) "I have never befouled the water."
Variant: I have not held back the water from flowing in its season.
—From Chapter 33 of the Ancient Egyptian Pert M Heru

Mother Teresa, when asked how she could stand to serve such severely ill people and not feel disheartened, repulsed or depressed, replied "I see only Jesus coming to me through people." This reply shows the saintly attitude towards humanity, and she also displayed the highest level of spiritual practice through the path of right action, which is known as Selfless Service. When Mother Teresa was asked how she was able to do all the work she has done, she would reply, "I do nothing…God does it all." Selfishness arises when a human being sees {him/her} self as separate from Creation and develops an egoistic selfishness, typified by the attitude of "I got mine you get yours." A mature and righteous person must develop sensitivity to the fact that all Creation is inexorably linked at all levels, the material and the spiritual. Therefore, a true aspirant feels empathy and compassion for all humanity and will work until all human beings have the essential needs of life, those being food, shelter and opportunity to grow and thrive. All social problems of the world can be traced to the selfishness and hoarding of precious basic necessities by certain segments of the population, and the subsequent development of resentments, greed, hatred and violence which lead to untold social strife.

However, a person who lives by Maat does not pursue the betterment of the world in a sentimental manner, but with deep understanding of the fact that people's ignorance of their true divine essence is the root cause that has led them to their current condition of suffering, and therefore simply sending money or aid will not resolve the issues. Where food, clothing or funds are needed, they should be given, but in addition to these, one must undertake an effort to promote mystical spiritual wisdom (which includes the complete practice of religion: myth, ritual and mysticism) in humanity. Beyond the basic necessities of life, the world needs mystical spiritual wisdom most of all. Technology, comforts of life, entertainments and other conveniences should come after. This is how a well-ordered society is structured along Maatian-Ubuntu principles: Mystical spiritual foundation which provides basic necessities (food and shelter) for its members, from which all else (development of technology, entertainment, etc.) will follow. Only in this way will the technological developments, entertainment and other aspects of society develop in a righteous (ethical), balanced and harmonious way. This can be contrasted with the current predicament of most modern day societies where the emphasis is foremost on the development of technology and entertainment, without giving much thought to spirituality (ethics, balance, harmony, truth, righteousness). Consequently, there are many people currently existing in communities all over the world who are deprived of the basic needs of life (food and shelter).

Studying the teachings of yogic mysticism and their subsequent practice through selfless service will promote the enlightenment of humanity, which will end the cycle of egoism and disharmony between peoples of differing cultures. Therefore, the act of helping others is extremely important and should be pursued. Working in service of other human beings allows a person who lives by Maat to apply the teachings and experience the results. It allows the a person who lives by Maat to develop the capacity to adapt and adjust to changing conditions of life, and to other personalities, while still maintaining the detachment and poise necessary to keep equal vision and awareness of the Divine, and thereby live by truth rather than favoritism. All of this promotes integration of the personality of the person who lives by Maat. Therefore, the results of one's selfless service actions are immediate and always good, because no matter what the results of those actions are, the service itself is the goal of a person who lives by Maat.

What are the disciplines of Selfless Service?

Service is an important ingredient in the development of spiritual life. In selfless service one adopts the attitude of seeing and serving the Divine in everyone and every creature, and one is to feel as an instrument of the Divine, working to help the less able. The following are some important points to keep in mind when practicing selfless service.

First, having controlled the body, speech and thoughts, a person who lives by Maat should see {him/her} self as an instrument of the Divine, being used to bring harmony, peace, and help to the world. All human beings and nature are expressions of the Divine. Serving human beings and nature is therefore serving the Supreme Divine Self (God).

In Chapter 34, Verse 10 of the Pert M Hru scripture, the initiate states that {he/she} has become a spiritual doctor: *There are sick, very ill people. I go to them, I spit on the arms, I set the shoulder, and I cleanse them.* As a servant of the Divine Self, a person who lives by Maat is also a healer. Just as it would be inappropriate for a medical doctor to become impatient with {his/her} patients because the they are complaining due to their illness, so too it is inappropriate for an initiate to lose their patience when dealing with the masses of worldly-minded people, suffering from the illness of ignorance of their true essence. As a servant of humanity one is a doctor, a healer, and the treatment needed to cure the disease of ignorance and its symptoms, the acts of unrighteousness, is Maat. Practicing Maat leads to self-knowledge and that is the cure for all problems of life. So, it must be clearly and profoundly understood that in serving, you are serving the true Self, not the ego.

Secondly, as discussed above, a person who lives by Maat should not expect a particular result from their actions. In other words one does not perform actions and wait for a reward or praises, and though working to achieve success in the project, one does not develop the expectation that one's efforts will succeed, because there may be failure in what one is trying to accomplish. If a person who lives by Maat focuses on the success of the project and failure occurs, the mind will become so imbalanced that it will negate the positive developments of personality integration, expansion and concentration which occurred as the project was pursued. Therefore, one's focus should be on doing one's part by performing the service, and letting the Divine handle the results. This provides a person who lives by Maat with peace and the ability to be more qualitative in the work being performed (without the egoistic content), and more harmonious, which will lead to being more sensitive to the needs of others and of the existence of the Spirit as the very essence of one's being.

Secular Maat Selfless Service Leads to Spiritual Maat Mysticism

The highly advanced and lofty teachings from Maat Philosophy of becoming one with the Supreme Being through righteous action is further augmented by the Hymn to Maat contained in the scripture now referred to as the Berlin papyrus below.

Maat Ankhu Maat
Maat is the source of life

Maat neb bu ten
Maat is in everywhere you are

Cha hena Maat
Rise in the morning with Maat

Ankh hena Maat
Live with Maat

Ha sema Maat
Let every limb join with Maat
(i.e. let her guide your actions)

Maat her ten
Maat is who you are deep down (i.e. your true identity is one with the Divine)

See the book *The Wisdom of Maati, The Prt M Hru (The Book of the Dead)*

Karma and Reincarnation

Many people know the term "Karma" and that is why it has been used here to introduce this concept in relation to Neterian Theology. However, most people do not truly understand the concept even from its most popular source, East Indian culture. Firstly, the Neterian (African religious term) is "*ari*." What is Ari? The answer to this question can be found in the *Ru Pert Em Heru* texts or "*Book of Enlightenment*" (also known as the *Book of Coming Forth by Day* and incorrectly as *Book of the Dead*). The goddess Maat presides over righteousness, order and truth. She has some associate divinities who carry forth the fate of an individual in accordance with their actions in life. The goddess *Meskhent* presides over the future birth of an individual, but she represents only the culmination of the process of reincarnation known as *Uhm-Ankh*. In reality it is the individual who determines his or her own fate by the actions they perform in life. However, the wisdom of the ancient Egyptian Sages dictated that the process should be explained in mythological terms to help people better understand the philosophy. The process works as follows:

The deities *Shai* and *Renunut* govern an individual's fate or destiny and their fortune. These deities are the "hands" of the great god Djehuti. Djehuti symbolizes the intellectual development of a human being. He inscribes a person's fate once they have faced the scales of Maat, that is, they are judged in reference to their past ability to uphold Maat in life. A person's intellectual capacity reflects in their actions. Thus, it is fitting for the intellect to judge its own actions. Further, God does not judge anyone because we are all essentially gods and goddesses, sparks of the same divinity, so God within us judges us. This is an objective judgment which only the individual is responsible for and it occurs at the unconscious level of the mind, beyond any interference from a person's personality or ego consciousness which is on the surface level of the mind. Therefore, one's conscious desire to go to heaven at the time of death or one's conscious repentance at he time of death for misdeeds in life cannot overcome the weight of the *ari* – (action thing done make something deed *Ari* -Karma) one has set up during a lifetime. So it is important to begin now to purify the heart and cleanse the soul so as to become *Maakheru* (true of speech-pure of heart) at the time of the judgment. The gods and goddesses are cosmic forces which only facilitate the process, but from a mythological and philosophical standpoint they are concepts for understanding the mystical philosophy of the teaching.

Once the judgment has been rendered the goddess Meskhent takes over and appoints the person's future family, place of birth, social status, etc. This is not meant as a punishment but as a process of leading the soul to the appropriate place where they can grow spiritually. If before you died you desired to be a musician, the goddess will send you to a country, family and circumstances where this desire can be pursued and resolved. If you were a mugger in a past life, you will end up in a place and situation where you will experience pain and suffering such as you caused to others. This experience will teach you to act otherwise in the future, thus improving your future birth. What you do after that is within the purview of your own free will and your actions in this new lifetime will engender and determine the next, and on and on. This process is *Meskhent*- "destiny of birth." Meskhent is the manifestation of one's *shai-nefer*, positive destiny, or one's *shai-mit*, negative destiny. This is one's harvest or what one reaps from one's actions.

This is the process leading to *Uhm Ankh* (reincarnation). The objective is to lead oneself on a process of increasingly better births until it is possible to have spiritual inclination and the company of Sages and Saints who can lead a person to self-discovery (*Rech-ab*). When a person achieves this self-discovery they are referred to as Akh (the enlightened).

First, a person must become virtuous because this purifies the person's actions and thus, also their Ari (karmic) basis. Negative Ari leads to negative situations, but also to mental dullness. When the mind is in a dull state, full of base thoughts, desires and feelings, it is hard to understand the teachings - this is the opposite of *rech-ab*, which may be referred to as *inj-Set* (mind afflicted by fetters of Set). There is much mental agitation and suffering in the dull state of mind. The positive karmic basis allows harmonious surroundings and birth into the family of spiritually minded people as well as the company of Sages, but most importantly the clarity of mind to understand the wisdom teachings. If the soul is judged to be pure enough in reference to Maat, it will not be led to Uhem Ankh (reincarnation), but to the inner shrine where it meets its own Higher Self, i.e. Asar, the soul, meets Asar the Supreme Being. This meeting ends any future possibility of reincarnation. It means becoming one with the Divine Self. It is termed *Nehast* (Resurrection), i.e. the Asarian Resurrection. This is the only way to break the cycle of reincarnation.

So *ari* (karma) is not a set destiny, but the impetus of the heart based on accumulated unconscious impressions from desires, thoughts and feelings of the past (from the present and previous lives). A person can change their *ari* by changing their present actions (thought process). The individual is always responsible for their present circumstances due to the actions they performed previously which led them to the place they are today, etc. External factors can affect one's life, but one is still in control ultimately of the response to those externalities of life (other people, circumstances, etc.). So, the present is not set. Otherwise people would not be able to change and would be destined to suffer or be happy based on some perverse cosmic joke. It is not like that. God has provided free will and with it a person can have a glorious life full of wisdom and prosperity or a life of strife, suffering and frustration based on egoism and egoistic desires, all depending on the actions one chooses.

The Ancient Egyptian word "Meskhent" is based on the word "*Mesken.*" *Mesken* means birthing place. Thus, *Meskhent* is the goddess (cosmic force) which presides over the *Mesken* of newborn souls. She makes a person's desires and unconscious inclinations effective by placing a person who is to reincarnate into the appropriate circumstance for their new life, based on previous actions and future potential.

I have detailed this information in the following book: *The Wisdom of Maati*.

The original Ancient Egyptian Hieroglyphic texts containing this teaching are:

Ru Pert Em Heru (especially Chap. 33 (125 and 125A))
Wisdom Texts of Ani
Wisdom Texts of Merikara
Temple of Aset in Agylkia Island (formally and Philae)
Temple of Asar in Abydos
And many other texts.

The Discipline of Neterian Tantric Philosophy

Tantra Yoga is one of the oldest systems of Yoga. Tantra Yoga is a system of Yoga which seeks to promote the re-union between the individual and the Absolute Reality, *"Neter"* (God), through the worship of nature. Since nature is an expression of *Neter*, it gives clues as to the underlying reality that sustains it and the way to achieve wisdom. The most obvious and important teaching that nature holds is the idea that creation is made up of pairs of opposites: Up-down, here-there, you-me, us-them, hot-cold, male-female, Ying-Yang, etc. The interaction of these two complementary opposites, we call life and movement.

Insight (wisdom) into the true nature of reality gives us a clue as to the way to realize the oneness of creation within ourselves. By re-uniting the male and female principles in our own bodies and minds, we may reach the oneness that underlies our apparent manifestation as a man or woman. The union of the male and female principles may be affected by two individuals who worship *Neter* through *Neter's* manifestation in each other or by an individual who seeks union with *Neter* through uniting with his or her male or female spiritual half. All men and women have both female and male principles within themselves.

In the Egyptian philosophical system, all neters or God principles emanate from the one God *(Neter)*. When these principles are created, they are depicted as having a **_male and female_** gender. All objects and life forms appear in creation as either male or female, but underlying this apparent duality, there is a unity which is rooted in the pure consciousness of oneness, the consciousness of *Neter*, which underlies and supports all things. To realize this oneness consciously deep inside is the supreme goal.

In Tantrism, sexual symbolism is used frequently because these are the most powerful images denoting the opposites of Creation and the urge to unify and become whole, for sexuality is the urge for unity and self-discovery albeit limited to physical intercourse by most people. If this force is understood, harnessed and sublimated, it can lead to unity of the highest order, which is unity with the Divine Self.

Figure 1: Above- the Kemetic god Geb and the Kemetic goddess Nut separate after the sexual union that gave birth to the gods and goddesses and Creation. Below: three depictions of the god Asar in tantric union with goddess Aset.

Figure 2: Above-The virgin birth of Heru (The resurrection of Asar - higher, Heru consciousness). Aset in the winged form hovers over the reconstructed penis of dead Asar. Note: Asar uses right hand.

Figure 3: Drawing found in an Ancient Egyptian Building of The Conception of Heru

For more teachings on the path of Tantra Yoga see the book *Egyptian Tanta Yoga* by Dr. Muata Ashby

Egyptian Mysteries Volume 1: Principles of Shetaut Neter

The Prt M Hru and The Mysteries of Life and Death

Mystery Of The Elements of the Human Personality

In order to properly practice the teachings of Neterianism, it is important to understand the architecture of the human constitution. This section will concentrate on the subtle human anatomy and the anatomy of all existence. Just as Neterian spiritual culture holds that the Creator, Lord Khepri, emerged from the primeval ocean with nine divinities, so too there are nine important aspects or elements of the individual human personality. The tenth is transcendental Self, the all-encompassing divinity: Neberdjer. Each holds important wisdom about the nature of the human personality beyond the physical aspect. Insight into the elements allows the aspirant to understand that:

1. There is more to the personality than the physical nature.
2. The personality exists on many planes at once. These aspects are the extension of the personality into those realms.
3. The higher aspects of the personality are related to different aspects of spirit.
4. If the nature of the elements of the personality are understood, the nature of the Divine personality, God, is also known. God has the same aspects of personality, as does everything that exists.
5. The pathway to comprehend the teachings and the ability to discern the secrets of Nehast (Spiritual Awakening) are opened.

The *Prt m Hru* makes a distinction between these because the human personality is a conglomerate or composite of several aspects or levels of existence. These elements are not readily discernible to the ordinary person due to the lack of spiritual sensitivity. Further, one element may not be effective in all planes of existence. For example, the Ka may not be discernible in the Ta or Physical Plane, while the Khat may not be discernible in the Pet or Heavenly Plane. It is necessary to know about these, because in knowing them, one gains greater insight into the higher planes of existence and the teachings of the *Prt m Hru*. This section will concentrate on the subtle human anatomy and the anatomy of all existence. It will discuss the Physical, Astral and Causal planes of existence and their inner workings as they relate to the elements that compose the human personality. First we will review the themes and essential wisdom developed in the book *Egyptian Yoga: The Philosophy of Enlightenment*. Then we will proceed to look into the nature of the subtle spiritual Self with more detail and depth. The Ancient Egyptian concept of the spiritual constitution recognized nine separate but interrelated parts that constitute the personality of every human being.

A two dimensional depiction of the elements of the personality.

The diagram above shows the Kemetic concept of the elements of the personality (bodies) with the grossest (human body) at the center, and the subtlest (Spirit, God) at the outer edge.

(1) THE KHU or AKHU:

The hieroglyph of the word Khu is the "crested ibis." The ibis is representative symbol of Djehuti, the god of reason and knowledge. As such it relates to the pure spiritual essence of a human being that is purified by lucidity of mind, that is, illumined intellect. The Khu or Akhu is the spirit, which is immortal; it is associated with the Ba and is an Ethereal Being. The Khu is also referred to as the "being of light" or "luminous being." The Khu illumines the personality and without this light, the personality and the mind cannot function. It is the light of consciousness itself.

(2) THE BA:

The hieroglyphic symbol of the Ba is the Jabiru bird. The Jabiru is a stork. It symbolizes the nature of the soul to spread its wings and take flight, and exist apart from the body. The Ba is the heart or soul, which dwells in the Ka with the power of metamorphosis. Sometimes described as the "Soul" and "Higher Self," it is seen as a spark from the Universal Ba (God). The Ba may be dialogued with and can be a spiritual guide to the developing individual. It is the indestructible, eternal and immortal spark of life. It is not affected by anything that may happen to the senses, body, mind or intellect (higher mind).

Through the mind, the Ba (soul-consciousness) "projects" and keeps together an aggregate of physical elements (earth, air, water, fire, ether) in a conglomerate that is called the psycho-physical personality. When the soul has no more use for the physical body, it discards it and returns to the Universal Ba if it is enlightened. If it is not enlightened, it will tune into another aggregate of elements to make another body (reincarnation).

There are two important forms of the Ba, the avian (A) and the ram (B). The avian symbolism of the Ba signifies its capacity to rise above the physical existence. The Ba comes from the higher regions (Heru) and settles the individual consciousness in the Khat (Physical body). At the time of death the avian quality allows the soul to escape physical mortal existence. The ram with horizontal antlers symbolizes the horizontal movement of the soul, i.e. reincarnation-rebirth. In the process of reincarnation the new physical body is fashioned by Khnum, the ram headed god (C). The scene below shows Djehuti writing the number of years that a person is to live on earth in that particular incarnation on the palm stem. Djehuti's hands represent Shai and Renunut, "destiny" and "fortune and harvest," respectively..

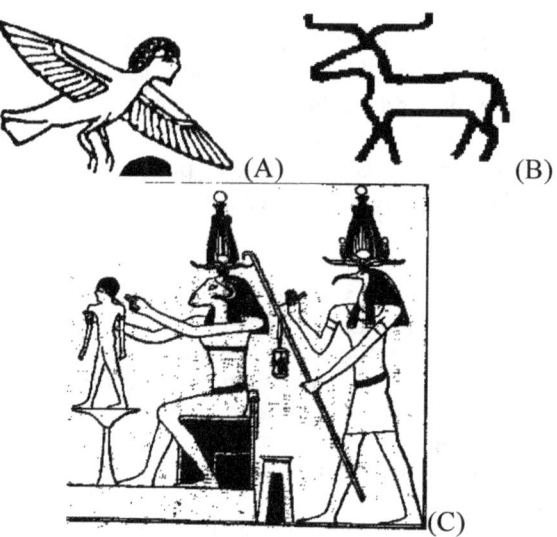

In *The Egyptian Book Of Coming Forth By Day* and in other hieroglyphic texts, the individual Soul is depicted either as a human headed hawk (Heru), or as a ram or ram-headed man (Amun). In this manner, we are led to understand that the individual soul is in reality a manifestation of the universal soul, the High God Heru or the High God Amun, who is the soul of everything. In its highest aspect, the individual soul cleanses itself from its association with the mortal body-consciousness achieves identification with the Universal Ba-Amun.

Above, from the papyrus of Nebseni, Nebseni's soul visits the mummy (physical body of Nebseni) in Nebseni's tomb. The Ba assumes the "Aset Position," a tantric sexual posture (sitting on top). Recall in the story of the Asarian Resurrection. Aset assumes this position and revives the body of Asar long enough to receive his seed and produce offspring, Heru-sa Asar sa Aset (Heru the son of Asar and Aset). This position of the soul hovering over the body signifies the transference of the life essence to the physical form. The soul is the intermediary aspect of the personality between the physical and the spiritual.

Above: Soul of Ani leaves the tomb.

Above: Soul of Ani hovers over the mummy with *shen* eternity amulet.

(3) THE SAHU:

The hieroglyphs of the word Sahu are the door bolt, meaning consonant "s" or "z," the arm, meaning the guttural sound "ain," the intertwined flax - consonant "h," the chick is the vowel "u," the determinative cylinder seal, meaning "treasure" or "precious," and the determinative of the "corpse" or "body." The Sahu is therefore sometimes referred to as the "glorious" spiritual body in which the Khu and Ba dwell. When the elements of a person are balanced (i.e., person moves towards or reaches enlightenment), the spiritual and mental attributes of the natural body are united and deified. The Sahu is the objective of all aspiration. It is the reason for human existence – to become Godlike while still alive by spiritualizing one's physical aspects and thereby allowing these to become proper vessels for the higher aspects of the personality to unfold.

(4) THE KHAIBIT:

The hieroglyphs of the word Khaibit are the "sunshade" and the consonant "t." The sunshade produces a shadow when the light is reflecting on it. Similarly, the shadow of a person, their personality, is produced when the light of their true essence (Akhu) is shining on the aspects of the personality. The Khaibit is therefore, an outline of the soul that is illumined by the light of the Spirit, which reflects in the mind as a subtle image of self (ego). In Chapter 31 of the *Prt M Hru*, it is stated *I (as the sundisk) fly away to illuminate the shades (in the Duat)*. The shades are the subtle reflection of the soul, which are not self-illuminating, and which therefore exist only due to the presence of light and an object. In this case, the object is the soul. The Khaibit is a subtle manifestation of the physical elements of the personality (earth, water, air, fire, ether, mind, soul) that acts somewhat as the resistor in an electronic component. A resistor causes a shadow in a manner of speaking, when it is placed in an electric circuit. In the same manner, the Khaibit and the other elements of the personality consume spiritual energy from the spirit and produce a particular image thereafter referred to as the individual personality of a human being. Another way to understand it is that the thought of individuality in the mind causes a congealing in the ocean of consciousness. That congealing is a wave in that ocean, a spot that is no longer clear, but opaque, and thus reflects when illumined by the higher aspects of the spirit (Akh). The Khaibit or Shadow is associated with the Ba from which it receives nourishment. It has the power of locomotion and omnipresence.

(5) THE AB:

"The conscience (Ab) of a man is his own God."

Egyptian Mysteries Volume 1: Principles of Shetaut Neter

The *Ab* or conscience is the source of Meskhenet (Ari, Karma) and the mother of reincarnation. The Ab represents the heart. It is the symbol of the deep unconscious mind, the conscience, and is also the repository of unconscious impressions gathered from past experiences in this and previous lives. As desires can never be fulfilled by experiences or from objects in the world of time and space, at death, the ignorant soul will harbor impressions of unfulfilled desires that will lead to further incarnations in search of fulfillment. This point is described in Chapter 36, from the *Egyptian Book of Coming Forth by Day (Prt m Hru)*: **"My heart, the mother of my coming into being."** The mind is seen as the source of incarnation (coming into being) because it contains the desires and illusions which compel a human being to be born to pursue the fulfillment of those desires. In the judgment scene from the *Book of Coming Forth By Day*, the Ab undergoes examination by Djehuti, the god of reason. In other words, one's own reasoning faculty will be the judge as well as that which is being judged. The heart (mind) itself metes out its own judgment based on its own contents. It is one's own heart which will fashion (*mother*) one's own fate (*come into being*) according to one's will and desires, which are based on one's understanding (wisdom) about one's true Self. Thus, the new embodiment is fashioned in accordance with what a person has done during previous lives and what they desire for the future. A desire for worldly experience will cause embodiment. A desire to go to the west and join with God will bring spiritual enlightenment.

(6) THE SEKHEM:

Sekhem is the Life Force or Power that exists in the universe. The symbol of Sekhem is the hand held staff pictured above. When used in worldly terms it refers to a scepter that means physical power, authority and strength. In spiritual terms, the Sekhem is the power or spiritual personification of the vital Life Force in humans, their vitality. Its dwelling place is in the heavens with the Khus, but all life draws upon this force in order to exist. Sekhem also denotes the potency, the erectile power or force used in fashioning one's own glorious new body for resurrection.

(7) The KA:

The hieroglyph of two upraised arms that are joined is the *Ka*. It is the abstract personality or ego-self and the conscious mind. It is the source from which subconscious desires emerge. It is also considered to be the ethereal body possessing the power of locomotion. It survives the death of the physical body. It is the ethereal double containing the other parts of the personality. The concept of the Ka was known in India, and the word was also known. The Indian God Brahma had a Ka (soul-twin). This teaching of the Ka in Ancient Egypt and in India shows that there is a keen understanding of the reflective quality of the personality. In reality the physical personality is a reflection or more accurately, a projection of the astral body. The Ka is associated with the Sekhem in that it is the dynamic aspect of a person's personality in the Astral Plane. It is the dynamic aspect of the vital force in the body of a human being.

(8) THE REN:

The Ancient Egyptian word Ren means "name." The name is an essential attribute to the personification of a being. You cannot exist without a name. Everything that comes into existence receives a name. This is an essential quality of that which comes into the realm of time and space. The Ancient Egyptian symbols that signify name are the "mouth" and "water." The name is sometimes found encircled by a rope of light called a cartouche, which is associated with the Shen (a symbol of eternity), the top part of the Ankh Symbol. The cartouche represents a rope of sunlight or Life Force harnessed into the form of a circle. It is the most impregnable structure to protect one's name against attack. The ⌒, means mouth.

Shen

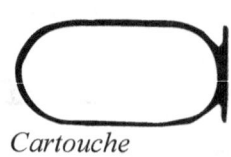

Cartouche

"R" and "N"
or "REN"

The symbol of the mouth is of paramount importance in Ancient Egyptian Mystical wisdom. The symbol of the mouth refers to the consonant sound "r," and it is a symbol of consciousness. It is the mouth which is used in two of the most important mystical teachings of Ancient Egyptian mysticism, *The Creation* and the *Opening of the Mouth Ceremony* of the *Book of Coming Forth By Day*. God created the universe by means of the utterance of his own name. In the *Book of Coming Forth By Day*, the mouth is manipulated so as to promote enlightenment. Why is the mouth so important to this mystical symbolism? This issue is discussed in more detail in the following section entitled "More Mystical Implications of Name and Word"

(9) THE KHAT:

The hieroglyphs of the word Khat are the fish meaning "dead body" and the consonant "k," the vulture meaning the vowel "a," the symbol of "bread" and the consonant "t," the egg-like determinative symbol of "embalming" and the determinative symbol of the "mummy," "corpse" or "body." The Khat is the concrete personality, the physical body. It refers to the solid aspect of a human being (bones, skin, blood, sense organs, etc.) that is transient and mortal.

More Mystical Implications of Name and Word

Consider the following. When you think of anything, you attach words to your thoughts. In fact, it is difficult for ordinary people (who have not undergone the mystical training) to think without words. Therefore, words are the symbols that the human mind uses to group thoughts and which constitute intellectual forms of understanding. However, thoughts are conditioning instruments. This means that when you think, you are actually differentiating. The differentiation process allows the mind to be conscious or aware of differences in matter. It labels these differences with different names based on the form or function of the object or the relationship it has to it. The mind learns to call objects by names. For example, a chair is an aggregate of matter just like a rock. However, the mind has learned to call it a particular name and associate the name "chair" with a particular kind of object which looks in a particular way and serves a particular function that is different from the rock.

When the mind goes beyond words, it goes beyond thoughts and thereby experiences undifferentiated consciousness. This is the deeper implication of the opening of the mouth ceremony. It signifies opening the consciousness and memory of the undifferentiated state of existence. At a lower state of spiritual evolution, consciousness appears to be differentiated, even though the underlying essence is undifferentiated. However, when intuitional realization or spiritual enlightenment dawns in the human mind, words are no longer viewed as differentiating instruments, but merely as practical instruments for the spirit to operate and interact with the world through a human personality in time and space. This is the difference between a human being who is spiritually enlightened and one who is caught in the state of ignorance and egoism.

The vocal capacity in a human being is intimately related to the unconscious level of the mind. This is why those who do not practice introspection and self-control often blurt out things they do not wish to say, and later regret. For this reason, the teachings enjoin that a spiritual aspirant should practice the disciplines of virtue and inner research which lead to self-control through right action and righteous living. In this manner, one's speech becomes *maakheru*, the highest truth. When one's speech becomes truth, one's consciousness is truth. When one's consciousness is truth, it is in harmony with the transcendental truth of the universe which is symbolized by the Ancient Egyptian goddess Maat. Thus, becoming true of speech is a primary objective for every spiritual aspirant. It is synonymous with coming into harmony with the universe and thus, refers to spiritual enlightenment itself.[liv]

The symbol of the water recalls the image of the Primordial Ocean of Consciousness. Thus, Ren relates to consciousness manifesting (the ocean that has taken a form, it has been differentiated temporarily) through names, words and sound itself.

The Importance of the Spiritual Name

In Ancient Egyptian Asarian mysticism, all initiates were given the spiritual name *"Asar"* regardless of if they were male or female. Thus, in the Papyrus of Ani, Ani, who was a human man, was renamed Asar Ani. Likewise, Nefertari, who was a woman, also received the name Asar Nefertari (see below). Thus, in the same manner, other papyruses of the *Prt m Hru* prepared for other initiates were not prepared for the man or woman, but for the spiritual aspirant. While Asar is usually seen as a male divinity, his higher attributes include those which relate him as an androgynous, transcendental Spirit. The term *"ren"* relating to the aspect of the personality of a human being therefore refers to the ego, the differentiated consciousness, and not to the Higher Self, the universal consciousness. So every human being has a Divine Name and an ego name.

Picture: (right) Queen Nefertari as initiate Asar.

The hieroglyphic inscription reads *"Asar Nefertari, the great queen, beloved of goddess Mut and Maakheru (spiritually victorious) is in the presence of Asar, the Great God"*

What is the deeper implication of this? This is a very important mystical teaching relating that the deeper Self within Ani and Nefertari is Asar, the Divine Self. That is, their true identity is not the birth name, but the Divinity which transcends mortal existence. In modern times, John would be Asar John, Cynthia would be Asar Cynthia, etc. It is an affirmation and acceptance of one's Divine true essential nature, not only as an expression of God, but as God in fact. Thus, the entire journey of self-discovery revolves around your discovering that the deeper reality within you is Neter, God. Therefore, in Ancient Egyptian terms as related in the *Book of Coming Forth By Day*, the deeper reality to be sought is Asar. So as you live your life, see your existence as a journey of discovery. Feel that you have come from a divine source and that as you practice the teachings, you are drawing ever closer to discovering that source. See your entire life as a ritual. When you wake up in the morning reflect on the majesty of the Sun (the Divine) just as Ani does with his prayer. When you eat, see this as an offering to the Divine Self (Asar) within you.

There are essentially three important teachings being imparted in the *Prt m Hru*. The first is the message that righteousness leads to spiritual realization. The second is that the process of purification is acting with righteousness. The third message of the text is the wisdom about the Divine. By learning about the nature of the Divine, acting, feeling and thinking as the Divine, it is finally possible to become one with the Divine. The spiritual name is an essential and powerful force linking the initiate to that spiritual source as well as a constant reminder of the true glory of the Higher Self.

The Prt M Hru and The Readings for the Guidance of the Dying Person and their Relatives

Before entering into a deep mystical study of the *Prt M Hru* or other Neterian texts such as the *Hymns of Amun* it is admonished that aspirants should study and have a firm grasp of the Shetaut Asar (Myth of Asar, Aset and Heru-see the book *Resurrecting Osiris*). There are at least three recognized uses of the *Prt m Hru* Chapters that can still be effective in modern times. In ancient times, the scriptures of the *Prt m Hru* were used by priests and priestesses to officiate at burials, which were actually rituals related to the guidance of the deceased. The scriptures chosen by the departed were read prior to their death, as they were on their deathbed, and another formal performance would have also taken place after they died. This one would have included the participation of the spouse of the deceased. For example, the wife of the deceased would assume the role of Aset, the resurrector.[lv] In this capacity, a dying person should be read all the appropriate Chapters selected for that person. The prepared text can be read (see the Book of the Dead), or it can be read as follows, beginning with the passages from Chapter 1, Part 1, related to the commencement of the movement into the higher plane of existence. At the time of death, the scriptures from Chapter 18, the movement through the Netherworld to discover the abode of Asar, and then Chapter 36, entry into the inner shrine, should be read to the dying person, or a dead person. Here, the commentary (glosses) of the spiritual preceptor can also be read. Then at the time of death and immediately afterwards, the attendees at the deathbed and later, the funeral or wake, should recite Chapter 1, Part 2, Hymn 1 (Hymn to Ra) and Hymn 2 (Hymn to Asar). In the reading of the scripture of *Prt m Hru* the deceased is to be guided by the readings to discover the abode of the Divine. Modern para-psychological experiments suggest the possibility that at the time of death, while an individual cannot move, they can still hear. Further, it is was believed in ancient times that the spiritual essence of a person, the astral body, would remain close to the body for a time and they would benefit from the readings.

The attendees should not be mourning at this time since the resurrection of the deceased's soul is a motive for rejoicing. The attendees should take comfort in the fact that the recitation of these verses is infallible for the person passing on if they had led a righteous life and turned their spiritual vision towards the Divine while they were still alive. The recitation will be helpful even if the person has not made these changes, but the help will be limited to experiencing less adversity in the Netherworld, and the next lifetime will be more propitious for attaining spiritual enlightenment. The recitation will benefit the attendees also. The attendees should by now realize that there is no real death. Therefore, mourning and fear are to be seen as irrational sentiments of those who are spiritually ignorant. The soul moves on, and they should free the soul by not regretting its passing and by wishing it a safe journey. This feeling helps the soul move on without the burden of attachments, and it allows the living to move on also in their own spiritual disciplines, leading up to their own passing.

In the case of those people who are in a coma or in a vegetative state, it must be understood that yogic philosophy holds that the soul is never in the body, but rather, it uses the body for a limited period of time. A person's death is determined by the higher aspects of the personality (Ba-Ka-Akhu) desire to move on even if the lower personality (Khat-Ren) of a person seems to be clinging to life. If there is clinging, then there is pain and sorrow for the dying person because they are going against the desire of the soul. Therefore, the family of the deceased should not try to hold on to the body and realize that the body is only an aggregate of elements that must go back to the nature where they came from (earth, air, water, fire). The soul is imperishable, and in this aspect we are all one and can never leave our loved ones. How can a wave leave the ocean? In deciding when to disconnect life support machines, the family should be guided by this wisdom along with the insight of health professionals, taking into account the factor of allowing other family members (those not initiated into this mystical teaching) sufficient time to grieve. It is degrading to the soul to be clinging to life in a limited state of health. Therefore, one should move on to the next life with a new body (reincarnation) or on to self-discovery and oneness with the Absolute, God, the Self.

The ideal of the practice of the *Prt m Hru* teachings is that by the time of the death of the physical body, the initiate should already have discovered that which is beyond. There should be no mystery about it, and the Divine should already have been discovered. This process of spiritual "awakening" is promoted through living in accordance with Maat Philosophy and practicing the metaphysics, rituals and meditations of the *Prt m Hru*. In the Valley of the Queens in Waset, Kamit (Thebes, Egypt) and in various papyri, there are depictions of parents making the offerings and readings of the Prt M Hru for children who are too young to present themselves for judgment. Thus, in this manner, the parent or guardian should perform the rituals, meditations, chanting and offerings with the child or for the dead child.

The Body of the Deceased, the Metaphysics of the Astral Plane and Transcending Beyond

Once a person dies, what should be done with the body? The body of the deceased was the instrument used by that person to perform actions in the physical realm. It is no longer needed now that the soul has flown away to continue its eternal journey. There are two main traditions within Neterian Theology, the Anunian and the Asarian. This implies solar and lunar, respectively. Ra is symbolized by the sun and Asar by the moon. Thus, there are two possibilities prescribed by the Kemetic teachings for attaining enlightenment and also for disposal of the physical body after its death. As there are two main paths to the Divine which are promoted in the *Prt m Hru*, the Asarian and the Atumian (Atum-Ra), so too there are two different traditions for the disposal of the body of the deceased. In the case of the Asarian, there is a tradition of burial (see Pyramid Texts Utterance 261/Coffin Texts 288, Coffin Texts 246 and Pyramid Texts Utterance 332 and Chapters 23 and 26) and in the case of the Atumian (Ra), cremation (see Coffin Invocation 246). Since Atum-Ra relates to the sun and to fire as well as to air, the indication for the disposal of the dead body is cremation. In order to "know" God, it is necessary to "BE" God. In the Egyptian *"Story of Sinuhe,"* the King (who is a symbol of a perfected human being, Heru), is said to have: **"*flown to heaven and united with the Sundisk, the divine body** (of the King) **merging with its maker."** This teaching implies a union and identification with Ra though dissolution of the individual personality into the essence of Ra as was explained in the myth of Ra and Aset. In the Asarian tradition, the pathway to Asar is identification through Self Knowledge; this is why all initiates get the name of Asar and are to make their given name secondary to the Divine name.

As Ra is the Divinity of Fire, cremation of the body is indicated in this tradition. The burnt body is to become subtle gasses that "rise up" to unite with the sundisk. The remaining ashes go back to rejoin the earth. In the fire tradition, the body is to become one with the fire and as subtle as air, and the soul is to have power over these elements as it escapes their grasp and moves towards the ultimate abode of the Higher Self. The higher elements of the personality become more powerful and that power expands consciousness, ultimately to the infinite, thereby allowing the personality to expand beyond its human confines, into its own higher nature. That higher nature is one with God. The earliest known mummies are believed to date from the early dynasties of Ancient Egyptian Culture. The technique of mummification was later adopted by the Assyrians, Hebrews, Persians and Scythians. Early Christian Sarcophagi were decorated with biblical scenes just as the earlier Neterian sarcophagi were decorated with scenes from the *Prt M Hru*. Christians forbade cremation because it was believed that the body would not be able to resurrect in the end times. Jews believed it was a desecration of the body and Muslims also forbade cremation.

As Asar is the god of vegetation, mythologically his dead body serves as fodder and fertilizer for all vegetation. Since every human being is essentially Asar, the indication for the disposal of the dead body in this tradition is burial. The burial should take into account ecological issues, and should not be done in such a way as to pollute the environment. Shrines or mausoleums can be created, but these should be in the form of Temples wherein family and others may come to perform religious rites, worship, etc. In other words, ideally, the tombs should be monuments not to the deceased, but sanctuaries exalting the teachings, containing segments of the scriptures in which the person believed, being displayed for all. Of course, the most profound teachings are to be reserved for the interior of the shrine. In Pre-dynastic times, the corpse of the deceased was not mummified. Mummification is defined as the maintenance of a corpse through artificial means. This practice grew out of a tradition attached to the practice of the Asarian religion. The idea was that if the images of life on earth were preserved, then the existence in the afterlife would be preserved as well. This idea is based in part on the teaching that everything in Creation is a form (image) and name. This great Ancient Egyptian teaching was the basis for much of Plato's work. If the form and name are given then, there is existence. Think about it. If you call an object to mind you, are giving it existence. This is what you do when you exercise the imagination, and even more so when you dream.

Egyptian Mysteries Volume 1: Principles of Shetaut Neter

Funerary mask of Tutankhamun

Funerary mask of Tuyu 1391 BCE

However, the extension of the idea into the conclusion that preserving the body guarantees existence in the afterlife with the image of the physical body, though true in part, is not the goal of the deeper aspects of Ancient Egyptian religion. This teaching is predicated upon the understanding of the Elements of the Human Personality that were introduced earlier. When the physical body dies, its physical elements disintegrate and dissolve into the earth. If that happens, the personality would have no concrete image to hold onto, so it too would eventually disintegrate. If one wanted to extend the time after death one could do so by having the physical body mummified and that would serve as an anchor for individual (ego) consciousness in time and space. With that anchor, the personality could then have an extended period in the Duat (astral plane) and more time to practice the teaching and attain enlightenment, instead of disintegrating after some time in the astral plane and then coming back to the earth in a new incarnation. However, this is only a tradition attached to the religion. It is not a mystical or spiritual ideal. Therefore, initiates should be striving to release all attachments to mortal existence while alive, in this lifetime. Families should strive to release the deceased and not promote sentimental attachments to that which is not real, and therefore, not abiding. Also, the deceased should not leave this world in anguish over what will happen to their families without them and so on. Grieving over the loss of a loved one is indicative of a life lived in delusion, where the very basic truth of life, that everyone will die, was never reflected upon. Not facing up to one's own mortality is another manifestation of the same problem. Those with true faith and/or true insight into the teachings will release that form of ignorant thought, and will work earnestly towards the goal of life, to discover that which lies beyond death, but before death actually comes to them. This is the basis of the *Shetaut Neter*.

Most people are familiar with the death mask of Pharaoh Tutankhamun. The idea of making the mask in the image of the person is to maintain the ideal likeness as a metaphysical icon. There are several masks that have survived which display a "contentment smile" much like the icons of Buddha, which display the peace and contentment of the soul, having moved on to the higher plane. The Funerary mask of Tuyu 1391 BCE is such an example.

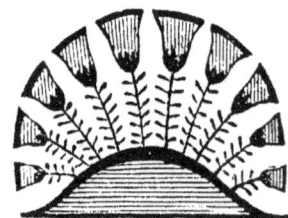

Figure: Burial mound with lotuses growing from it, symbolizing the spiritual resurrection.

In ancient times (Neolithic period – beginning 10,000 B.C.E.), the deceased were wrapped in a reed mat and placed in simple graves with the body in a prenatal position, lying on its left side, and not stretched out on the back as in later times. They were buried with vessels (pottery) that were painted black and red. This pottery is almost identical to that which was found by archeologists in India, from the ancient period (Dravidian c. 2,500 B.C.E). While it is possible to be extravagant with funerals, it is not necessary or prudent in view of the mystical teachings. The use of coffins, tombs and elaborate structures came later in the Dynastic period. Many of the upper class began to think that they could "take it all with them," so they had *ushabti* (slave amulets), food, jewelry, etc., buried with them, only to have them robbed by grave-robbers or their tombs emptied by Egyptologists, museums, etc., and their mummified bodies destroyed. There is no security in this world or any other. Indeed, at any moment a passing comet or accidental nuclear war, or other possible disasters can destroy this world. It therefore behooves the wise aspirant to begin right away to exert effort in the spiritual disciplines, so as not to fall prey to the world of illusions. There is no truth or security except in that Divinity which transcends Creation.

Below: Sarcophagus of the 19th Dynasty in Memphis now making use of (human form) anthropoid art.

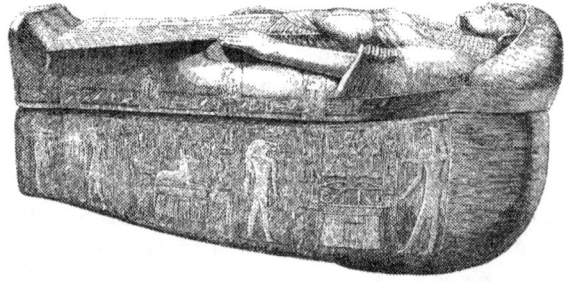

See *The Book of the Dead: Prt M Hru*, by Muata Ashby

Egyptian Mysteries Volume 1: Principles of Shetaut Neter

Architecture of Heaven, Hell and the Transcendental Realms

In order to attain the highest goal of life, it is necessary to make a mystical spiritual journey into higher realms of consciousness. The Neterian Conception of that journey is presented in the Prt M Hru texts. One of the most important teachings relates the wisdom of the Duat and the regions that are to be traversed. This is known as the Sekhetu or Fields. These fields are to be traversed by an aspirant with the assistance of the Divinity Anpu, who represents right discernment, and with Hekau, the words of power that open the mouth and wield the power that control the inimical forces of the ego consciousness. The details and disciplines to master this art are not given here as this is an introductory volume. The reader is directed to our books *Initiation Into Egyptian Yoga*, *Resurrecting Osiris* and *The Book of the Dead* (*Prt M Hru*).

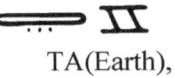
TA (Earth),

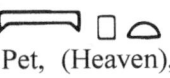
Pet, (Heaven),

and the Duat

The Duat - Sekhet-Hetepet of Anhai from the *Prt m Hru* of Initiate Anhai. The Duat is illustrated as two-dimensional registers or sections (1-to 4).

1- Lady Anhai pays homage to her parents and divine beings (uppermost register).
2- Anhai binds wheat into bundles, then praises exalted souls.
3- Anhai is seen ploughing.
4- The Celestial Boat in the form of a headrest containing a shrine with seven steps.

While there is no single Neterian[lvi] scripture wherein all the aspects of this concept are discussed, they are described in various texts. Foremost among these are Chapter 18 of the various editions of the *Prt m Hru* and the *Book of Am Duat* (Book of What is in the Duat). The Ancient Egyptian concept of creation recognized three realms of existence, *Ta* (Earth), *Pet* (Sky-Heavens) and the *Duat* (Astral Plane). The Duat is the realm where the nine primordial gods and goddesses of the Ennead were birthed, the residence of astral beings, the lower gods and goddesses as well as the demons and fiends that dwell there alongside the departed souls. It is also within this realm that Asar can be discovered. The Duat is to be understood as a parallel plane of existence in reference to the physical plane of ordinary physical human experience. It is a mental plane which human beings visit temporarily, during the dream state of consciousness or during meditation when experiencing a vision. Unlike a dream, at the time of death, there is no coming back to the waking state of the previous birth. After death, the unenlightened remain in the "dream world" of their own making, which, while on the astral level of consciousness, is unconscious of the path to discover God. Due to ignorance, they are not able to discover the path to the Divine Self, but only experience situations (hellish or heavenly) based on their level of ignorance, and then return to the physical plane by being born again into another family (reincarnation). The conscious state of mind is a level used by a human being to experience the physical world. In order to experience the Duat or Astral plane consciously, it is necessary to enter into the subconscious levels of mind, which is within one. This is a deeper level of mind. Thus, as one explores the depths of mental existence, one gradually moves towards more subtle planes until one reaches the subtlest, God, the Divine Self. Thus, while these realms are understood as levels of Creation, they are also understood as planes of consciousness within the personality of a human being. Therefore, creation is a projection inward. A detailed view of the architecture of existence may look as follows. The physical plane is within the Astral, which is within the Causal, which is in turn within the Spirit (God) from the subtlest essence, the Spirit, to the grossest, the physical world. An advanced soul can have an astral existence in the Duat and not come back to the physical world, but rather move on and discover God from that higher plane.

Seen from the perspective of the physical world, a three dimensional diagram of Creation, based on the teachings of the *Prt M Hru* (Book of the Dead) and the *Book of Am Duat* (Book of What is in the Duat) looks as follows. It contains the Ancient Egyptian concept of Creation which includes three realms. These are the TA, (Earth), Pet, (Heaven), and the Duat (the Netherworld). Notice that the earth plane is the smallest with the more subtle planes being larger, and that the abode (Aset) of Asar is in the center of Creation. Though depicted as a small object in the center of the Duat, it is actually all-encompassing (Asar, Neberdjer or Pa-Neter) of the other planes. The Physical Plane is a reflection of the Astral Plane, which itself is a reflection of the Sekhet Hetep, which is itself and emanation from God, who dwells in the special region known as Yanrutf, within the Sekhet Yaru region.

Figure: The Architecture of Creation.

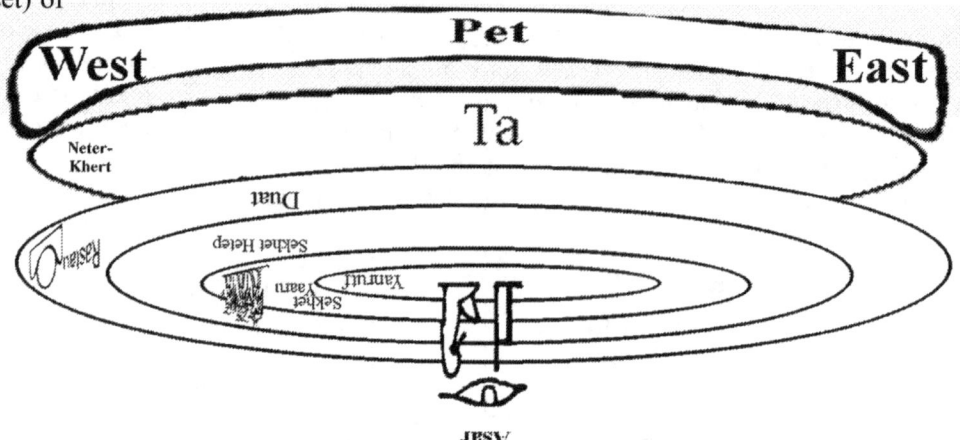

The Amenta, The Beautiful West

In the context of Neterian philosophy, the earth is set up in an order determined by the sun, which is the sustainer of Creation, from east to west. In the east there is a beginning and in the west, an end, just as in life there is birth and death. The goal of life is to lead a life of righteousness and spiritual enlightenment, so as to enter into the western horizon, through the valley of Manu[lvii], into the Amentet ("hidden" region in the west), which is the final destination of the soul. The term Amentet (Ament, Amenta) may be understood as a region of the Duat or also as the Duat itself. Those who are enlightened and have come to understand their oneness with Asar, go to rejoin Asar in the *Beautiful West* (the Land of the Setting Sun- Ra) also known as Amenta, and become one with him. This is the most desirable attainment for any aspirant. When you succeed in cultivating an intuitive intellect (*Saa* or *Sia*) which understands the nature of creation and the oneness of all things in the one "Hidden God," then you will achieve *Saa-Amenti-Ra,* the intelligence or knowledge of the Amenti of Ra, the hidden world. Those who do not achieve this level of spiritual realization are subjected to the various experiences which can occur in the Duat. Notice that the teaching of the Duat incorporates the main characters of the Ancient Egyptian religion, Amun, Ra and Asar, thus showing the uniformity of its understanding and the synchronicity of its teaching throughout Ancient Egypt. When the Ta (Physical Plane) and the Duat (Astral Plane) are placed end to end, the wisdom of the Kemetic conceptualization of the realms of existence can be seen. **Note:** The original drawings presented in this volume as well as those contained in the ancient versions of the *Prt m Hru* are given only as a means to promote understanding of the principles of Kemetic mysticism. They are not to be understood as actual physical locales, but rather as representations of psychological realms within the mind to assist the mind in finding its path to the Divine Self, the ultimate abode. Further, they should also not be understood as levels as in an ordinary educational system wherein a student must go to kindergarten, elementary, junior high, high school and then college. Rather, they are venues wherein the soul obtains experiences in time and space. The needs of the soul at a given point determine the realms of experience. Thus, the soul may have experiences on earth, and then in the Astral Plane, and then back to the earth again, and if enlightened at that point, jump to the Plane of Asar directly.

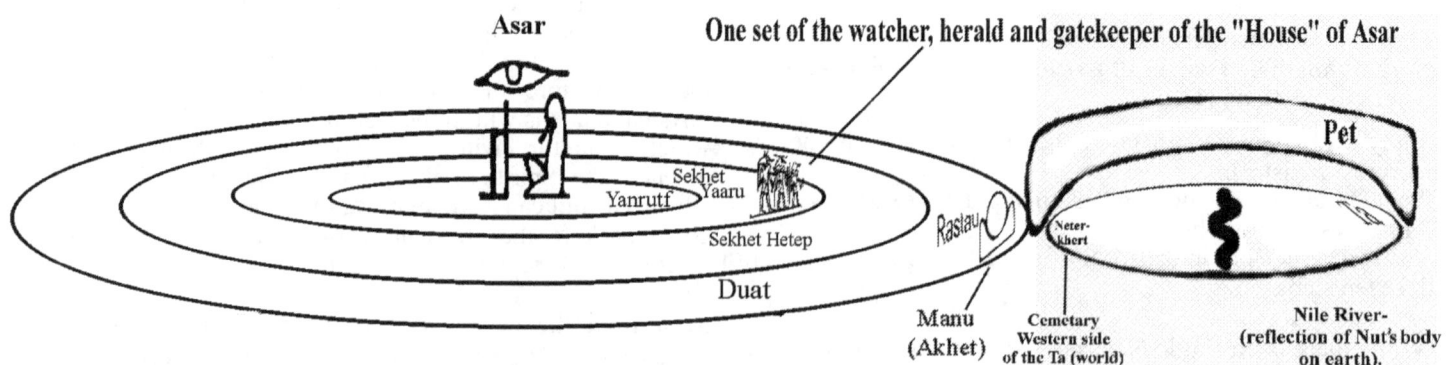

Figure above: The Architecture of Creation introduced previously but now when viewed two horizontally.

Part 4: Initiation Into Shetaut Neter

The Ancient Egyptian Precepts of Initiatic Education

An Aspirant must learn to achieve the following capacities:

(1) "Control your thoughts,"
(2) "Control your actions,"
(3) "Have devotion of purpose,"
(4) "Have faith in your master's ability to lead you along the path of truth,"
(5) "Have faith in your own ability to accept the truth,"
(6) "Have faith in your ability to act with wisdom,"
(7) "Be free from resentment under the experience of persecution" (Bear insult)
(8) "Be free from resentment under experience of wrong," (Bear injury)
(9) "Learn how to distinguish between right and wrong,"
(10) "Learn to distinguish the real from the unreal."

How is this to be accomplished? The following sections provide insight into how the process of following the teachings works and what is necessary to develop the necessary qualities to be a successful aspirant.

The Importance of Good Association

One of the most important ways of promoting awareness and constant reflection is keeping the company of wise teachers or Sages. In ancient Egypt, the Temple system served the purpose of instructing aspirants in the wisdom teachings and then allowing them back into the world on a regular basis in order to test their level of understanding and self control by practicing the teachings when confronted with ordinary, worldly minded people. The Temple was a place where the initiate could go on a regular basis to receive instruction and counseling on the correct application of the teachings in day to day life. The idea is reflected in the Ancient Egyptian *Stela of Djehuti-Nefer*:

> "Consume pure foods and pure thoughts with pure hands, adore celestial beings; become associated with wise ones: sages, saints and prophets; make offerings to GOD..."

The association with Sages and Saints (Good Association) is seen as a primary way to accelerate the spiritual development of the aspirant. Again, this is because it is the nature of the mind to imitate that which it focuses on. An important definition of the symbols associated with *Sma* or Sema is *to render clear or visible*. In ancient Egypt, the *gathering, assembly or reunion* was called *Smait* and *Smai* is a name for the Temple, the gathering place. In Kamit, the priest assumed the role of preceptor, *Sbai*, leading the initiate to understand the teachings of the hieroglyphs, to purification of the mind and body and eventually to intuitional realization through the practice of mental exercises and the application of the wisdom teachings. In ancient Egyptian this is symbolized by the scenes where deities such as *Heru, Djehuti, Anpu, Hetheru, Aset,* etc. lead the initiate to meet Asar (his/her Higher Self). This teaching was adopted in the Greek Mysteries. In India, this process is known as *"Satsanga"* where the aspirant receives teaching from the *Guru* (Spiritual Preceptor) on a continuous basis. In Buddhism the process is known as *Sanga*. In Christianity, this idea was reflected in the relationship between Jesus and John the Baptist, and later between Jesus and his disciples. Keeping the company of wise people or those seeking wisdom is an important and powerful tool for spiritual development because the nature of the unenlightened (ignorant) mind allows it to make subtle mistakes that can lead the aspirant astray from the correct interpretation of the teachings. Thus, it is the receiving of the teaching that is the real force which causes transformation through a baptismal ritual, and not the ritual itself.

Therefore, the teacher, guru, priest, etc., who is "close" to God (enlightened) as it were, is seen as greater than God because he or she can lead the aspirant toward God (knowing who and where God is and how God is to be discovered). Otherwise it would be a very difficult, long and arduous process for the aspirant to realize the truth. It would take millions of incarnations, wherein untold sufferings would occur in the process of gaining experiences which would teach the proper way to discover the Self.

Your journey through this volume will impart one most important point about true spirituality, namely, that you are transcendental, immortal and eternal and as such, you are endowed with all the qualities necessary to achieve the highest level of spiritual realization regardless of your background or country of origin.

Another important point is to try to become the best possible disciple you can while still performing your every day duties of life. Do not engage in fancies about spirituality, or extremes either. That will disrupt the real spiritual movement. Once you honestly set in motion the mystical process of your own spiritual aspiration, you will one day encounter more advanced personalities from whom you can learn and progress further in your understanding. In every country, there exist more advanced personalities who can lead you further along your path of self-discovery. Have you known anyone who is able to control their emotions? Have you known anyone who has lived through a bad situation such as the loss of a loved one or a serious illness and has moved forward with composure, without losing enthusiasm for life? Have you met anyone who has been like a pillar for others, whom others go to in times of trouble or need? If you have the good fortune to know someone like this, get close to them and ask them to show you how they came to possess those advanced spiritual qualities. Ask their permission to spend time with them so that you may benefit from their knowledge and experience in living. You may find that some people are well developed in some areas, but not in others. Learn what you can and emulate their virtuous characteristics. If you get to a point where you feel there is no more to learn from that person, continue seeking and you will discover the steps which lead upward on the ladder of spiritual aspiration.

There is no greater blessing than to meet Sages and or Saints who have attained Nehast, Higher Consciousness, Nirvana, Moksha, Christhood, Buddhahood, Heruhood, Salvation, Liberation, etc., themselves while at the same time being well versed in the written teachings. They can best help you to understand the subtlety of the teachings and lead you to greater and greater awareness and comprehension which will lead to your own higher mystical realization in a shorter time than through any other method. They cannot transform you into a spiritual personality; you must do that yourself. However, they can direct you on the correct path and point out your mistakes if you are willing to listen. You should not become distracted by different religions or teachers, rather set your attention on the highest goal, Enlightenment, then all else will fall into place. Only one path and one teacher are needed and advisable.

A disciple who does not practice the teachings of their spiritual preceptor with the notion that the preceptor will provide for his/her spiritual development is like a person who expects to become physically fit by merely going to a gymnasium without doing any exercise. The preceptor provides the mental food in the form of the wisdom teachings and then it is up to you to take this food, consume it, digest it, absorb it and allow it to become part of your being.

Since your innermost self (God) is your Supreme Preceptor, all of the situations you find yourself involved with are divinely inspired to provide for your spiritual education. The same Divine Self is instructing you through the spiritual preceptor, and it is this same Divine Self which aids your reflecting and understanding process.

How to Approach a Spiritual Preceptor

**(Left) Sem Priest making an offering.
(Right) Ancient Egyptian Sem Priestess.**

The Sem (officiating) priest(ess) wear a leopard skin, as a symbol of identification with *Mafdet*, the leopard goddess, who has the power to dispel the evil of death and to open the mouth (mind) of the initiate.

There are many orders of priests and priestesses. A detailed description of them will be given in a future volume of this Egyptian Mysteries Series. The Seba is the imparter of the teaching. The Sebai is the sage of the mysteries. This is a special personality, someone who has achieved Divine Consciousness, which is the goal of all spiritual efforts. Those personalities have chosen to maintain the initiatic tradition and instruct new aspirants who will become initiates, and eventually priests and priestesses, as well as Preceptors. Gaining an insight into who they are and how to approach them is of paramount importance in achieving the higher goals of spiritual development. You may begin by reading the books of those personalities so as to have a partial communion with their minds, and then you will want to meet them in person in order to truly understand what you have read!

There are many people who do their own research and believe they have discovered the "mysteries." Thus they go around teaching others, and sometimes even starting new religions. But in the end their lack of authenticity emerges in the form of egoism, unrighteousness, inability to espouse the teachings through books based on the original scriptures, inability to answer certain questions, inability to handle crisis, inability to resist worldly temptations, inability to show others the path to spiritual realization beyond slogans, exuberant rantings or emotional appeals. Many preachers use exciting methods to talk about their scriptures and may even sound authentic, but the excitement soon dies down and the aspirant is left without a viable understanding or path to follow. Also, many self-styled spiritual leaders are not interested in showing others a higher path because then they would loose their source of income. An authentic Spiritual Preceptor is not interested in developing cults, slaves, servants or keeping people at an ignorant level.

An authentic teacher is and should be treated as a precious resource, even more so than millions of dollars in the bank. Why? Because that person will free you from untold miseries over many future lifetimes, as they lead you to enlightenment in this lifetime, so that you can truly enjoy whatever wealth you have by placing it in the service of the Divine. Even if you are poor you will also be led to enjoyment of life since the successful aspirants transcend all good or bad conditions in the world.

You should approach the preceptor with humility and not insolently. As soon as the authentic teacher hears arrogance, conceit, self-importance, vanity, snobbishness, etc., their lips close and the flow of the enlightening stream of the wisdom ceases to flow towards you. Even if you egoistically sought to attend their class you would not understand or benefit from the teaching. Respect, humility, deference and obedience are keys to approaching a preceptor. Without these your relationship cannot exist. For this reason you should practice Maat to remove the gross (overt) impurities (anger, hatred, greed, jealousy, lust, envy, etc.) in your personality. The preceptor will show you how to get rid of the more subtle (unconscious) impurities so that you may progress in the teaching.

(4)"Have faith in your master's ability
to lead you along the path of truth"
-Ancient Egyptian Precept for the initiates.

Once you have recognized an authentic teacher, do not doubt him/her. Do not become arrogant and think you know as much as them. Also, never take the preceptor for granted. Never treat or refer to the preceptor as you would a "friend" or a "buddy" or as "one of the guys." Also, as the preceptor is elevated in consciousness but operating through a physical body, there will be occasional human error or faults in areas outside of the teachings. An ignorant aspirant would look at this with the idea that enlightenment means absolute perfection in everything, and in this manner dismiss the teacher as inadequate, thus loosing out on the benefits that would otherwise be derived from the association. Therefore, as in ordinary relations, there should never be gossiping about faults or petty foibles or minor eccentricities.

"It takes a strong disciple to rule over the mountainous thoughts and constantly go to the essence of the meaning; as mental complexity increases, thus will the depth of your decadence and challenge both be revealed."
-Ancient Egyptian Proverb

Ordinary friendships, based on egoism, are burdened with egoistic desires and expectations. A preceptor is not interested in fulfilling your egoistic desires but rather in dispelling these and fulfilling your true spiritual desire. Therefore, if you do not have the understanding as to what is the nature and purpose of the initiatic affiliation, your relationship is doomed. You will be the one leaving the relationship without transforming, without growing and without enlightening yourself. Never treat the preceptor as an ordinary person, who like, others has an "opinion" you can accept or disregard. If you want to be a "free spirit," to exercise "free will," you have no need of the preceptor. If you are a sincere aspirant, you will have no need to exercise free will to commit sinful acts or unrighteous schemes, pursue egoistic desires, hurt others or delude yourself. Therefore, your free will can be surrendered to the Divine without a second thought or reservation. Once you are secure in the authenticity of the person you have chosen as your teacher, you must realize that that person is a representative of the Divine on earth and should be accorded the same respect and admiration as a facilitator who will help you on the path. You have come to that person because you recognize your ignorance and the elevation of the teacher. Therefore, cease all thoughts of pride and self-importance. Otherwise you are only toying at being an aspirant and have no chance to be a real initiate. In the beginning, as you check out a spiritual teacher, yes you should be cautious and slow to ally yourself, but once you choose to do so your allegiance should be complete and unreserved, unconditional and wholehearted. The unrighteous, and therefore limited ways of relating thwart the spiritual process of the teacher-disciple relationship and will render it fruitless. They cause rifts in the mind of the aspirant and prevent them from pursuing the teaching in the correct manner. Sometimes as children, they may keep themselves from facing the preceptor after they have made some transgression, due to pride and shame. At those times when life humbles the aspirant it is even more important that they should trust in the teacher who will never rub their noses in it or turn them away. A preceptor is like the sun in that he/she witnesses the good and the bad while remaining aloof and dispassionate, but yet is in touch, sending warmth to all regardless. So the preceptor understands how tough it is to make it

Egyptian Mysteries Volume 1: Principles of Shetaut Neter

through the gross and subtle temptations, fancies, notions and desires of life, and is thus prepared to forgive all. Even though a transcendent master is beyond personal hang-ups, desires, attachments and so on, an aspirant should never disrespect the preceptor, steal from the preceptor (objects or knowledge) or speak out of turn or test the patience of the preceptor. Some aspirants, due to ignorance, believe they can go around taking knowledge from different teachers without giving anything in return. They are acting against the laws of the universe (giving and receiving). So they remain unchanged because they do not give themselves, their allegiance, trust and support to the cause of the teacher. Subsequently, they never get the opportunity to form a long-term relationship with the teacher which they need in order to develop deeper understanding of the teaching. Their understanding remains superficial, and thereby they develop delusions of grandeur as advanced initiates when in reality they are setting themselves up for a great fall.

> "Sacrifice the first portions of the harvest, that your strength and faith to bring about what you desire may be increased; give the FIRST portion, to avoid danger of worldly indulgence; Give that you may receive. Fulfill the requirements of the universal law of equilibrium"
>
> -Ancient Egyptian Proverb

Every aspirant must offer his or her ego, pride and ignorance on the divine altar of wisdom. They must sacrifice the egoistic notions and vanities in order to attain insight and wisdom. They must pledge their service to the preceptor in the form of physical, mental and spiritual support and devotion. Further, an aspirant should not hesitate to beg the preceptor's forgiveness for any transgression. While the preceptor is not personally bothered by transgressions or insolence, etc., the preceptor's voice is silenced in the presence of such ignorant aspirants; this hurts them severely, allowing the cycle of ignorance, pain and suffering in life and reincarnation after death to continue unabated. Disrespect and callousness as well as ill manners and rudeness are symptoms of spiritual immaturity, i.e., ignorance. Spiritual teachings to such a personality will be as effective as instructing a dog or a cat on the finer principles of brain surgery. This unrighteous way of relating closes the door to real spiritual instruction. And this closing has been the fault of the aspirant. Take care to not be two-faced and burn your bridges, thinking that you have attained some higher level and no longer need your teacher or have discovered a better teacher, thus disrespecting the old. The old brought you to the new you think you have arrived at and is therefore worthy of the same respect and gratitude that was supposed to have been there all along. While the teacher exists in transcendental bliss regardless of the aspirant's righteous conduct or lack thereof, the aspirant is severely affected by their actions. Even the subtlest unrighteous act is a pathway to strengthening of the ego, Egoism leads to impaired intellect and degraded feeling. Unrighteous behavior reverberates in the consciousness of an aspirant and forms negative impressions in the mind that cloud understanding and may take lifetimes to erase. Therefore, take care to make sure that your relationship with the preceptor is righteous, if not in the beginning, certainly in the end. But there is only one true ending if it can be referred to as such, and that is the attainment of enlightenment. Does a river end when it joins the ocean? In like manner the true end of the road of the teacher-disciple relationship is the aspirant's attainment of enlightenment. However, this is not the end, but a merging of the aspirant's consciousness with that of the teacher's, the beginning of conscious experience of the transcendental Spirit, and also the transformation of the aspirant into a preceptor; this is the initiatic tradition, which stretches back into the far reaches of antiquity, all the way back to the first aspirants, those who learned from God (Asar) directly, and became preceptors to those who followed next, and so on up to the present.

You must treat a Spiritual Preceptor even better than you treat someone you love. Ordinary love affairs are fraught with strife. Periods of love alternate with periods of hate, sprinkled with passionate moments and dashes of exuberant flights of fancy. People develop possessiveness and attachments and call this love. Also they fall in out of love as if it were a disease. This of course is not true love. True love transcends even the capacity to feel anger or disdain. If you truly love something you stick with it through thick or thin, and there is no "falling out" of it. True love is not defined by physical proximity or by actions. Therefore, one can love a person but not what they do. And one can love a person but not live with them. True love, Divine Love, *Neter Merri,* is an upward and expanding movement that is all encompassing and eternal. So unless you have loved in this way, do not believe that you have truly loved anything. Your relationships are only training you for the true love which must learn that from the preceptor.[lviii]

You must attempt to never treat the preceptor unrighteously or with resentment. You must learn to receive whatever the teacher says and apply it in your life. Many aspirants have learned to do things "their own way," and have difficulty following instructions from the teacher. You may question for deeper understanding, but not to challenge in order to get out of your duty or to discredit what has been said so that you may feel justified in disobeying the edict. That is the path of the weak minded and the ignorant. Never attempt to put emotional guilt trips on elevated personalities. These are immature attempts at getting the desires of your ego met, and they will be impotent in the face of the elevated preceptor. Gossiping about the preceptor or any other person is also a sign of degraded consciousness and will eventually lead you away from the teacher as well as true spiritual knowledge. Bouncing around from one teacher to another is also a way to go astray, as you cannot find water if you dig several superficial wells, but rather a single deep well. Therefore, even though you may read the books of many teachers or see many teachers, there should be one special one with whom you may develop a rapport that will cause the flow of divine wisdom to move in your direction. Therefore, seek out a teacher who has a personality that is in harmony with your own and who teaches in the way that is compatible with your learning style. That is, if you are an intellectual person, look for a teacher who emphasizes the wisdom aspect of the disciplines. However, while you may have a special resonance in some aspect of the teachings, there should always be practice of the other disciplines so that you may develop your entire personality and not be like the fanatical ignorant masses. Also, you must strive to never say you will do something for the teacher and then not do it or develop excuses. All of these things and more are worldly ways and will not bring you the favor of the preceptor. Favor is attention, and when you have this, the lips of the preceptor move for you as they will not for others; you will receive the grace of insight into Divine Consciousness that is the objective of all aspirants the world over.

Aspirants should take care to pay their dues. This means that at no time should they allow themselves to believe that they have achieved anything on their own or without the assistance of mentors and teachers. There are many unrighteous writers who take the writings of others and give no credit to them and even act as if they themselves wrote the information. In like manner some aspirants conduct discourses on the teachings and do not give the proper credit for what they have learned and thereby develop egoism as they dazzle others with their "wisdom." However, as they fatten their own ego, they are actually leading people to a place that they will not be able to lead them beyond. Here is where stagnation in the teachings commences. Some preachers rely on drama or exuberant performances while giving sermons. This distracts people and may even make people believe that these preachers or lecturers know what they are talking about, but the listeners will not be able to transform themselves because the teaching is dishonest and incomplete. If an aspirant does not pay homage to the teacher, they are committing an injustice and the higher wisdom will escape them, even if it is presented to them in person or if they come across it in a book.

Approach with a spirit of service and do not practice the mysteries as a part-time dabbler. In order to progress you must work diligently and learn how every waking moment is to be dedicated to the Divine. This is the only way to succeed in dispelling the veil of ignorance. The world is a very powerful force against the ignorant mind, and therefore an aspirant must fight hard to overcome the yoke of worldly consciousness. Only complete dedication and service towards the Divine will open the doors of the House of Asar (palace of enlightenment). Therefore, you must understand that being an initiate means complete devotion to spiritual life. This translates to reverence and service towards the Spiritual Preceptor. Never allow the preceptor to do work that you can do since their time should be reserved for the higher dissemination of the teachings. So again, in serving the teacher you are facilitating the teacher's time and availability to teach you and others. The teacher may not always ask for help because he/she wants to give you room to act on initiative. Thereby the initiatic process cannot be one-sided. The aspirant who hopes to become an *initiate* needs to *initiate* the contact with the teacher and have the *initiative* to make good use of the teaching.

You may find a Spiritual Preceptor who has all the qualifications to lead you, someone who is not only elevated but also who is capable of teaching you how to elevate yourself, for the two capacities are not the same, nor are they always found in the same personality. A person may be elevated but not versed in the scripture or the ways to develop aspirants. Therefore, if you feel a burning desire to grow spiritually and you have dealt with your worldly responsibilities so that you can be free to pursue the teaching, seek out a teacher. That person may be in your hometown, but if not you must go to them and touch the floor with your face before them and humbly ask for their permission to be accepted as a student. First though, develop a keen understanding of what it means to be an aspirant and become familiar with and practice the disciplines of Maat which purify the heart. Do not present to God a dirty vessel. Wouldn't you wash a bowl before placing food in it as an offering to God? In the same manner, properly cleanse your personality before approaching a preceptor as if to God herself. Therefore, be clean in your body, mind and soul to the best of your ability, then, even if you have to go around the world to meet and work with your teacher, the trip will not be a waste of time, but a glorious start on the golden road to enlightened experience.

The Tradition of Initiation

Priest as the God Heru Leads the Aspirant to the Initiation Hall

Those who are seriously interested in pursuing spiritual life should follow the instructions given in the previous section,

Egyptian Mysteries Volume 1: Principles of Shetaut Neter

seeking to purify themselves so as to become proper vessels to recognize and understand the teacher when he or she arrives. There is a tendency sometimes to engage in the flights of emotionality and in the psychic contacts that can be made when you begin to discover the inner dimensions of the mind. Sometimes aspirants believe they have encountered genuine divine personalities not realizing that these are expressions of their own mental creations as in a dream. Others believe that since they have experienced certain psychic "energies" or have developed certain psychic abilities that this in and of itself constitutes spiritual enlightenment.

You must clearly understand that psychic phenomena do not necessarily signify or accompany spiritual enlightenment such as we are discussing here. Spiritual enlightenment is nothing short of mystical union with God. Therefore, while people may exhibit great feats of psychic nature or amazing control of bodily functions such as living without food for weeks or months or holding the breath for hours, etc., these are not to be automatically equated with spirituality, and indeed may not have anything to do with spirituality in regard to the particular person who possesses such powers. Nevertheless, a spiritually enlightened personality may possess some such powers or may not. In any case, only one who is a genuinely advanced or an advancing spiritual personality can discern the difference. Thus, you must strive to purify yourself and dispel the illusions and misconceptions in your mind as to what constitutes true spirituality so that you may be led to the true spiritual teacher. Seek out those who exhibit compassion, patience, dispassion, equanimity of mind and selflessness. These are advanced psychic powers although they are not normally considered in this way. A stark contrast can be seen between ordinary egoistic human beings who think only of providing for themselves and the pleasures of the body at the expense of others (the ignorant and worldly minded), and the more spiritually advanced individuals. The qualities of the ignorant: discontent, desire, hard-heartedness, distraction, mental agitation, restlessness, selfishness, etc., lead to experiences of pain, disappointment and frustration in life, whereas the qualities of a spiritually advancing personality, selflessness, contentment, peacefulness, detachment from worldly possessions and relationships, etc., lead to greater levels of inner peace and self-discovery. These allow the mind to experience deeper and deeper levels until the true nature of one's own being is revealed.

In the spiritual realm, you may encounter the divine in the form of God, Goddess, or an archetypal divine being. You may also experience this realm as wholeness, light, freedom, an awakening, etc. You need to understand that as you tread the path of initiatic science, you will need to gradually let go of all your mental concepts and notions of spirituality. This means that whatever you discover is to be understood as a relative reality because it is being perceived through the mind and senses, which are limited.

If you do not have a specific spiritual preceptor who is versed in the spiritual disciplines of the mysteries, the most important point you need to keep in mind is your conviction to attain the highest. You must honestly and ardently ask for assistance and guidance while offering all of your activities and feelings to the Divine. As you learn about the various yogic paths, you will begin to develop a feeling for which course suits your personality. This is the reason why there are so many paths (devotional, wisdom, action, life force development, etc.). The process of becoming established on your personal path may involve many ups and downs, trial and error, however you must be assured that if you follow through you will eventually reach the goal you have set.

Thus, initiation involves your decision to make the mystic path your life's endeavor. You must develop a strong desire to discover who you are and what the world is and you must have a deep rooted conviction that it is possible for you to understand and apply the principles and disciplines of yoga to your life, regardless of your life situation. At some point you may want to become formally initiated by a particular spiritual preceptor. This means that you have decided to come into closer association with the teaching as espoused by that teacher, and that you are desirous of aligning yourself with the spiritual tradition of that teacher.

There are teachers who specialize in certain aspects of the disciplines. For example, a spiritual preceptor may focus on yoga through the wisdom teachings. This implies, studying, reflecting and rationalizing in order to develop a subtle intellect that will be able to discover the spiritual truth. Another spiritual preceptor may focus on developing and disciplining the physical body through physical and breathing exercises in order to achieve the same goal. Another may focus on prayer, and another on meditation, etc. However, if you find a preceptor who is well versed in Integral Yoga, which is the combination of these main yogic paths, you should not need to search further for other teachers.

In the mean time, apply yourself to the teachings to the best of your understanding and if possible, associate with others who are honest seekers on the path of self-discovery. Finding those around you who are sincerely interested in practicing yoga for spiritual development can be a powerful means to spiritual growth. When people come together, their energies are multiplied toward the task which they have chosen to undertake. This is also true of spiritual practice. Therefore, those who meet and help each other can keep the enthusiasm and level of interest up in prosperous as well as hard times. Also, in a group setting, the subtle vibrations are more strongly attuned to the study process which in turn helps the process of concentration and understanding for each aspirant. The group learning process is a powerful practice which aids the goal of purification of the heart, especially when it is conducted under the guidance of a spiritual preceptor.

Initiation With a Spiritual Preceptor

The Priestess Leads the Aspirant to the Initiation Hall

In essence the entire program of study in Yoga is an initiatic ritual. However, a specific ritual of initiation is additionally efficacious since it serves to establish a subtle connection between teacher and disciple, which fosters greater understanding through personal contact. It allows the aspirant to develop a devotional feeling toward the teacher and the teachings that relate to the *Self*. It engenders a mystic force towards spiritual aspiration even when done alone. Essentially, initiation is an expression of a person's personal conviction and desire to engage in a lifestyle which will lead to spiritual transformation. It is a commitment to a process of learning spiritual teaching and its practice. The initiation ritual performed with a Spiritual Preceptor also fosters a mystic link between an aspirant and his or her hekau and everything else related to the spiritual practice because it causes a deeper mental impression of the understanding of their divine nature. This is especially important in the practice of chanting or hekau repetition. The hekau acts to cleanse the heart (mind) and it sets up positive vibrations that calm the mind and awaken spiritual feeling. Chanting elevates the mind and lifts it to transcendental levels.

The initiation ritual is usually accompanied by certain ceremonial rites, specific instruction on how chanting works and the procedure for uttering words of power. A specific hekau is given to an initiate based on the individual's spiritual inclination, attitudes and level of evolution. A spiritual aspirant will be drawn to a Spiritual Preceptor on the basis of internal spiritual sensitivity. At some point in life a person will look for someone who can understand him or her and lead them on the spiritual path.

In ancient times those desiring to learn from a spiritual teacher would come to them with humility and reverence. They would bring fruits or firewood to help sustain the teacher and his or her efforts in disseminating the teaching. In Ancient Egypt the people and the government would support the Temples so that the spiritual upliftment of the country might be insured. Therefore, when you approach a teacher bring an offering. This may be a symbolic object but realizing that it represents your inner desire to grow spiritually and respect for the teachings you will receive. Also, come with patience and a spirit of joy. Then you will discover the true meaning of the teachings. This does not happen overnight. Fanaticism is not a part of real spiritual evolution. It is a hindrance. True spiritual evolution occurs in degrees. There is a Yoga parable given to illustrate this point. An aspirant went to a spiritual preceptor and asked for initiation into the teachings. The preceptor said "Alright, come to the Temple and study the scriptures, attend my lectures and practice what I tell you." The aspirant said, "Oh no, I don't have time for that. I want liberation from this miserable world now. Why will you withhold the teachings from me?" The preceptor replied, "Very well, I will give you initiation into the teachings this evening. I will come to your house this evening but you must prepare the special food offering to your preceptor." That evening, the preceptor came and was greeted by the aspirant. The aspirant had set everything up and offered the preceptor a seat. The aspirant brought the food offering to the preceptor and the preceptor took out a bowl for the aspirant to put the food into. The aspirant was about to place the food in the bowl when he noticed that it was full of muck and insects, so he said: "Please oh venerable sir, let me wash your bowl and then I will place the food into it." The preceptor replied: "No, that's alright, I will eat from this bowl the way it is." The aspirant was astonished and replied: "How can you expect me to put my wonderfully prepared food into your dirty bowl; I cannot do that." The preceptor replied: "How can you expect me to teach you the highest spiritual wisdom if you will not cleanse the vessel of your mind?" Immediately the aspirant understood the teaching and fell at the feet of the preceptor and pledged to follow his instruction from then on. The aspirant should realize that any endeavor in life requires instruction. Many fall under the delusion that the spiritual path can be accomplished without the help of a spiritual preceptor. All means should be used to learn, but there is no better way than attending classes and receiving instruction from an authentic spiritual teacher. Then only through humility and total devotion is it possible to truly advance.

What are You Being Initiated Into?

Those who wish to become *Shemsu Neter,* followers of the Kamitan spiritual teaching (Neterianism), are initiated into *Shetaut Neter* and *Smai Tawi*. Shetaut Neter is the religion and its mythic teachings based on the varied traditions of the different gods and goddesses. Smai Tawi are the yogic disciplines, techniques or technologies used to transform a human being. These disciplines promote a transformation through a movement that purifies the personality and renders it subtle enough to perceive the transcendental spiritual reality beyond time and space. This is a movement from ignorance to enlightenment, from mortality and weakness to immortality and supreme power, to discover the Absolute from whence the gods and goddesses and all Creation arose. This is a movement towards becoming one with the universe and the consciousness behind it, which is eternal and infinite. This is the lofty goal of initiation. So those who tread this path must be mature and virtuous, as well as physically, mentally and emotionally strong. The purpose of the religion and disciplines is to promote purity of heart and virtue; these lead to higher realization and spiritual enlightenment.

What is the Philosophy of Shems?

Shems

{to follow }

What does it mean to follow something? Why should some things be followed and others not? What should be followed in life and why? These are certainly some of the most important questions in life, because if serious thought is put to them, they involve the crucial questions of life which are or should be the most important concerns in life, "Who am I? Why am I here? What is my purpose?, etc.". This book holds some answers. They are offered from the perspective of an Ancient Egyptian concept and its attendant teachings as developed by the sages of Shetaut Neter-African religion in ancient times.

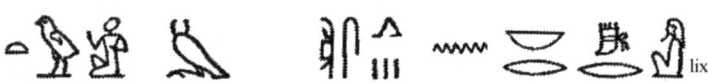

tu-a m shems n Neberdjer

"I am a follower of Neberdjer[lix]

er sesh n Kheperu

in accordance with the writings of Lord Kheperu"

The answer to these important questions of life was given by the sages of ancient times: follow the spiritual path. In ancient times that path was known as *Shetaut Neter*. The "teachings" were given by the Creator, *Kheperu* in the form of outward appearances, shapes and objects of creation. *Lord Djehuti* codified those into the hieroglyphic texts and these teachings were passed on through history to succeeding generations of sages, priests and priestesses of Neterian Religion. Why is it important for you to become a member of the Shetaut Neter tradition and what does it mean to be a follower of the Shetaut Neter spiritual teaching? If you are reading this, it is because at one time or another you have come to the recognition of the important work being conducted by those who currently are following *Shetaut Neter* for the betterment of humanity, and that you also desire to promote your own *Nehast* {spiritual awakening and emancipation, resurrection}. In order to reach the state of consciousness known as *Nehast,* there must first be *Nehas* {wakefulness, being awake}. Being awake implies wakefulness towards the teaching, that is, attentiveness, spending time, desire, etc., for spiritual pursuits. This means being mature enough to have grown beyond childish pursuits and interests, the worldly ideals of life. It is easy to think one is mature when one hears the Ancient Egyptian Proverb: *"Searching for one's self in the world is the pursuit of an illusion."* However, why is it that these same ones who have heard and agree continue to pursue worldly illusions instead of applying themselves fully to the teaching? Needing to have a job to support oneself and one's family should not be an impediment to intensive practice. However, it will become an obstacle if that job or career is the main objective in life. The teaching should be the main objective and the job should be a means to finance the intensification of the practice of the teachings. We must conclude that until the action follows the thought, the thought is not being held as a reality or a priority. So there is insufficient maturity in such a person to pursue the teaching in an intensive and advanced way. Their choice of action reveals their lower state of maturity and aspiration. Such people should follow the teaching at the level of that includes devotional practices, rituals, and the study of *Maat* teachings to develop purity or heart until a higher level of aspiration develops. The focus here is to develop *arit maat* {"offering righteous actions, living life righteously"}.

The opposite of *nehas* is *Nem* {"sleep, slumber, slothfulness, immaturity"}. A person who is immature cannot adopt the teaching properly, and will thus not be able to follow it rightly. What is needed is wakefulness towards the higher perspectives in life, and slothfulness towards what is degraded. This means an aspirant should be awake to real spirituality as opposed to ordinary worldly people who are asleep towards the higher perspective and wakeful towards what is base, degraded and illusory in life. Once there is wakefulness, spiritual sensitivity, spiritual aspiration, respect for the sages and reverence towards the spiritual teaching and the Divine, there should be *Snehas* {"Wakefulness, watchfulness, alertness, vigilance"}. There are many who follow spiritual teachings of all traditions who

Egyptian Mysteries Volume 1: Principles of Shetaut Neter

at times appear to have grown and at others seem to have fallen back to their old habits and degraded passions and desires, *aba*. In order to truly follow an ideal one must be steady on the path and watchful so that negative behaviors and patterns do not draw one back into earlier, lower states of consciousness. However, the spiritual movement will never be in one direction. There will be ups and downs, but the downs should be of short duration and less in frequency; d the aspirant should not indulge in those, but rather learn from them and continue striving.

The work of following a spiritual teaching requires the follower's financial support, but also their psychic support as well as their physical support. When a person becomes a member of the Shetaut Neter Community they are taking an important step in sustaining the dissemination of the *shetit*, "teachings" of *Shetaut Neter*- "Ancient Egyptian-African Religion" for themselves and for the world. It is important to take the step of membership in the Neterian community because this shows to oneself, the world and to others of like mind that there are others who believe, feel and aspire as they do. This develops *udja*, spiritual strength and in a mysterious way allows individual members to have a subtle means of support that urges them on to success on the spiritual path, wherever they may be. So *shems* really means the need to have *knumt-nefer* – "good association, divine association, joining others, together". This is a special association, unlike the worldly kinds of groups that have worldly goals and objective or religious goals and objectives. *Shems* is the coming together of Neterian followers of the Divine for the purpose of promoting righteousness and order in society, and also spiritual awakening and enlightenment for those who are ready to tread the path to *rech-m-ab* –"self-knowledge, higher consciousness" and *an-menit* –"immortality."

This has been a summary of the Egyptian Mysteries and the means to practice them today. May you find the path to awaken the higher consciousness within you and may you discover the glory of the Divine, the infinite peace of life after death and the infinite nature of Creation as one with God.

HTP

Sebai Maa

Egyptian Mysteries Volume 1: Principles of Shetaut Neter

INDEX

Aahs, 23
Ab, 128, 129
Abdu, 12, 83, 93
Absolute, 42, 75, 114, 125, 132, 143, 153
Africa, 4, 8, 10, 11, 12, 13, 17, 18, 19, 20, 22, 26, 27, 36, 40, 41, 43, 59, 73, 76, 83, 91, 95, 114, 143
African Religion, 10, 13, 30, 52, 58, 59, 63, 144
Akhenaton, 90, 91
Akhnaton, 12, 76, 89
Akhus, 56, 90, 95
Alexander the Great, 26
Alexandria, 42
Allah, 76
Amenta, 25, 135, 155
Amentet, 25, 38, 135, 156
Americas, 8, 76
Amun, 2, 12, 20, 22, 23, 42, 57, 58, 60, 63, 77, 81, 84, 85, 90, 109, 114, 116, 127, 135, 153
Amunhotep, 109
Amun-Ra-Ptah, 12, 57, 63, 153
Ancient Egypt, 1, 3, 4, 11, 12, 13, 16, 17, 19, 20, 22, 23, 24, 25, 26, 28, 30, 32, 33, 34, 35, 36, 38, 40, 44, 48, 49, 50, 55, 57, 61, 67, 73, 74, 76, 77, 78, 84, 90, 91, 97, 101, 106, 107, 111, 114, 115, 118, 121, 124, 125, 126, 129, 130, 131, 132, 133, 134, 135, 136, 137, 138, 139, 142, 143, 144, 151, 152, 153, 154, 155, 156, 157, 158, 159
Ancient Egyptian Pyramid Texts, 23, 38
Ancient Nubian, 25
Anger, 50
Ani, 18, 96, 97, 124, 128, 130, 131
Ankh, 85, 109, 122, 123, 129
Annunciation, 85
Anu, 12, 33, 35, 57, 78, 79, 116, 156
Anu (Greek Heliopolis), 12, 33, 35, 57, 78, 79, 116, 156
Anubis, 79, 84, 136
Anunian Theology, 42, 57, 58, 59, 73, 77, 79, 109
Apep serpent, 70
Arabs, 25, 101
Architecture, 134, 135

Ari, 23, 75, 118, 119, 121, 123, 129
Ari Hems Nefer, 23
Arit Maat, 119
Aryan, 30, 153
Asar, 12, 15, 17, 18, 20, 22, 23, 24, 25, 34, 38, 39, 40, 42, 56, 58, 60, 67, 68, 76, 77, 79, 83, 84, 85, 86, 87, 93, 94, 95, 96, 115, 116, 117, 121, 123, 124, 125, 128, 130, 131, 132, 134, 135, 140, 156, 157, 159
Asarian Resurrection, 42, 86, 87, 123, 155, 157
Asclepius, 38
Aset, 1, 4, 10, 12, 15, 17, 18, 23, 24, 25, 39, 44, 55, 58, 60, 63, 67, 68, 78, 79, 82, 83, 84, 85, 86, 87, 90, 91, 100, 101, 102, 105, 109, 115, 124, 125, 128, 131, 132, 135, 136, 156, 157, 159
Aset (Isis), 1, 4, 10, 12, 15, 17, 18, 23, 24, 25, 39, 44, 55, 58, 60, 63, 67, 68, 78, 79, 82, 83, 84, 85, 86, 87, 90, 91, 100, 101, 102, 105, 109, 115, 124, 128, 131, 132, 135, 136, 156, 157, 159
Asia, 8, 13, 22, 25, 30, 41, 68, 91, 114
Asia Minor, 13, 25, 30, 41
Asiatic, 25, 35
Aspirant, 97, 136, 140, 142
Assyrian, 26
Assyrians, 26, 132
Astral, 37, 83, 106, 126, 129, 132, 134, 135, 155
Astral Plane, 37, 83, 106, 126, 129, 132, 134, 135, 155
Aten, see also Aton, 159
Aton, 12, 76, 77, 89, 90, 116
Atonism, 89
Augustus, 20, 42
Axum, 25
Ba (also see Soul), 84, 127, 128, 131
Babylon, 33, 36
Badarian culture, 26
Bas, 22, 23, 87
Basu, 22, 23, 24
Being, 15, 16, 40, 42, 43, 58, 59, 61, 68, 70, 71, 72, 74, 75, 76, 78, 79, 80, 81, 83, 89, 91, 92, 116, 121, 122, 123, 127, 142, 143, 153, 156

Benben, 15
Berossos, 33
Bible, 31, 91, 92, 156, 157
Big Dipper, 32, 38, 39
Black, 11, 25, 76
Black and red pottery, 25
Blackness, 11, 76
Book of Coming Forth by Day, 129
Book of Coming Forth By Day, 42, 88, 129, 130, 131, 155
Book of Enlightenment, 38, 75, 120, 123
Book of the Dead, see also Rau Nu Prt M Hru, 18, 38, 42, 75, 94, 120, 121, 122, 123, 133, 134, 156
Brahma, 114, 129
Brahman, 114
Buddha, 54, 76, 133
Buddhism, 4, 13, 30, 31, 43, 48, 68, 136
Bull, 38
Campbell, Joseph, 33
Caribbean, 4
Cartouche, 129
Catholic, 156
Causal Plane, 83, 126, 134
Chanting, 117, 142
Cheops, see also Khufu, 35
Chepesh, 38, 39, 40
China, 41, 83, 114, 120
Christ, 31, 137, 155
Christ Consciousness, 137
Christhood, 137
Christianity, 25, 26, 30, 31, 42, 43, 48, 73, 85, 92, 97, 136, 152, 156
Chronology, 25
Church, 156
Civilization, 41, 101, 114
Coffin Texts, 42
Company of gods and goddesses, 15, 78, 79
Conception, 85, 125, 134
Conflict, 70
Confucianism, 120
Consciousness, 130, 137, 140, 155
Copper Age, 34
Coptic, 42, 155
Cosmogony, 78
Cosmos, 107
Cow, 82
Creation, 14, 15, 24, 25, 42, 60, 65, 71, 73, 74, 76, 77, 78, 79, 80, 81, 82, 83, 85, 87, 89, 121, 125, 130, 132, 133, 134, 135, 143, 144, 153, 155, 156

Cross, 65
Culture, 8, 14, 28, 35, 41, 132, 153, 154
Cymbals, 158, 159
Death, 126
December, 156
Delta, 13
Denderah, 12, 24, 36, 39, 155
Dharma, 120
Diet, 4, 106, 107, 113, 152
Diodorus, 19, 20, 34, 114
Discipline, 4, 116, 117, 118, 119
Disease, 106
Divine Consciousness, 137, 140
Djehuti, 16, 17, 18, 34, 38, 42, 74, 79, 84, 85, 86, 87, 115, 123, 127, 129, 136, 139, 143
Djehutimes IIII, 35
DNA, 102
Dogon, 31, 71
Drum, 158, 159
Duat, 25, 84, 128, 133, 134, 135
Dudun, 23
Dynastic period, 42, 133
Dynastic Period, 16, 24, 25, 26, 36, 42
Earth, 32, 37, 59, 134, 135
Eastern religions, 43, 59
Ecstasy, 63
Edfu, 12, 83, 155
Egyptian Book of Coming Forth By Day, 42, 88, 155
Egyptian civilization, 36, 111
Egyptian Mysteries, 1, 2, 8, 120, 144, 152, 157
Egyptian Physics, 156
Egyptian proverbs, 154
Egyptian religion, 17, 26, 133, 135
Egyptian Yoga, 4, 63, 77, 81, 101, 107, 108, 113, 114, 115, 126, 130, 134, 151, 152, 153, 154, 155, 158, 159
Egyptian Yoga Book Series, 4
Egyptian Yoga see also Kamitan Yoga, 4, 63, 77, 81, 101, 107, 108, 113, 114, 115, 126, 130, 134, 151, 152, 153, 154, 155, 158, 159
Egyptologists, 19, 35, 36, 133
Elements, 126, 133

Egyptian Mysteries Volume 1: Principles of Shetaut Neter

Enlightenment, 4, 17, 38, 56, 75, 90, 106, 111, 114, 118, 120, 123, 126, 137, 153, 154, 157
Ennead, 79, 86, 134
Ethics, 119
Ethiopia, 11, 12, 19, 20, 114
Eucharist, 88, 155
European explorers, 99
Exercise, 4, 155
Eye of Heru, 40
Eye of Ra, 85
Forgiveness, 48
Form, 161
Geb, 14, 15, 22, 34, 59, 79, 125, 155
Giza, 21, 36, 38
Giza Plateau, 38
God, 14, 17, 22, 23, 24, 35, 43, 45, 48, 49, 50, 51, 52, 54, 55, 59, 61, 62, 63, 65, 70, 71, 72, 73, 75, 76, 77, 85, 90, 91, 92, 95, 97, 109, 114, 115, 117, 120, 121, 122, 123, 124, 125, 126, 127, 128, 129, 130, 131, 132, 134, 135, 136, 137, 139, 140, 141, 144, 153, 155, 156, 159
Goddess, 24, 42, 43, 65, 67, 77, 82, 91, 116, 119, 121, 122, 125, 141, 156, 158, 159, 160
Goddesses, 22, 79, 81, 82, 108, 154
Gods, 22, 27, 70, 72, 79, 81, 108, 114, 120, 154
Good, 77, 136
Good Association, 136
Gospels, 156
Great Months, 33
Great Pyramid, 21, 32, 38, 39
Great Pyramids, 21, 39
Great Spirit, 56, 61
Great Truths, 75
Great Year, 32, 33, 34, 35, 36
Greece, 19, 36, 114, 152
Greek philosophy, 152
Greeks, 11, 23, 24, 26, 32, 78
Guru, 136
Haari, 159
Hapi, 13, 59, 61, 84
Harmony, 120
Hatha Yoga, 4
Hathor, 42, 79, 85, 136, 155, 156, 157
Health, 4, 106, 152
Heart, 95, 117, 157
Heart (also see Ab, mind, conscience), 95, 117, 157
Heaven, 38, 50, 134, 135, 156
Hekau, 114, 117, 134, 159
Heliopolis, 12, 33, 78
Hell, 50, 134
Hermes, 38
Hermes (see also Djehuti, Thoth), 38
Hermes (see also Tehuti, Thoth), 38
Hermetic, 38
Herodotus, 19, 32, 114
Heru, 12, 13, 18, 22, 23, 24, 25, 34, 35, 36, 38, 39, 40, 42, 45, 55, 56, 58, 60, 72, 75, 79, 83, 84, 85, 86, 87, 90, 94, 95, 96, 101, 102, 105, 106, 109, 115, 121, 123, 124, 125, 127, 128, 136, 140, 155, 156, 157, 159
Heru (see Horus), 12, 13, 18, 22, 23, 24, 25, 34, 35, 36, 38, 39, 40, 42, 45, 55, 56, 58, 60, 72, 75, 79, 83, 84, 85, 86, 87, 90, 94, 95, 96, 101, 102, 105, 106, 109, 115, 121, 123, 124, 125, 127, 128, 136, 140, 155, 156, 157, 159
Heru in the Horizon, 36
Hetep, 2, 38, 39, 50, 135
Hetheru, 12, 15, 17, 39, 55, 60, 72, 78, 79, 82, 85, 87, 108, 115, 136, 157, 158
Hetheru (Hetheru, Hathor), 12, 15, 17, 39, 55, 60, 72, 78, 79, 82, 85, 87, 108, 115, 136, 157, 158
Het-Ka-Ptah, see also Men-nefer, Memphis, 24, 73
Hidden, 135
Hidden God, 114, 135
Hieroglyphic Writing, language, 124, 154
Hindu, 60, 84
Hinduism, 13, 30, 31, 43, 48, 68
Hindus, 76
History of Manetho, 33
Holy of Holies, 62, 63, 65, 85
Holy Spirit, 85
Horus, 34, 36, 40, 42, 58, 79, 83, 84, 85, 86, 87, 114, 115, 125, 132, 136, 159
Horushood, 137
Hyksos, 20, 26
Hymn to Ra, 131
Hymns of Amun, 90
Hymns to Aton, 76, 90
Ibis, 16
Ignorance, 74, 91
Imhotep, 38, 55, 108
Imperishable stars, 38
India, 4, 13, 19, 30, 33, 41, 60, 73, 83, 111, 114, 120, 129, 133, 136, 152, 153, 154, 159
Indian Yoga, 4, 151, 153, 159
Indus, 25, 26, 30, 114, 153
Indus Valley, 25, 26, 114, 153
Initiate, 40, 134, 152
Iron Age, 34
Isis, 24, 39, 42, 58, 60, 67, 78, 79, 83, 84, 85, 86, 106, 125, 155, 156, 159
Isis, See also Aset, 24, 39, 42, 58, 60, 67, 78, 83, 106, 155, 156
Islam, 26, 30, 31, 43, 48, 152
Jesus, 18, 25, 31, 52, 59, 85, 121, 136, 155, 156, 157
Jesus Christ, 155
Jews, 31, 76, 91, 92, 132
John the Baptist, 136
Joseph, 33, 85
Joseph Campbell, 33
Judaism, 25, 26, 30, 31, 43, 92, 152
Ka, 24, 73, 126, 127, 129, 131
Kabbalah, 152
Kali, 34
Kamit, 10, 11, 12, 13, 15, 18, 19, 20, 22, 23, 24, 25, 26, 30, 31, 40, 41, 57, 61, 68, 77, 82, 83, 84, 85, 92, 94, 108, 109, 115, 117, 118, 120, 132
Kamit (Egypt), 10, 11, 12, 13, 15, 18, 19, 20, 22, 23, 24, 25, 26, 30, 31, 40, 41, 57, 61, 68, 77, 82, 83, 84, 85, 92, 94, 108, 109, 115, 117, 118, 120, 132
Kamitan, 4, 10, 11, 13, 20, 22, 23, 24, 31, 32, 38, 39, 41, 42, 44, 46, 47, 52, 53, 54, 59, 60, 61, 68, 70, 72, 73, 74, 77, 90, 91, 93, 100, 106, 107, 108, 111, 113, 119, 120, 142, 152, 156, 158, 159
Karma, 4, 75, 123, 129, 154
Karmah, 20, 25
Karmah Period, 20, 25
Kemetic, 4, 32, 38, 42, 125, 126, 132, 134, 135, 158, 159
Kerma, 20
Khaibit, 128
Khat, 126, 127, 130, 131
Khepri, 14, 15, 16, 17, 18, 71, 89
Khu, 114, 127, 128
Khufu, 35
Khufu, see also Cheops, 35
Kingdom, 20, 21, 22, 26, 35, 62, 65, 81, 89, 112, 156
Kingdom of Heaven, 156
Kmt, 84
Know thyself, 55, 90
Know Thyself, 49
Knowledge, 132
Knum, 23, 85
Krishna, 18, 76, 114, 157
Kundalini, 4, 109, 111
Kundalini XE "Kundalini" Yoga see also Serpent Power, 4, 111
Kush, 11, 12, 13, 19, 25, 26, 40, 41
Liberation, 137
Life Force, 25, 36, 79, 85, 87, 111, 115, 118, 129, 154
Listening, 63, 103, 109, 113, 116, 117
Little Dipper, 32
Lord of the Perfect Black, 25, 76
Lotus, 115
Love, 3, 77, 99, 106, 117, 154
Lower Egypt, 13, 26, 34, 42, 115
Luxor, 85
M, 129
Maakheru, 16, 17, 74, 75, 76, 101, 123, 131
Maat, 34, 38, 40, 49, 50, 51, 68, 69, 70, 73, 76, 77, 79, 93, 94, 95, 97, 98, 106, 109, 113, 118, 119, 120, 121, 122, 123, 130, 132, 138, 140, 143, 154, 156, 157
MAAT, 42, 73, 85, 120, 153, 154
Maati, 67, 95, 122, 124
MAATI, 154
Maat-Ubuntu, 40
Madonna, 24
Manetho, 19, 33, 34, 35
Manetho, see also History of Manetho, 19, 33, 34, 35
Mantras, 114
Manu, 135
Mars, 32
Matter, 156
Matthew, 85
Meditation, 63, 77, 103, 106, 109, 110, 113, 117, 118, 152, 153, 154, 159
Mediterranean, 13, 100
Medu Neter, 10, 16, 17, 44, 74, 75, 77
Mehurt, 82
Memphis, 12, 24, 34, 133
Memphite Theology, 42, 77, 80
Menes, 34
Men-nefer, see also Het-Ka-Ptah, Memphis, 12, 24
Merikara, 124
Meril, 23
Meroe, 20
Meroitic Period, 21
Mesken, 85, 124
Meskhenet, 129
Mesopotamia, 32, 38, 41
Metaphysics, 63, 132, 156
Middle East, 30, 152
Middle Kingdom, 26
Min, 86, 155

Egyptian Mysteries Volume 1: Principles of Shetaut Neter

Mind, 4, 77, 97
Moksha, 137
Moon, 32
Mortals, 65
Moses, 31, 91, 92
Mother Mary, 25
Mother Teresa, 121
mummy, 130
Music, 4, 68, 117, 159
Muslims, 26, 75, 76, 101, 104, 132
Mysteries, 1, 17, 61, 77, 106, 113, 114, 126, 144, 152, 156, 157
Mystical religion, 76
Mysticism, 4, 63, 122, 153, 155, 156, 157
N, 130
Napata, 25
Native American, 73
Neberdjer, 22, 23, 70, 71, 75, 76, 135, 143, 153
Nebethet, 79, 83, 84, 159
Nebthet, 67, 79
Nefer, 23, 136, 158, 159
Nefertari, Queen, 130, 131
Nefertem, 80
Nehast, 17, 56, 60, 61, 74, 75, 77, 90, 113, 123, 126, 137, 143
Nekhen (Hierakonpolis), 42
Neolithic, 25, 42, 133
Neolithicxe "Neolithic" Period, 25
Nephthys, 79, 84
Net, goddess, 12, 22, 42, 78, 82, 160
Neter, 1, 4, 8, 10, 11, 13, 14, 16, 17, 29, 31, 43, 44, 45, 46, 50, 52, 55, 57, 61, 64, 68, 69, 70, 71, 72, 74, 75, 76, 77, 89, 90, 91, 105, 107, 113, 114, 116, 117, 118, 135, 136, 142, 143, 144, 155
Neterian, 2, 9, 14, 16, 18, 30, 31, 32, 44, 45, 48, 53, 56, 58, 59, 60, 61, 62, 64, 68, 69, 70, 73, 74, 75, 82, 84, 87, 88, 90, 92, 97, 104, 107, 108, 116, 117, 119, 123, 126, 132, 134, 135, 143, 144
Neterianism, 8, 10, 11, 14, 44, 52, 71, 75, 83, 86, 87, 88, 92, 103, 104, 113, 119, 126
Neters, 71, 125
Neteru, 4, 22, 56, 58, 60, 61, 70, 72, 75, 90, 91, 97, 154, 158, 159
Netherworld, 25, 53, 94, 96, 131, 135
New Age, 9
New Kingdom, 20, 21, 22, 26, 62, 65, 81, 89, 112
New Testament, 85
Nile River, 11, 13, 84
Nirvana, 137
Nomarchs, 26
Nomes, 26
Nu, 79
Nubia, 11, 12, 19, 20, 22, 23, 24, 25, 26
Nubian, 12, 21, 22, 23, 24, 25, 26, 42
Nubian divinity – see Dudun, Meril, Aahs, Ari Hems Nefer, 23
Nubians, 19, 20, 22, 25, 26
Nun, 14, 15, 71, 72, 73
Nun (primeval waters- unformed matter), 14, 15, 71, 72, 73
Nun (See also Nu), 14, 15, 71, 72, 73
Nut, 14, 15, 22, 24, 59, 79, 125, 155
Nutrition, 4
Obelisk, 15
Old Kingdom, 21, 35
Om, 2, 57, 159
One God, 90
Oneness, 90
Opening of the Mouth Ceremony, 38, 39, 40, 88, 130
Opposites, 42
Orion Star Constellation, 38, 39, 156
Orthodox, 36, 48, 73, 76, 101
Orthodox religions, 48
Osiris, 12, 38, 58, 77, 79, 83, 84, 85, 86, 87, 88, 114, 125, 135, 136, 155, 159
Pa Neter, 70, 75
Paleolithic, 42
Papyrus of Turin, 34
Paut, 4, 22, 58
Pautti, 58, 78, 79
Peace (see also Hetep), 4, 117
Per-Aah, 35
Persians, 132
Pert Em Heru, See also Book of the Dead, 75, 115, 123, 124, 155
phallus, 84, 85, 86
Pharaonic headdress, 36, 111
Philae, 12, 23, 124, 155
Philosophy, 3, 4, 46, 54, 69, 94, 95, 97, 108, 114, 115, 119, 121, 122, 126, 132, 143, 153, 155, 156, 157
Physical body, 127
Physical Plane, 126, 135
Pigmy, 24
Plato, 132
Pole Star, 32, 38
Presbyterians, 57
Priests and Priestesses, 40, 61, 100, 152
Ptah, 2, 12, 23, 24, 34, 42, 57, 58, 63, 73, 77, 80, 116, 153, 156
PTAH, 156
Ptahotep, 42, 55
Ptah-Seker-Asar – see, 23, 24
Ptolemy, Greek ruler, 36
Puerto Rico, 4
Purity of heart (see purity of mind), 76
Pyramid, 12, 14, 15, 16, 21, 22, 23, 32, 38, 42, 55, 97
Pyramid texts, 16, 97
Pyramid Texts, 12, 16, 22, 23, 38, 42, 55
Pyramids, 21, 39
Pyramids at Giza, 21
Qamit, 11, 12
R, 130
Ra, 2, 12, 14, 15, 17, 22, 23, 24, 33, 34, 35, 36, 40, 42, 54, 57, 58, 63, 70, 71, 77, 79, 81, 83, 84, 85, 86, 89, 92, 105, 109, 116, 118, 131, 132, 135, 153, 155, 158, 159
Ram, 22, 38
Rameses II, 20
Reality, 125
Realm of Light, 42
Reflection, 63, 103
reincarnation, 127, 129
Reincarnation, 123
Religion, 4, 9, 10, 13, 27, 30, 44, 48, 53, 57, 58, 59, 60, 63, 65, 90, 113, 115, 143, 144, 155, 157, 159
Ren, 129, 130, 131
resurrection, 129, 131
Resurrection, 17, 42, 86, 87, 123, 155, 156, 157
Righteous action, 118
Righteousness, 113, 119
ritual, 131
Ritual, 63, 66, 103, 119
Rituals, 64, 103, 114, 119, 156
Roman, 26
Rome, 42
S, 143
Saa (spiritual understanding faculty), 135
Sacrifice, 139
Sages, 50, 76, 109, 123, 136, 137, 153, 155, 156, 157
Sahu, 38, 128
Saints, 50, 123, 136, 137, 156
Sais, 12, 42
Sakkara, 12, 16
Salvation, 52, 71, 137
Salvation . See also resurrection, 137
Salvation, See also resurrection, 52, 71, 137
Sanskrit, 114
Satan, 31, 91, 92
Satsanga, 136
Schwaller de Lubicz, 32, 34, 35, 36
Seba Ur, 53
Sebai, 1, 4, 89, 102, 144
See also Egyptian Yoga, 4
Sekhem, 110, 111, 118, 129
Sekhmet, 42, 78
Self (see Ba, soul, Spirit, Universal, Ba, Neter, Heru)., 16, 39, 48, 49, 50, 51, 59, 77, 78, 91, 114, 115, 118, 122, 123, 126, 127, 129, 131, 132, 134, 135, 136, 137, 142, 153, 154, 155
Self (seeBasoulSpiritUniversal BaNeterHorus)., 39, 114, 115, 117, 118, 122, 125, 126, 127, 129, 131, 132, 134, 135, 136, 137, 142
Selfless service, 122
Sema, 1, 3, 4, 10, 48, 49, 63, 77, 87, 108, 113, 115, 136, 151, 161
Sema XE "Sema" Paut, see also Egyptian Yoga, 4
Sema Tawi, 4, 49, 63, 87, 113
Serpent, 42, 65, 106, 109, 110, 111, 118
Serpent Power, 42, 65, 106, 109, 110, 111, 118
Serpent Power (see also Kundalini and Buto), 42, 65, 106, 109, 110, 111, 118
Serpent Power see also Kundalini Yoga, 42, 65, 106, 109, 110, 111, 118
Set, 18, 34, 38, 70, 73, 74, 76, 79, 83, 84, 85, 86, 87, 91, 92, 115, 119, 123
Seti I, 93, 154, 159
Sex, 90, 155
Shadow, 128
Shai, 123, 127
Shen, 129
Sheps, 17
Shetaut Neter, 1, 8, 10, 11, 13, 14, 16, 17, 29, 31, 43, 44, 45, 46, 49, 52, 55, 57, 64, 68, 69, 70, 72, 76, 77, 90, 91, 105, 107, 113, 114, 116, 117, 136, 142, 143, 144, 155
Shetaut Neter See also Egyptian Religion, 1, 8, 10, 11, 13, 14, 16, 17, 29, 31, 43, 44, 45, 46, 49, 52, 55, 57, 64, 68, 69, 70, 72, 76, 77, 90, 91, 105, 107, 113, 114, 116, 117, 136, 142, 143, 144, 155
Shiva, 114
Shu (air and space), 14, 22, 34, 59, 79

Sirius, 33, 39, 42, 156
Sky, 42, 134
Sma, 115, 118, 136
Smai, 4, 63, 114, 115, 136, 142
Smai Tawi, 114, 115, 142
Soul, 4, 96, 127, 128
Sphinx, 13, 14, 26, 28, 34, 35, 36, 37, 42, 110, 111
Spirit, 14, 36, 37, 42, 64, 85, 87, 121, 122, 126, 128, 130, 134
Spiritual discipline, 152
Stellar Symbolism, 32
Story of Sinuhe, 132
Storytelling, 63
Sublimation, 155
Sudan, 11, 12, 100
Sumer, 30, 114
Sun, 32, 131, 135
Sun XE "Sun" and Moon, 32
Sundisk, 132
Supreme Being, 15, 16, 40, 43, 58, 59, 61, 67, 68, 70, 71, 72, 74, 75, 76, 78, 79, 80, 81, 82, 83, 89, 92, 116, 121, 122, 123, 153, 156
Supreme Divinity, 23, 48, 70
Syria, 20, 84
Taharka, 21
Tantra, 84, 125, 155
Tantra Yoga, 125, 155
Taoism, 30, 43, 48, 152
Tawi, 4, 23, 49, 63, 87, 113, 114, 115, 142
Tefnut, 14, 15, 22, 59, 79
Tefnut (moisture), 14, 15, 22, 59, 79
Tem, 24, 79, 89, 105
Temple of Aset, 4, 10, 17, 63, 67, 83, 87, 100, 109, 124, 161
Ten Commandments, 103
The Absolute, 153
The God, 22, 42, 59, 65, 79, 82, 95, 120, 154
The Gods, 42, 79, 154
The Hymns of Amun, 90
The Pyramid Texts, 22
The Self, 78, 118
Theban Theology, 42
Thebes, 12, 42, 132, 153, 154
Theodosius, 42
Thoth, 79
Time, 39
Timeline, 42
Tomb, 19, 20, 118, 154, 159
Tomb of Huy, 19
Tomb of Seti I, 118, 154, 159
Tradition, 32, 58, 77, 80, 81, 82, 83, 89, 116
Tree, 109
Tree of Life, 109
Triad, 153
Trinity, 12, 42, 57, 78, 80, 81, 83, 86, 105, 114, 153, 155, 159
Truth, 34, 70, 73, 74, 75, 101, 105
Turin Papyrus, 34
Tutankhamon, 112
Tutankhamun, 36, 112, 133
Tutankhamun, Pharaoh, 36, 112, 133
Ubuntu, 40, 119, 121
Uganda, 100
Union with the Divine, 77
Universal Ba, 127
Universal Consciousness, 155
Upanishads, 156
Upper Egypt, 13, 115
Ur, 53, 69, 79
Vedic, 153
Vishnu, 60, 76, 114
Waset, 12, 116, 132, 153
Water, 59, 95
Will, 95
Wisdom, 42, 68, 76, 94, 95, 106, 116, 118, 120, 122, 124, 153, 154
WISDOM (ALSO SEE DJEHUTI), 42, 117
Wisdom (also see Djehuti, Aset), 42, 68, 76, 94, 95, 106, 116, 118, 120, 122, 124, 153, 154
Wisdom texts, 94
Yoga, 1, 3, 4, 34, 48, 63, 77, 81, 101, 107, 108, 111, 113, 114, 115, 117, 125, 126, 130, 141, 142, 151, 152, 153, 154, 155, 156, 157, 158, 159, 161
Yoga Exercise, 4
Yoga of Action, 117
Yoga of Devotion (see Yoga of Divine Love), 117
Yoga of Wisdom (see also Jnana Yoga), 117
Yogic, 121
Yoruba, 10, 31, 71
Yuga, 34
Yuga (Kali, Maha, Dwarpar, Treta, Satya), 34
Zodiac, Kamitan, 32
Zoomorphic, 60
Zoroastrianism, 31, 92

Egyptian Mysteries Volume 1: Principles of Shetaut Neter

SEMA UNIVERSITY

CURRICULUM FOR THE SEMA UNIVERSITY ASSOCIATE DEGREE PROGRAM

CORRESPONDENCE (DISTANCE LEARNING) DEGREE PROGRAM CLASSES ARE SCHEDULED ON TRIMESTER BASIS:
Register to begin January, May or September

✓ Those completing the Associate Degree will receive the title Basu (Teacher of Kemetic Culture)
Basu (school teacher)

Associate Degree   15 Credits $500 PER COURSE   (curriculum/prices subject to change)

KEMETIC DIET – INTRODUCTION TO NETERIANISM AND SEMA PHILOSOPHY, NATURAL LIVING AND SELF HEALING FOR ASPIRANTS
1) AS101 Class Subject: Kemetic Diet Level 1: Natural Living –

INTRODUCTION TO SEMA-YOGA AND NETERIAN THEOLOGY and METAPHYSICS
1) AS102 Class subject: Introduction to Neterian Spirituality and Philosophy

INTRODUCTION TO SEMA-YOGA DISCIPLINES and METAPHYSICS
1) AS103 Class Subject: Initiation into Shetaut Neter And Sema Tawi

INTRODUCTION TO MAAT PHILOSOPHY
1) AS104 Class subject: Introduction to Maat Philosophy and Metaphysics

AFRICAN ORIGINS & HISTORY OF RELIGION, YOGA AND PHILOSOPHY LEVEL 1
1) AS105 Class Subject: Level 1: *African Origins of African Civilization-*

Sema Institute of Yoga, P.O.Box 570459, Miami, Florida, 33257, (305) 378-6253 Fax: (305) 378-6253

© 2004 By Sebai Muata Abhaya Ashby

For Detailed program description and policies: Main Site of The Sema University go to www.Egyptianyoga.com or call Sema Institute

www.Egyptianyoga.com

Egyptian Mysteries Volume 1: Principles of Shetaut Neter

How to Become A Unut-Minister of Shetaut Neter

Unut - "priests and priestesses that serve part time"

Udja -(Greetings),

Many of you have inquired about becoming more deeply involved with the work of the Temple of Shetaut Neter. Some of you have expressed the desire to teach some of the disciplines of Shetaut Neter (Ancient Egyptian-African Religion) and Sema Tawi (Ancient Egyptian-African Yoga). The following has been added for your orientation.

Unut (minister) is the first level of Kamitan clergy. An Unut is one who takes care of the needs of rekhyt (lay people-congregation) on behalf of a higher authority of the Temple. In this capacity, the ministers assist in the dissemination of the teachings and disciplines of Shetaut Neter and Sema Tawi. They assist the community by giving classes in the disciplines to help people better their lives. They also assist in the work of the higher authorities of the Temple as they conduct programs for aspirants, the general public and for the priesthood. In so doing they develop spiritual merit through service and the enlightening effect of teaching others what they know. In this manner they become more proficient and hasten their own movement towards enlightenment.

Therefore, those of you who are interested in serving the Temple and the community, this is a good first step. Also if you are interested in applying for higher levels of practice in the Temple, such as the priesthood, this is also the first step.

For those aspirants desiring to complete the Unut (Priesthood Ordination) Program attendance at the monthly online meetings is mandatory and in addition to completing the Associate Degree Program attendance at the Unut Training Seminar is also mandatory. There will be a $500 attendance fee to be paid to the Sema Institute in addition to your other expenses for transportation and accommodation and food.

The Duties of the Unut include:
• Assist the priests and priestesses as they disseminate the teachings of Shetaut Neter and Sema Tawi and assist the general public in the practice of the disciplines of Sema Tawi (Egyptian Yoga). The first and main duty of Ministers is to lead weekly Shedy meetings where the basic worship and sema disciplines are practiced:
1. Assist incoming aspirants to work through the initiation-orientation series lectures
   i. Listen to etiquette for aspirants
   ii. Introduction to Sema Tawi (Egyptian Yoga) Series
   iii. Video Recovering the African Civilization, Religion and Culture
   iv. Video Intro to Shetaut Neter
   v. Initiatic Practice series
2. Lead Shedy group meetings where the daily worship program is practiced.
3. Lead Shedy group meetings in chant and divine singing-Devotion
4. Lead Shedy group meetings in Uaah (meditation)
5. Lead in adoption of the Kemetic Diet program
6. Transcribing lectures as direct service to the temple for future publishing.
7. Organize and Coordinate seminars and workshops to present Shetaut Neter to the public.
8. Lead in selfless service to humanity
   ▪ Organize monthly charity – ***Maat Ari***
   • Food for the hungry, shelter for the homeless, hospice service, children in distress, or other approved program.
9. Help support the vision of Shetaut Neter:
   ▪ Promote spiritual awakening for individuals and humanity.
   ▪ Promote order, truth and righteousness in society.

In order to be considered for appointment as a *Unut* – with minister status you need to meet the following criteria: Become a member of the Sema Institute and the Shetatu Neter Community, Complete the Associate Degree academic Studies, and Be initiated as a Shemsu (Follower of Shetaut Neter)
1. Complete the Sema Institute/Temple of Shetaut Neter Minister Training Certification Course:
Class detailing the history, metaphisics, discipline and duties of Unut ministry.
2. The Aspirant must successfully complete the Associate Degree Program as outlined in the Sema University catalog
3. The Aspirant must participate in the daily worship program.
4. Attend Annual Synod (clergy meeting) conference.
5. Annual certification and licensure as Unut (Minister) will be given to those individuals that meet and uphold all of the requirements set forth here.
6. As minister of Shetaut Neter and Sema Tawi the practitioner agrees to promote and teach the philosophy and disciplines of Shetaut Neter and Sema Tawi EXCLUSIVELY. All aspirants who desire to become Unut of Shetaut Neter will be asked to refrain from studying and or teaching other forms of religion or spiritual disciplines during and after their training at the Temple of Shetaut Neter.
7. For more details on What do Priests and Priestesses of Shetaut Neter do? Contact the Sema Institute/Temple of Shetaut Neter or view web site: www.egyptianyoga.com

Egyptian Mysteries Volume 1: Principles of Shetaut Neter

Other Books by Muata Ashby

P.O.Box 570459
Miami, Florida, 33257
(305) 378-6253 Fax: (305) 378-6253

This book is part of a series on the study and practice of Ancient Egyptian Yoga and Mystical Spirituality based on the writings of Dr. Muata Abhaya Ashby. They are also part of the Egyptian Yoga Course provided by the Sema Institute of Yoga. Below you will find a listing of the other books in this series. For more information send for the Egyptian Yoga Book-Audio-Video Catalog or the Egyptian Yoga Course Catalog.

Now you can study the teachings of Egyptian and Indian Yoga wisdom and Spirituality with the Egyptian Yoga Mystical Spirituality Series. The Egyptian Yoga Series takes you through the Initiation process and lead you to understand the mysteries of the soul and the Divine and to attain the highest goal of life: ENLIGHTENMENT. The *Egyptian Yoga Series*, takes you on an in depth study of Ancient Egyptian mythology and their inner mystical meaning. Each Book is prepared for the serious student of the mystical sciences and provides a study of the teachings along with exercises, assignments and projects to make the teachings understood and effective in real life. The Series is part of the Egyptian Yoga course but may be purchased even if you are not taking the course. The series is ideal for study groups.

THE EGYPTIAN MYSTIERIES BOOK SERIES

Coming Soon

EGYPTIAN MYSTERIES VOLUME 2: Shetaut Neteru- The Mysteries of the Gods and Goddesses

EGYPTIAN MYSTERIES VOLUME 3: Shemsu Heru- The Mysteries of Initiation and Discipleship

EGYPTIAN MYSTERIES VOLUME 4: Hemu Neter- The Ancient Egyptian Priests and Priestesses

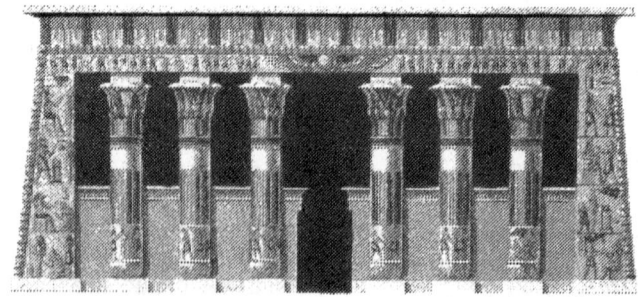

Egyptian Mysteries Volume 1: Principles of Shetaut Neter

Prices subject to change.

Prices subject to change.

1. EGYPTIAN YOGA: THE PHILOSOPHY OF ENLIGHTENMENT An original, fully illustrated work, including hieroglyphs, detailing the meaning of the Egyptian mysteries, tantric yoga, psycho-spiritual and physical exercises. Egyptian Yoga is a guide to the practice of the highest spiritual philosophy which leads to absolute freedom from human misery and to immortality. It is well known by scholars that Egyptian philosophy is the basis of Western and Middle Eastern religious philosophies such as *Christianity, Islam, Judaism,* the *Kabala,* and Greek philosophy, but what about Indian philosophy, Yoga and Taoism? What were the original teachings? How can they be practiced today? What is the source of pain and suffering in the world and what is the solution? Discover the deepest mysteries of the mind and universe within and outside of your self. 8.5" X 11" ISBN: 1-884564-01-1 Soft $19.95

2. EGYPTIAN YOGA II: The Supreme Wisdom of Enlightenment by Dr. Muata Ashby ISBN 1-884564-39-9 $22.95 U.S. In this long awaited sequel to *Egyptian Yoga: The Philosophy of Enlightenment* you will take a fascinating and enlightening journey back in time and discover the teachings which constituted the epitome of Ancient Egyptian spiritual wisdom. What are the disciplines which lead to the fulfillment of all desires? Delve into the three states of consciousness (waking, dream and deep sleep) and the fourth state which transcends them all, Neberdjer, "The Absolute." These teachings of the city of Waset (Thebes) were the crowning achievement of the Sages of Ancient Egypt. They establish the standard mystical keys for understanding the profound mystical symbolism of the Triad of human consciousness.

3. THE KAMITAN DIET GUIDE TO HEALTH, DIET AND FASTING Health issues have always been important to human beings since the beginning of time. The earliest records of history show that the art of healing was held in high esteem since the time of Ancient Egypt. In the early 20th century, medical doctors had almost attained the status of sainthood by the promotion of the idea that they alone were "scientists" while other healing modalities and traditional healers who did not follow the "scientific method' were nothing but superstitious, ignorant charlatans who at best would take the money of their clients and at worst kill them with the unscientific "snake oils" and "irrational theories". In the late 20th century, the failure of the modern medical establishment's ability to lead the general public to good health, promoted the move by many in society towards "alternative medicine". Alternative medicine disciplines are those healing modalities which do not adhere to the philosophy of allopathic medicine. Allopathic medicine is what medical doctors practice by an large. It is the theory that disease is caused by agencies outside the body such as bacteria, viruses or physical means which affect the body. These can therefore be treated by medicines and therapies The natural healing method began in the absence of extensive technologies with the idea that all the answers for health may be found in nature or rather, the deviation from nature. Therefore, the health of the body can be restored by correcting the aberration and thereby restoring balance. This is the area that will be covered in this volume. Allopathic techniques have their place in the art of healing. However, we should not forget that the body is a grand achievement of the spirit and built into it is the capacity to maintain itself and heal itself. Ashby, Muata ISBN: 1-884564-49-6 $24.95

4. INITIATION INTO EGYPTIAN YOGA Shedy: Spiritual discipline or program, to go deeply into the mysteries, to study the mystery teachings and literature profoundly, to penetrate the mysteries. You will learn about the mysteries of initiation into the teachings and practice of Yoga and how to become an Initiate of the mystical sciences. This insightful manual is the first in a series which introduces you to the goals of daily spiritual and yoga practices: Meditation, Diet, Words of Power and the ancient wisdom teachings. 8.5" X 11" ISBN 1-884564-02-X   Soft Cover $24.95 U.S.

5. *THE AFRICAN ORIGINS OF CIVILIZATION, MYSTICAL RELIGION AND YOGA PHILOSOPHY* HARD COVER EDITION ISBN: 1-884564-50-X $80.00 U.S.   81/2" X 11"   Part 1, Part 2, Part 3 in one volume 683 Pages Hard Cover First Edition Three volumes in one. Over the past several years I have been

Egyptian Mysteries Volume 1: Principles of Shetaut Neter

asked to put together in one volume the most important evidences showing the correlations and common teachings between Kamitan (Ancient Egyptian) culture and religion and that of India. The questions of the history of Ancient Egypt, and the latest archeological evidences showing civilization and culture in Ancient Egypt and its spread to other countries, has intrigued many scholars as well as mystics over the years. Also, the possibility that Ancient Egyptian Priests and Priestesses migrated to Greece, India and other countries to carry on the traditions of the Ancient Egyptian Mysteries, has been speculated over the years as well. In chapter 1 of the book *Egyptian Yoga The Philosophy of Enlightenment,* 1995, I first introduced the deepest comparison between Ancient Egypt and India that had been brought forth up to that time. Now, in the year 2001 this new book, *THE AFRICAN ORIGINS OF CIVILIZATION, MYSTICAL RELIGION AND YOGA PHILOSOPHY,* more fully explores the motifs, symbols and philosophical correlations between Ancient Egyptian and Indian mysticism and clearly shows not only that Ancient Egypt and India were connected culturally but also spiritually. How does this knowledge help the spiritual aspirant? This discovery has great importance for the Yogis and mystics who follow the philosophy of Ancient Egypt and the mysticism of India. It means that India has a longer history and heritage than was previously understood. It shows that the mysteries of Ancient Egypt were essentially a yoga tradition which did not die but rather developed into the modern day systems of Yoga technology of India. It further shows that African culture developed Yoga Mysticism earlier than any other civilization in history. All of this expands our understanding of the unity of culture and the deep legacy of Yoga, which stretches into the distant past, beyond the Indus Valley civilization, the earliest known high culture in India as well as the Vedic tradition of Aryan culture. Therefore, Yoga culture and mysticism is the oldest known tradition of spiritual development and Indian mysticism is an extension of the Ancient Egyptian mysticism. By understanding the legacy which Ancient Egypt gave to India the mysticism of India is better understood and by comprehending the heritage of Indian Yoga, which is rooted in Ancient Egypt the Mysticism of Ancient Egypt is also better understood. This expanded understanding allows us to prove the underlying kinship of humanity, through the common symbols, motifs and philosophies which are not disparate and confusing teachings but in reality expressions of the same study of truth through metaphysics and mystical realization of Self. (HARD COVER)

6. AFRICAN ORIGINS BOOK 1 PART 1 African Origins of African Civilization, Religion, Yoga Mysticism and Ethics Philosophy-Soft Cover $24.95 ISBN: 1-884564-55-0

7. AFRICAN ORIGINS BOOK 2 PART 2 African Origins of Western Civilization, Religion and Philosophy(Soft) -Soft Cover $24.95 ISBN: 1-884564-56-9

8. EGYPT AND INDIA (AFRICAN ORIGINS BOOK 3 PART 3) African Origins of Eastern Civilization, Religion, Yoga Mysticism and Philosophy-Soft Cover $29.95 (Soft) ISBN: 1-884564-57-7

9. THE MYSTERIES OF ISIS: The Path of Wisdom, Immortality and Enlightenment   Through the study of ancient myth and the illumination of initiatic understanding the idea of God is expanded from the mythological comprehension to the metaphysical. Then this metaphysical understanding is related to you, the student, so as to begin understanding your true divine nature. ISBN 1-884564-24-0 $24.99

10. EGYPTIAN PROVERBS: TEMT TCHAAS *Temt Tchaas* means: collection of ——Ancient Egyptian Proverbs How to live according to MAAT Philosophy. Beginning Meditation. All proverbs are indexed for easy searches. For the first time in one volume, ——Ancient Egyptian Proverbs, wisdom teachings and meditations, fully illustrated with hieroglyphic text and symbols. EGYPTIAN PROVERBS is a unique collection of knowledge and wisdom which you can put into practice today and transform your life. 5.5"x 8.5" $14.95 U.S   ISBN: 1-884564-00-3

11. THE PATH OF DIVINE LOVE The Process of Mystical Transformation and The Path of Divine Love This Volume will focus on the ancient wisdom teachings and how to use them in a scientific process for self-transformation. Also, this volume will detail the process of transformation from ordinary

Egyptian Mysteries Volume 1: Principles of Shetaut Neter

consciousness to cosmic consciousness through the integrated practice of the teachings and the path of Devotional Love toward the Divine. 5.5"x 8.5" ISBN 1-884564-11-9 $22.99

12. INTRODUCTION TO MAAT PHILOSOPHY: Spiritual Enlightenment Through the Path of Virtue Known as Karma Yoga in India, the teachings of MAAT for living virtuously and with orderly wisdom are explained and the student is to begin practicing the precepts of Maat in daily life so as to promote the process of purification of the heart in preparation for the judgment of the soul. This judgment will be understood not as an event that will occur at the time of death but as an event that occurs continuously, at every moment in the life of the individual. The student will learn how to become allied with the forces of the Higher Self and to thereby begin cleansing the mind (heart) of impurities so as to attain a higher vision of reality. ISBN 1-884564-20-8 $22.99

13. MEDITATION The Ancient Egyptian Path to Enlightenment   Many people do not know about the rich history of meditation practice in Ancient Egypt. This volume outlines the theory of meditation and presents the Ancient Egyptian Hieroglyphic text which give instruction as to the nature of the mind and its three modes of expression. It also presents the texts which give instruction on the practice of meditation for spiritual Enlightenment and unity with the Divine. This volume allows the reader to begin practicing meditation by explaining, in easy to understand terms, the simplest form of meditation and working up to the most advanced form which was practiced in ancient times and which is still practiced by yogis around the world in modern times. ISBN 1-884564-27-7 $24.99

14. THE GLORIOUS LIGHT MEDITATION TECHNIQUE OF ANCIENT EGYPT ISBN: 1-884564-15-1 $14.95 (PB) New for the year 2000. This volume is based on the earliest known instruction in history given for the practice of formal meditation. Discovered by Dr. Muata Ashby, it is inscribed on the walls of the Tomb of Seti I in Thebes Egypt. This volume details the philosophy and practice of this unique system of meditation originated in Ancient Egypt and the earliest practice of meditation known in the world which occurred in the most advanced African Culture.

15. THE SERPENT POWER: The Ancient Egyptian Mystical Wisdom of the Inner Life Force.   This Volume specifically deals with the latent life Force energy of the universe and in the human body, its control and sublimation. How to develop the Life Force energy of the subtle body. This Volume will introduce the esoteric wisdom of the science of how virtuous living acts in a subtle and mysterious way to cleanse the latent psychic energy conduits and vortices of the spiritual body. ISBN 1-884564-19-4 $22.95

16. EGYPTIAN YOGA MEDITATION IN MOTION Thef Neteru: *The Movement of The Gods and Goddesses* Discover the physical postures and exercises practiced thousands of years ago in Ancient Egypt which are today known as Yoga exercises. This work is based on the pictures and teachings from the Creation story of Ra, The Asarian Resurrection Myth and the carvings and reliefs from various Temples in Ancient Egypt 8.5" X 11" ISBN 1-884564-10-0 Soft Cover $18.99   Exercise video $21.99

17. EGYPTIAN TANTRA YOGA: The Art of Sex Sublimation and Universal Consciousness This Volume will expand on the male and female principles within the human body and in the universe and further detail the sublimation of sexual energy into spiritual energy. The student will study the deities Min and Hathor, Asar and Aset, Geb and Nut and discover the mystical implications for a practical spiritual discipline. This Volume will also focus on the Tantric aspects of Ancient Egyptian and Indian mysticism, the purpose of sex and the mystical teachings of sexual sublimation which lead to self-knowledge and Enlightenment. 5.5"x 8.5" ISBN 1-884564-03-8 $24.95

Egyptian Mysteries Volume 1: Principles of Shetaut Neter

18. ASARIAN RELIGION: RESURRECTING OSIRIS The path of Mystical Awakening and the Keys to Immortality NEW REVISED AND EXPANDED EDITION! The Ancient Sages created stories based on human and superhuman beings whose struggles, aspirations, needs and desires ultimately lead them to discover their true Self. The myth of Aset, Asar and Heru is no exception in this area. While there is no one source where the entire story may be found, pieces of it are inscribed in various ancient Temples walls, tombs, steles and papyri. For the first time available, the complete myth of Asar, Aset and Heru has been compiled from original Ancient Egyptian, Greek and Coptic Texts. This epic myth has been richly illustrated with reliefs from the Temple of Heru at Edfu, the Temple of Aset at Philae, the Temple of Asar at Abydos, the Temple of Hathor at Denderah and various papyri, inscriptions and reliefs. Discover the myth which inspired the teachings of the *Shetaut Neter* (Egyptian Mystery System - Egyptian Yoga) and the Egyptian Book of Coming Forth By Day. Also, discover the three levels of Ancient Egyptian Religion, how to understand the mysteries of the Duat or Astral World and how to discover the abode of the Supreme in the Amenta, *The Other World* The ancient religion of Asar, Aset and Heru, if properly understood, contains all of the elements necessary to lead the sincere aspirant to attain immortality through inner self-discovery. This volume presents the entire myth and explores the main mystical themes and rituals associated with the myth for understating human existence, creation and the way to achieve spiritual emancipation - *Resurrection.* The Asarian myth is so powerful that it influenced and is still having an effect on the major world religions. Discover the origins and mystical meaning of the Christian Trinity, the Eucharist ritual and the ancient origin of the birthday of Jesus Christ. Soft Cover ISBN: 1-884564-27-5 $24.95

19. THE EGYPTIAN BOOK OF THE DEAD MYSTICISM OF THE PERT EM HERU $26.95   ISBN# 1-884564-28-3 Size: 8½" X 11" I Know myself, I know myself, I am One With God!–From the Pert Em Heru "The Ru Pert em Heru" or "Ancient Egyptian Book of The Dead," or "Book of Coming Forth By Day" as it is more popularly known, has fascinated the world since the successful translation of Ancient Egyptian hieroglyphic scripture over 150 years ago. The astonishing writings in it reveal that the Ancient Egyptians believed in life after death and in an ultimate destiny to discover the Divine. The elegance and aesthetic beauty of the hieroglyphic text itself has inspired many see it as an art form in and of itself. But is there more to it than that? Did the Ancient Egyptian wisdom contain more than just aphorisms and hopes of eternal life beyond death? In this volume Dr. Muata Ashby, the author of over 25 books on Ancient Egyptian Yoga Philosophy has produced a new translation of the original texts which uncovers a mystical teaching underlying the sayings and rituals instituted by the Ancient Egyptian Sages and Saints. "Once the philosophy of Ancient Egypt is understood as a mystical tradition instead of as a religion or primitive mythology, it reveals its secrets which if practiced today will lead anyone to discover the glory of spiritual self-discovery. The Pert em Heru is in every way comparable to the Indian Upanishads or the Tibetan Book of the Dead." Muata Abhaya Ashby

20. ANUNIAN THEOLOGY THE MYSTERIES OF RA The Philosophy of Anu and The Mystical Teachings of The Ancient Egyptian Creation Myth Discover the mystical teachings contained in the Creation Myth and the gods and goddesses who brought creation and human beings into existence. The Creation Myth holds the key to understanding the universe and for attaining spiritual Enlightenment. ISBN: 1-884564-38-0 40 pages $14.95

21. MYSTERIES OF MIND AND MEMPHITE THEOLOGY Mysticism of Ptah, Egyptian Physics and Yoga Metaphysics and the Hidden properties of Matter   This Volume will go deeper into the philosophy of God as creation and will explore the concepts of modern science and how they correlate with ancient teachings. This Volume will lay the ground work for the understanding of the philosophy of universal consciousness and the initiatic/yogic insight into who or what is God? ISBN 1-884564-07-0 $21.95

22. THE GODDESS AND THE EGYPTIAN MYSTERIESTHE PATH OF THE GODDESS THE GODDESS PATH The Secret Forms of the Goddess and the Rituals of Resurrection The Supreme Being may be worshipped as father or as mother. *Ushet Rekhat* or *Mother Worship*, is the spiritual process of worshipping

Egyptian Mysteries Volume 1: Principles of Shetaut Neter

the Divine in the form of the Divine Goddess. It celebrates the most important forms of the Goddess including *Nathor, Maat, Aset, Arat, Amentet and Hathor* and explores their mystical meaning as well as the rising of *Sirius,* the star of Aset (Aset) and the new birth of Hor (Heru). The end of the year is a time of reckoning, reflection and engendering a new or renewed positive movement toward attaining spiritual Enlightenment. The Mother Worship devotional meditation ritual, performed on five days during the month of December and on New Year's Eve, is based on the Ushet Rekhit. During the ceremony, the cosmic forces, symbolized by Sirius - and the constellation of Orion ---, are harnessed through the understanding and devotional attitude of the participant. This propitiation draws the light of wisdom and health to all those who share in the ritual, leading to prosperity and wisdom. $14.95 ISBN 1-884564-18-6

23. *THE MYSTICAL JOURNEY FROM JESUS TO CHRIST* $24.95   ISBN# 1-884564-05-4 size: 8½" X 11" Discover the ancient Egyptian origins of Christianity before the Catholic Church and learn the mystical teachings given by Jesus to assist all humanity in becoming Christlike. Discover the secret meaning of the Gospels that were discovered in Egypt. Also discover how and why so many Christian churches came into being. Discover that the Bible still holds the keys to mystical realization even though its original writings were changed by the church. Discover how to practice the original teachings of Christianity which leads to the Kingdom of Heaven.

24. THE STORY OF ASAR, ASET AND HERU: An Ancient Egyptian Legend (For Children)   Now for the first time, the most ancient myth of Ancient Egypt comes alive for children. Inspired by the books *The Asarian Resurrection: The Ancient Egyptian Bible* and *The Mystical Teachings of The Asarian Resurrection, The Story of Asar, Aset and Heru* is an easy to understand and thrilling tale which inspired the children of Ancient Egypt to aspire to greatness and righteousness. If you and your child have enjoyed stories like *The Lion King* and *Star Wars you will love The Story of Asar, Aset and Heru.* Also, if you know the story of Jesus and Krishna you will discover than Ancient Egypt had a similar myth and that this myth carries important spiritual teachings for living a fruitful and fulfilling life. This book may be used along with *The Parents Guide To The Asarian Resurrection Myth: How to Teach Yourself and Your Child the Principles of Universal Mystical Religion.* The guide provides some background to the Asarian Resurrection myth and it also gives insight into the mystical teachings contained in it which you may introduce to your child. It is designed for parents who wish to grow spiritually with their children and it serves as an introduction for those who would like to study the Asarian Resurrection Myth in depth and to practice its teachings. 41 pages 8.5" X 11"   ISBN: 1-884564-31-3 $12.95

25. THE PARENTS GUIDE TO THE AUSARIAN RESURRECTION MYTH: How to Teach Yourself and Your Child the Principles of Universal Mystical Religion.   This insightful manual brings for the timeless wisdom of the ancient through the Ancient Egyptian myth of Asar, Aset and Heru and the mystical teachings contained in it for parents who want to guide their children to understand and practice the teachings of mystical spirituality. This manual may be used with the children's storybook *The Story of Asar, Aset and Heru* by Dr. Muata Abhaya Ashby. 5.5"x 8.5"   ISBN: 1-884564-30-5 $14.95

26. HEALING THE CRIMINAL HEART BOOK 1 Introduction to Maat Philosophy, Yoga and Spiritual Redemption Through the Path of Virtue   Who is a criminal? Is there such a thing as a criminal heart? What is the source of evil and sinfulness and is there any way to rise above it? Is there redemption for those who have committed sins, even the worst crimes?   Ancient Egyptian mystical psychology holds important answers to these questions. Over ten thousand years ago mystical psychologists, the Sages of Ancient Egypt, studied and charted the human mind and spirit and laid out a path which will lead to spiritual redemption, prosperity and Enlightenment.   This introductory volume brings forth the teachings of the Asarian Resurrection, the most important myth of Ancient Egypt, with relation to the faults of human existence: anger, hatred, greed, lust, animosity, discontent, ignorance, egoism jealousy, bitterness, and a myriad of psycho-spiritual ailments which keep a human being in a state of negativity and adversity. 5.5"x 8.5"   ISBN: 1-884564-17-8 $15.95

Egyptian Mysteries Volume 1: Principles of Shetaut Neter

27. THEATER & DRAMA OF THE ANCIENT EGYPTIAN MYSTERIES: Featuring the Ancient Egyptian stage play-"The Enlightenment of Hathor' Based on an Ancient Egyptian Drama, The original Theater - Mysticism of the Temple of Hetheru $14.95   By Dr. Muata Ashby

28. GUIDE TO PRINT ON DEMAND: SELF-PUBLISH FOR PROFIT, SPIRITUAL FULFILLMENT AND SERVICE TO HUMANITY Everyone asks us how we produced so many books in such a short time. Here are the secrets to writing and producing books that uplift humanity and how to get them printed for a fraction of the regular cost. Anyone can become an author even if they have limited funds. All that is necessary is the willingness to learn how the printing and book business work and the desire to follow the special instructions given here for preparing your manuscript format. Then you take your work directly to the non-traditional companies who can produce your books for less than the traditional book printer can. ISBN: 1-884564-40-2 $16.95 U. S.

29. Egyptian Mysteries: Vol. 1, Shetaut Neter ISBN: 1-884564-41-0 $19.99 What are the Mysteries? For thousands of years the spiritual tradition of Ancient Egypt, S*hetaut Neter,* "The Egyptian Mysteries," "The Secret Teachings," have fascinated, tantalized and amazed the world. At one time exalted and recognized as the highest culture of the world, by Africans, Europeans, Asiatics, Hindus, Buddhists and other cultures of the ancient world, in time it was shunned by the emerging orthodox world religions. Its temples desecrated, its philosophy maligned, its tradition spurned, its philosophy dormant in the mystical *Medu Neter*, the mysterious hieroglyphic texts which hold the secret symbolic meaning that has scarcely been discerned up to now. What are the secrets of *Nehast* {spiritual awakening and emancipation, resurrection}. More than just a literal translation, this volume is for awakening to the secret code *Shetitu* of the teaching which was not deciphered by Egyptologists, nor could be understood by ordinary spiritualists. This book is a reinstatement of the original science made available for our times, to the reincarnated followers of Ancient Egyptian culture and the prospect of spiritual freedom to break the bonds of *Khemn,* "ignorance," and slavery to evil forces: *Såaa* .

30. EGYPTIAN MYSTERIES VOL 2: Dictionary of Gods and Goddesses ISBN: 1-884564-23-2 $19.99 This book is about the mystery of neteru, the gods and goddesses of Ancient Egypt (Kamit, Kemet). Neteru means "Gods and Goddesses." But the Neterian teaching of Neteru represents more than the usual limited modern day concept of "divinities" or "spirits." The Neteru of Kamit are also metaphors, cosmic principles and vehicles for the enlightening teachings of Shetaut Neter (Ancient Egyptian-African Religion). Actually they are the elements for one of the most advanced systems of spirituality ever conceived in human history. Understanding the concept of neteru provides a firm basis for spiritual evolution and the pathway for viable culture, peace on earth and a healthy human society.   Why is it important to have gods and goddesses in our lives? In order for spiritual evolution to be possible, once a human being has accepted that there is existence after death and there is a transcendental being who exists beyond time and space knowledge, human beings need a connection to that which transcends the ordinary experience of human life in time and space and a means to understand the transcendental reality beyond the mundane reality.

31. EGYPTIAN MYSTERIES VOL. 3 The Priests and Priestesses of Ancient Egypt ISBN: 1-884564-53-4 $22.95 This volume details the path of Neterian priesthood, the joys, challenges and rewards of advanced Neterian life, the teachings that allowed the priests and priestesses to manage the most long lived civilization in human history and how that path can be adopted today; for those who want to tread the path of the Clergy of Shetaut Neter.

32. THE KING OF EGYPT: The Struggle of Good and Evil for Control of the World and The Human Soul ISBN 1-8840564-44-5 $18.95   Have you seen movies like The Lion King, Hamlet, The Odyssey, or The Little Buddha? These have been some of the most popular movies in modern times. The Sema Institute of Yoga is dedicated to researching and presenting the wisdom and culture of ancient Africa. The Script is

Egyptian Mysteries Volume 1: Principles of Shetaut Neter

designed to be produced as a motion picture but may be addapted for the theater as well. 160 pages bound or unbound (specify with your order) $19.95   copyright 1998 By Dr. Muata Ashby

33. FROM EGYPT TO GREECE: The Kamitan Origins of Greek Culture and Religion ISBN: 1-884564-47-X $22.95 U.S. FROM EGYPT TO GREECE   This insightful manual is a quick reference to Ancient Egyptian mythology and philosophy and its correlation to what later became known as Greek and Rome mythology and philosophy. It outlines the basic tenets of the mythologies and shoes the ancient origins of Greek culture in Ancient Egypt. This volume also acts as a resource for Colleges students who would like to set up fraternities and sororities based on the original Ancient Egyptian principles of Sheti and Maat philosophy. ISBN: 1-884564-47-X $22.95 U.S.

34. THE FORTY TWO PRECEPTS OF MAAT, THE PHILOSOPHY OF RIGHTEOUS ACTION AND THE ANCIENT EGYPTIAN WISDOM TEXTS <u>ADVANCED STUDIES</u> This manual is designed for use with the 1998 Maat Philosophy Class conducted by Dr. Muata Ashby. This is a detailed study of Maat Philosophy. It contains a compilation of the 42 laws or precepts of Maat and the corresponding principles which they represent along with the teachings of the ancient Egyptian Sages relating to each. Maat philosophy was the basis of Ancient Egyptian society and government as well as the heart of Ancient Egyptian myth and spirituality. Maat is at once a goddess, a cosmic force and a living social doctrine, which promotes social harmony and thereby paves the way for spiritual evolution in all levels of society. ISBN: 1-884564-48-8 $16.95 U.S.

Music Based on the Prt M Hru and other Kemetic Texts

Available on Compact Disc $14.99 and Audio Cassette $9.99

Adorations to the Goddess

Music for Worship of the Goddess

**NEW Egyptian Yoga Music CD
by Sehu Maa
Ancient Egyptian Music CD**

Instrumental Music played on reproductions of Ancient Egyptian Instruments– Ideal for <u>meditation</u> and
reflection on the Divine and for the practice of spiritual programs and <u>Yoga exercise sessions.</u>

©1999 By Muata Ashby
CD $14.99 –

Egyptian Mysteries Volume 1: Principles of Shetaut Neter

MERIT'S INSPIRATION
NEW Egyptian Yoga Music CD
by Sehu Maa
Ancient Egyptian Music CD
Instrumental Music played on reproductions of Ancient Egyptian Instruments– Ideal for meditation and reflection on the Divine and for the practice of spiritual programs and Yoga exercise sessions.
©1999 By Muata Ashby
CD $14.99 –
UPC# 761527100429

ANORATIONS TO RA AND HETHERU
NEW Egyptian Yoga Music CD
By Sehu Maa (Muata Ashby)
Based on the Words of Power of Ra and HetHeru
played on reproductions of Ancient Egyptian Instruments **Ancient Egyptian Instruments used: Voice, Clapping, Nefer Lute, Tar Drum, Sistrums, Cymbals –** The Chants, Devotions, Rhythms and Festive Songs Of the Neteru - Ideal for meditation, and devotional singing and dancing.
©1999 By Muata Ashby
CD $14.99 –
UPC# 761527100221

SONGS TO ASAR ASET AND HERU
NEW
Egyptian Yoga Music CD
By Sehu Maa
played on reproductions of Ancient Egyptian Instruments– The Chants, Devotions, Rhythms and
Festive Songs Of the Neteru - Ideal for meditation, and devotional singing and dancing.
Based on the Words of Power of Asar (Asar), Aset (Aset) and Heru (Heru) Om Asar Aset Heru is the third in a series of musical explorations of the Kemetic (Ancient Egyptian) tradition of music. Its ideas are based on the Ancient Egyptian Religion of Asar, Aset and Heru and it is designed for listening, meditation and worship. ©1999 By Muata Ashby
CD $14.99 –
UPC# 761527100122

HAARI OM: ANCIENT EGYPT MEETS INDIA IN MUSIC
NEW Music CD
By Sehu Maa

The Chants, Devotions, Rhythms and Festive Songs Of the Ancient Egypt and India, harmonized and played on reproductions of ancient instruments along with modern instruments and beats. Ideal for meditation, and devotional singing and dancing.

Haari Om is the fourth in a series of musical explorations of the Kemetic (Ancient Egyptian) and Indian traditions of music, chanting and devotional spiritual practice. Its ideas are based on the Ancient Egyptian Yoga spirituality and Indian Yoga spirituality.

©1999 By Muata Ashby
CD $14.99 –
UPC# 761527100528

RA AKHU: THE GLORIOUS LIGHT
NEW
Egyptian Yoga Music CD
By Sehu Maa

The fifth collection of original music compositions based on the Teachings and Words of The Trinity, the God Asar and the Goddess Nebethet, the Divinity Aten, the God Heru, and the Special Meditation Hekau or Words of Power of Ra from the Ancient Egyptian Tomb of Seti I and more... played on reproductions of Ancient Egyptian Instruments and modern instruments - **Ancient Egyptian Instruments used: Voice, Clapping, Nefer Lute, Tar Drum, Sistrums, Cymbals**

– The Chants, Devotions, Rhythms and Festive Songs Of the Neteru - Ideal for meditation, and devotional singing and dancing.

©1999 By Muata Ashby
CD $14.99 –
UPC# 761527100825

GLORIES OF THE DIVINE MOTHER
Based on the hieroglyphic text of the worship of Goddess Net.
The Glories of The Great Mother
©2000 **Muata Ashby**
CD $14.99 UPC# 761527101129`

Egyptian Mysteries Volume 1: Principles of Shetaut Neter

Order Form

Telephone orders: Call Toll Free: 1(305) 378-6253. Have your AMEX, Optima, Visa or MasterCard ready.

Fax orders: 1-(305) 378-6253   E-MAIL ADDRESS: Semayoga@aol.com

Postal Orders: Sema Institute of Yoga, P.O. Box 570459, Miami, Fl. 33257. USA.

Please send the following books and / or tapes.

ITEM

_____Cost $_____
_____Cost $_____
_____Cost $_____
_____Cost $_____
_____Cost $_____

Total $_____

Name:_____
Physical Address:_____
City:_____ State:_____ Zip:_____

Sales tax: Please add 6.5% for books shipped to Florida addresses
_____Shipping: $6.50 for first book and .50¢ for each additional
_____Shipping: Outside US $5.00 for first book and $3.00 for each additional

_____Payment:_____
_____Check -Include Driver License #:
         _____

_____Credit card: _____ Visa, _____ MasterCard, _____ Optima,
_____ AMEX.

Card number:_____
Name on card:_____ Exp. date:_____/_____

Copyright 1995-2005 Dr. R. Muata Abhaya Ashby
Sema Institute of Yoga
P.O.Box 570459, Miami, Florida, 33257
(305) 378-6253 Fax: (305) 378-6253

www.ingramcontent.com/pod-product-compliance
Lightning Source LLC
Chambersburg PA
CBHW081112080526
44587CB00021B/3560